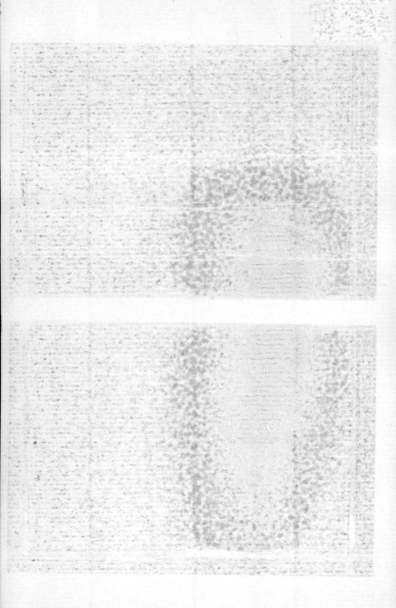

ENGLISH RECUSANT LITERATURE
1558–1640

Selected and Edited by
D. M. ROGERS

Volume 233

FRANCOIS COSTER
Meditations
1616

FRANCOIS COSTER
Meditations of the Whole Historie
of the Passion of Christ
1616

The Scolar Press
1975

ISBN 0 85967 219 0

*Published and printed in Great Britain by
The Scolar Press Limited, 59-61 East Parade,
Ilkley, Yorkshire and
39 Great Russell Street,
London WC1*

NOTE

Reproduced (original size) from a copy in the library of Ushaw College, by permission of the President. In this copy pages 573–4 have been damaged, and these pages are reproduced as an appendix from a copy in the British Library, by permission of the Board.

References: Allison and Rogers 262; STC 5827.

✠
I H S.

MEDITATIONS
of the whole Historie
of the Passion of
CHRIST.

Written by the Reuerend Father,
F. Francis Costerus, Doctor of
Diuinity, of the Society
of *IESVS*.

Translated out of Latine into
English by *R. W*. Esquire.

I. Pet. 4. 1.

*Christo igitur passo in carne, & vos
eadem cogitatione armamini.*

Christ therefore hauing suffered in the
flesh, bee you also armed with the
same cogitation.

Printed at Doway.
1 6 1 6.

The Preface.

*To the Sodality of the most
blessed Sacrament in A-
quicincts Colledge, in
the Vniuersity of
Doway.*

Of the best manner of Meditation of the Passion of Christ.

I *is manifest, that the
end, for which Almighty
God created Man, was,
that beeing indowed not
onely with that inferiour part,
which is common to him with o-
ther Creatures; but also with the
peculiar priuiledge and prehe-
minence of a Cælestiall minde ;*

A 3   hee

hee should onely imploy his exte-
riour sences in the mannaging of
outward and transitory thinges,
and with his minde surpassing all
humane affaires should aspire
wholy to God, and bee carryed
to him, as to his first beginning.
Wherefore it is wonderfull, and
much to bee lamented, that some
being vnmindefull of their condition and end, doe with such
earnestnes follow these temporall
Vanityes. as if they wanted this
diuine vnderstanding; hauing
not their mindes eleuated on
high, but fixed on the earth, and
creeping like Wormes vpon the
ground, so as the very brute
Beastes accuse them of ingratitude, which by a certain vstinct
of Nature seeme to retaine a
memory of the benefite they haue
receiued.

received. Whom least you should seeme (deare brethren) to resemble, you are accustomed together with the frequent participation of the holy Sacraments, to giue your selues daily to the pious meditation of Heauenly thinges : That although in your bodyes you bee heere on Earth, yet your minde is transported into Heauen, where you conuerse with the blessed Saints, and with Christ himselfe, labouring to vnite your minde to him, from whome at first it did proceed. This Godly endeauour both of you, and all pious persons, that I might in some sort promote and further, I haue gathered together diuers Meditations of the Passion of our blessed Sauiour, which may minister vnto you

A 4　　　occasion

The Preface.

occasion and matter of many deuoute and profitable contemplations. Which Meditations I haue thought good to commend vnto you for diuers reasons: First, because nothing is of such force to moone mens mindes, and to inflame them with the fire of the loue of God, as the serious cogitation of benefites, especially such as are so great, and proceed from so great a Lord and God. Some indeede, whose consciences are oppressed with the burthen of sinne, are oftentimes reclaimed from their wickednes with the horror of Death, Iudgement, and the paines of Hell: but the vertuous sort, and such as serue Almighty God rather for loue then feare, are wholy set on fire with the loue of their

Redeemer

Redeemer through the remembrance and meditation of his
Death and Passion. Secondly,
because nothing doth so easily
present it selfe vnto our vnderstanding, as the meditation of
the paines, torments, sorrowes,
and tribulations, wherewith in
our whole life we are enuironed,
and beset on euery side. As for
Heauen, Hell, and the last Iudgment, because they are not subiect to our sight, and seeme to be
a farre off, we doe not sufficiently
conceiue or apprehend the same:
but for the afflictions of the body
and the anguishes of the minde,
we vnderstand oftentimes by experience more then wee would.
Thirdly, because I know no meditation to be more acceptable to
our blessed Sauiour, then that
which

which wee conceiue of the bitter
passion, that hee suffered for vs.
For as a *Conqueror* doth reioyce
at the remembrance of his bat-
taile, so we may well thinke, that
Christ our Lord is delighted,
when wee doe often remember his
Passion; both because by so bloudy a combat hee hath obtained
a perpetuall and renowned victory both for himselfe and vs; and
also because herein hee seeth our
thankefulnes which wee render
vnto him for so great a benefite.
Fourthly, because I perceiued
that the meditation of no other
thing could bee so necessary for
Man-kinde, as of that, from
which alone is deriued vnto vs
the remission of our sinnes, our iustification, our workes of merite,
and our whole saluation: Which
certainly

certainly is the principall cause,
why the Catholike Church, according to the institution of the
Apostles, hath ordained that the
memory of this Passion should by
sundry wayes be so ofte iterated;
as, by making the signe of the
Crosse with our handes; by Pi-
ctures and Images of the Passion, which the Laye people are
accustomed to vse in stead of
Bookes; by fasting on Fridayes
and Saterdayes; by the yearely
celebritry of the Passion in the
end of Lent; by Sermons, by
Lessons, by sounding of Bells and
such like, yea Christ himselfe
hath instituted a most sacred and
daily remembrance of his Passion, to wit the holy Sacrifice of
the Masse, wherein his death,
and shedding of his bloud is most
clearly

clearly reprefented vnto vs.
Fiftly, becaufe greater vtility
redoundeth vnto vs by thefe
Meditations, then by the contemplation of any other thing
whatfoeuer. For as all good
thinges are purchafed for vs by
the merites of our Sauiours Paf-
fio, fo in the fame as in a wel fur-
nifhed fhop all precious wares of
vertues and good examples are
to bee found.

But that you may more eafily
reape thefe fruites; I thinke it
requifite to propofe vnto you certaine aduertifements touching
the beft manner of Meditation.
For many ar· deceiued, which
thinke it is fufficient to repeat in
their mindes the hiftory of the
Paffion, or by confideration therof to feele an inward delight;
whereas

whereas notwithstanding, that auaileth little to their saluation, if withall, the affection and will bee not thereby mooued. For meate neuer satisfieth a man, if hee onely looke vpon it, and doe not put it into his mouth, chewe it with his teeth, and let it downe into his stomacke. The knowledge indeed of the History is the ground of Meditation, and the discourses of the vnderstanding doe affoord the matter, but all the profite consisteth in this, that the will, which beareth the greatest sway in man, bee moued with many affections : for she onely meriteth, she onely loueth, she onely directeth all our thoughtes, and actions towards God.

Therefore to comprehend all in fewe wordes, those which haue
treated

treated best of this matter of Meditation, haue designed and set downe vnto vs seauen affections of the minde, which may bee moued with this consideration of the Passion : To wit; Compassion, Compunction, Imagination, Thankesgiuing, Admiration, Hope, and the Loue of God. Which I will explicate vnto you briefly and in fewe wordes, to the end you may vnderstand, after what manner you may bee imployed with profite in these ensuing Meditations. For by these seauen wayes, as by seauen teeth, the matter ministred by these Meditations may bee chewed, and with the affection tasted, and disgested.

Compassion.

The first therefore is Compassion, that is, an affection of the

the minde, by which we participate of other mens griefes, and
afflictions, feeling the same
though not in body yet in minde:
by which affection, the griefe of
the Patient seemeth to bee diuided and communicated with another, and is thereby greatly
mittigated and asswaged; as on
the contrary side it is much augmented and increased, if either
we deride him, or bee not moued
with his afflictions. Christ our
Sauiour, to diminish our sorrowes, would suffer for vs, and
condole also with vs, as the A-
postle saith : Wee haue not a
High Priest, that cannot haue
compassió on our infirmities,
but tempted in all thinges by
similitude, except sinne. And
truly although we cannot lessen

by

by this our sorrowe the most grieuous and exessiue sorrowes that
our Sauiour suffered for vs; yet
this our compassion is most gratefull to him, whereby we make his
dolours ours, and apply his suf-
frings vnto our selues. Wherefore
the Apostle hath said very rightly: We are coheires of Christ,
yet if we suffer with him, that
we may be also glorified with
him. For hee that will not bee
a partaker with Christ in his
sufferings, cannot be a partaker
with him in his kingdome. There
are two thinges which are most
availeable to prouoke this commiseration: First the condition
of the person, that is to say, his
nobility, his goodnesse, his piety
towards men, and such other
things, which doe aggrauate the
indignity

The Preface.

indignity of his inflicted miserie.
Secondly, the cruelty and immanity of his torments. If therefore
we desire to feele in our hearts
this comiseration, we must consider in euery article, First, who
it is that suffereth: As first,
that it is God, who with his Maiesty filleth Heauen and Earth;
secondly, a most honorable man,
descended of the house of Dauid,
and conceiued by the holy Ghost
in the wombe of the Virgine;
thirdly, one most learned in his
vnderstanding, and most holy in
his will, who by no error or sinne,
did euer offend either God or
man; fourthly, most graue and
sober in his conuersation, being
neuer seene to laugh, but often
to weepe, and that for our sinnes;
fiftly, more beautifull in his body
                                    then

then all the sonnes of men, and
of a more tender and delicate
complexion. Secondly wee must
set before our eyes the greatnes
of his torments, and with what
particular payne euery member
was afflicted. Considering first,
that all the sences of his body, and
all the powres of his soule sustayned their proper and peculiar tortures. Secondly, that his torments were most grieuous, both
by reason of the most tender con-
stitution of his body, and also because he wanted all interior comfort to indure the same. Certainly it is the vndoubted opinion of
all Diuines, that neuer any creature indured such paynes and
torments as our blessed Sauiour
did. If we see a wicked man suffer such punishment, as he hath

most

The Preface.

most iustly deserued, we cannot but be moued to compassion and griefe: and if we see but a Dogge or an Asse cruelly whipped or beaten, we are presently touched with commiseration. Ought we not then to condole with the Son of God, suffering so vnspeakable tortures, and that for our sakes?

The second affectiō is, Compunction, or sorrowe for our sinnes, when we are induced to an horror and detestation of our sinnes by the remembrance of our Sauiours passion: which may easily be done, if we ponder what the malice of sinne is, and what torments it hath drawne vpon Christ our Sauiour. As God is infinite, so the malice of sinne, which is committed against God, is also infinite: and this malice

in

Compun-
ction.

in the iustice of God (which ought
not to be violated) could not by
any satisfaction be taken away,
but by that, which was infinite.
Wherfore either an infinite paine
was to be endured, which no finite
creature could endure; or for an
infinite time, which the damned
in hell endure; or by an infinite
person, which is God himselfe.
Hence let vs proceede, and consider, what it was that drewe
God from Heauen to earth. and
induced him to vndergoe his
passion; which was nothing else
but our sinnes. For if man had
neuer sinned, God had neuer
been incarnated, neuer suffered,
neuer dyed. Wherefore, like as
for the sinner, his sinnes prepare
a place in hell; & for the thiefe,
his theft prepareth his punishment:

ment: *so for our bleſſed Sauiour our grieuous ſins haue procured a neceſſity of ſuffering death. The malice therefore of ſinne is aboue all things to bee deteſted, which cauſed euen our Lord God himſelfe to bee crucified. But leaſt thou ſhouldeſt imagine per-happs, that the grieuouſneſſe of ſinne is heereby extenuated, be-cauſe Chriſt did not ſuffer for thy ſinnes alone, but for the ſinnes of all the world; be thou aſſured of this, that the malice of ſinne is not thereby diminiſhed or impai-red, but the ſingular vertue of our Sauiours paſſion is declared, which hath waſhed away the ſins not of this or that man, but of all the men in the world. For the me-rite of his paſſion is infinite, and no malice whatſoeuer is able to*

counter-

counteruaile it : which thing a-
lone doth sufficiently discouer
the grieuousnes of sinne, because
without the infinite merite of
Christ it could not be forgiuen.
As therefore if one only man see
the Sunne, it will shine no more
to him alone, then it would doe to
him, and all other men together ;
and as a man doth no lesse kill
another when alone he stabbeth
him to the heart, then if he should
take ten or twelue others to assist
him in the same : so euen one
mortall sinne (for redeeming
whereof the death and passion of
the Sonne of God was necessary)
is no lesse the cause of our Sauiours death, then all the sinnes of
the world ioyned together. Neither doth the passion of our Sauiour bring vs lesse profite, being
vnder-

The Preface.

vndertaken for the vniuersall saluation of the world, then if it had beene vndertaken for mee alone.

    The third affection is Imitation, *whereby wee desire to followe and imitate those rare excellencies, which we discouer in* Christ, *as the Apostle teacheth vs :* Christ suffered for vs, leauing you an example, that you may followe his steppes. *And againe :* Christ hauing suffered for vs in the flesh, be you also armed with ȳ same cogitatiō. *There are two thinges principally to bee imitated in our Saniours Passion. The one is a desire to suffer for vs. The other is, a great heap of vertues, which appeared so plainly in this his Passion, that though our Saniour*

our

Imitation.

1Pet. 2.

1Pet.4.

our spake nothing, yet by his example from the Pulpit as it were
of the Croſſe he taught all kinde
of vertues; yea and taught them
moſt perfectly, both for that hee
was deſtitute of all interior comfort, which doth ordinarily ac-
company our vertuous acts ; and
alſo becauſe there wanted not
meanes, whereby hee might haue
reſiſted his Paſſion. Wherefore
in euery Meditation wee muſt
ſearch out, Firſt, what vertue is
chiefly cōmended vnto vs therein ; Secondly, how our Sauiour
exerciſed the ſame ; And laſtly
wee muſt ſtirre vp a deſire, and
firme purpoſe to obtaine that
vertue , deuiſing the meanes
whereby it may bee acquired, &
imploring the aſſiſtance of our
Sauiour to accompliſh our intēt.
Chriſt

The Preface.

Christ in his *Passion gaue vs a patterne of all vertues, but especially of those which the Scriptures doe so often commend vnto vs.* Of which the first is Humility, *whereby being most bitterly scoffed at, cloathed in a white and purple garment, crowned with a crowne of thornes, lesse esteemed then the murtherer* Barrabas, *crucified betwixt two Theeues, and suffering many other mockings and contempts, he alwaies humbly behaued himselfe.* The second is Meekenes, *whereby he euer shewed himselfe milde and gentle to all men, endured torments most patiently, was silent in all reproches and iniuries; neuer vsed any excuses, neuer offended any body with his language or froward actions.*

The

The Preface.

The third is Obedience, *which then deserueth greatest commendation, when hard things are commanded, & by wicked men. Christ was not onely obedient to*

Phil. 2.

his Father euen vnto death, yea the death of the Crosse; but also to wicked Iudges and torturers, whome he obeyed simply, cheare-fully, and constantly, when hee put off his garments, put on the purple, receiued the Crowne of Thornes, caryed his owne Crosse, stretched out his hands and feete to be nayled, and did many other things that they cōmanded him. The fourth is Charity, *which then onely seemeth to be perfect, when as for Gods sake wee loue, not onely our friends, but also our enemies, esteeming them not our enemies, but our friendes.*

Which

Which our Lord *seemeth to haue performed most abundantly,* when *speaking of his most perfect loue towards vs, hee* said, No man hath greater charity then this, that a man giue his life for his friends. *For albeit, it may seeme greater charity to yeild our life for our enemies; yet that charity is indeed most perfect which acknowledgeth no enemies, but reputeth those for our friends, which are our enemies, and doth good no lesse to them then to our friends.* Now Christ was *so tenderly affected towards his enemies, that the more iniuries and wrongs he receiued at their hands, the more his loue encreased towards them, and the greater benefites he bestowed vpon them; like vnto fire,*

¶ 2   *which*

which the more it is blowed, the hotter it burneth. Therefore in the whole time of his passion he prayed vnto God his Father for his enemies. For this that they should loue me, they detracted from me, and I prayed in minde but not in voyce, *But whē he was fastned to the Crosse, and the bloud ranne out of thē foure fountaiues of his hands & feete, then with a loud voyce he prayed for them that crucified him: & at the last when he yeilded vp his spirite, he moued with exceeding charity the heartes of the standers by to faith and penaunce.* The *first* is Mercy, which is the daughter of charity. By this our Lord gaue vnto vs his garments, honour, fame, estimatiō, flourishing age, strēgth, health,

Psal. 108

fifth

The Preface.

health, & life. The sixt is Contempt of the world, *by which he refused all thinges which the world admireth, and accounteth good; and tooke vpon him those things which the world abhorreth; for riches choosing pouerty, for honours contempt, for pleasures paines, for comme dations mockings. The seauenth is* Perseuerance, *through which being neither ouercome by his Mothers sorrowes, nor moued by the heauines of his friends, nor conquered by the derision of his enemies, nor wearied with the torments of his body, he would not come down from the Crosse, which he had ascended for thy saluatiõ.*

The fourth is Thanksgiuing, *by which, pondering the benefites bestowed vpon vs, wee breake*

¶ 3   *foorth*

The Preface.

foorth into praiſes, not in wordes
onely, which is the leaſt praiſe,
and action of thankes, but rather
in heart and workes; that weighing in our mindes the great benefite beſtowed vpon vs, we ſhould
eſteeme much thereof, and take
heede of all offending our Benefactor, and omitt no occaſion in
all things to requite it. There are
fiue thinges, which doe moone
much vnto this thankefulneſſe.
Firſt, the euill, which we haue eſ-
caped. Secondly, the good, which
we haue receiued by the benefite.
Thirdly, the worthineſſe of our
Benefactor. Fourthly, the manner of the benefite beſtowed. And
fiftly, the condition of the perſon
vpon whome the benefite is beſtowed. Therefore that we may
be moued to thankefulneſſe, wee
muſt

must consider : first, the euills,
which we haue escaped through
this passion of Christ ; as sinne the
greatest of all euills ; blindnes of
minde ; hardnes of heart ; bon-
dage of the druill ; fowlenes of the
soule ; the present perill of eter-
nall fire, so grieuous, as can-
not be conceiued ; so long, as it
hath no end ; so certaine, as
without Christ it cannot bee a-
voyded. Secondly, the goods,
which we haue gayned; as grace.
iustice, the adoption to bee the
sonnes of God, Sacraments, Sa-
crifice, vertues, the promise of
euerlasting life, and to be briefe,
all the goods both of body and
minde. For there is no good thing
in mans life, which the passion of
Christ hath not either giuen or
preserued. Thirdly, the dignity

of the person : for euen as we vse
to allowe a greater stipend to a
Nobleman, or Doctor, for a
small office, then to a plaine country man, for a great labour : so
we ought to be more thankefull
to the more worthy person. How
thankefull then shall we bee to
Christ, who is of infinite dignity?
Fourthly, the manner of the benefite bestowed, to wit, gratis,
and not without great labour.
God made Heauen and Earth
without any trouble by his onely
word : but thee he redeemed with
paynes, bloud, and his owne life :
and for all these benefites he requireth nothing of thee, but
praise and thankefulnes. Fiftly,
the condition of the person, vpon
whome the benefite is bestowed ;
if base, if an enemy, if ingrateful.

What

The Preface.

What are we then ? If (as the wise man sayeth) The whole world before God is as a drop of the morning deawe, which falleth vpon the earth : *What in comparison of God shall one silly man be, who being compared with the whole world, & with all the multitude of men is nothing.* Holy Iob *hath expressed our basenesse* : I said to rottennes, thou art my Father; and to the wormes, my Mother & my Sister. *Now, we are not only base, but we were also enemies, estranged, & averted frō God, neither seeking, nor desiring his grace, but rather reiecting it, when it was offered. When therefore thou shalt consider, first, that thou art deliuered from the greatest, most certain, & euerlasting miseries ;*

Eccle.11.

Iob.17.

¶ 5 *second-*

secondly, that thou art indued with most high and infinite goods: thirdly, by the most mighty God, of infinite maiestie ; fourthly, with so great labours and paines, as neuer any mortall creature sustayned: thou canst not choose but thinke, whether it is fit, that so abiect a creature should bee dissolued into praise & thankesgiuing.

Hope. *The fift is conceiuing* Hope. *By the consideration of three things our hope is much shaken and weakened. First of the purity which is required for eternall* **Apoc. 21.** *life, into which nothing defiled or vncleane shall enter. Secondly, of the strict examination of the Iudge, who will demaund an accompt of euery idle worde, and will reach euen vnto the diuision of*

The Preface.

of the soule and the spirit, and will search out the cogitations & intentions of the heart. Thirdly, of our basenes, who both offend the iustice of God with our dayly sinnes, & liue full of concupisence & imperfections, & do not enter into the inward cogitations of our hearts. And if I be simple (saith Iob,) euen this my soule shall not knowe. To this diffidence the Passion of Christ giueth help and remedy, and lifteth vp the hart of a sinner to confidence and hope. For first, as the glory of eternall life requireth great cleannes : so the Passion & blood of Christ washeth away all our iniquities; it causeth our soules to be more bright then the Sunne; it maketh vs the sonnes of God, it giueth vs right vnto euerlasting life,

Heb. 4.

Iob. 6.

life, that now we goe not into a strange, but into our owne inheritance. Secondly, the iudgement of Christ is very strict; but the merits of the Passion of Christ can wel beare the seuerity therof; because the satisfaction is greater then the debt; and our sinnes being in number infinite, his merits are in value infinite; and to be briefe, he shall be our Iudge, which was our Aduocat, Mediator, and Redeemer, who, that he might giue vs heauen, payd the price thereof for vs, that is to say, his bloud, which he shed for our sinnes, being not ignorant of the value and dignity of that which he shed with so great paine and labour. Thirdly our basenes is very great, being able to doe nothing of our selues; but

his

The Preface.

his grace being communicated vnto vs through the merite
of his Passion, addeth an admirable splendor and brightnes to our
soules, remitteth all our sinnes,
giueth vs strength and power to
worke, and addeth such dignity
to our workes, as to bee able to
merit euerlasting life. Therefore
our hope will be much confirmed,
if we consider, that all the wealth
of Christ, all his merits, all his
fastings, labours, paines, and, to
be briefe, all that euer he did, or
suffered, is ours, no lesse then the
goods of the husband belong vnto
the wife, which she may vse for
the payment of her debtes, and
her other necessities.

The sixt is, the Loue of God.
And first the nobility & beauty
of the thing beloued stirreth vp
the

Loue of
God.

The Preface.

the affection of Loue; euen as we
are enflamed with the defire of
vertues and fciences through
their beauty and excellency. Secondly, Loue, when we fee our
felues firft beloued. And to increafe this Loue, it anayleth
much: Firft if wee fee the loue of
our Louer prooued, not onely by
wordes, but alfo by great benefites. Secondly, if hee procured
thefe benefites for vs by his owne
great labour and difcommodity.
Thirdly, if we often repelled him,
and did him iniuries, and yet his
loue was not diminfhed thereby.
Fourthly, if by all his labours &
troubles he defireth nothing but
to bee beloued againe. All thefe
hath Chrift done for vs in his
Paffion. Firft hee loued vs in
deede and truth, and gaue vs all
                            good

The Preface.

good thinges. Secondly, hee to his
great discōmodity became poore,
that hee might inrich vs; and
tooke vpon himselfe all euills,
that hee might replenish vs with
all goodnes. Thirdly, being so
often repelled by vs, hee abated
nothing of his Loue. Fourthly,
hee requireth nothing of vs, but
our Loue. Loue (saith hee)and
it is enough. Moreouer, that
thou mayest loue, thou must obserue the Lawes and conditions
of a Louer, which Christ expressed in this his Passion. The first
is, that we alwayes thinke of that
which we Loue; and this by the
example of Christ himselfe, who,
because hee would neuer forget
vs, ingraued vs in his owne
handes. Secondly, that we speake
often of it : for Out of the a-
                    boun-

Mat. 12.

boundance of the heart the mouth speaketh : *and this also by the example of Christ, who on the very Crosse spake to his Father of vs, and prayed vnto him for vs.* Thirdly, *that we feare nothing more, then to offend him whome wee loue, as Christ hath taught vs, who referred his Passion, and all that hee had to this end, that hee might induce vs to loue him.* Fourthly, *that we bestow all our labours and indeauours to helpe our freind : for Christ laboured not for himselfe, but for vs.* Fiftly, *that we should desire to bee alwayes with our friend : for* The delight of Christ is, to bee with ỹ sonnes of men, *who hath sought vs, in Sea and Land, in the Ayer, & in Hell; that hauing fonnd vs hee might*

The Preface.

might ioyne vs with him in euerlasting blisse, and communicate
his Diuinity vnto vs.

The seauenth and last māner
of meditating vpon the Passion
proceedeth from Admiration.
This Admiration is commonly
prouoked by some newe, strange,
and incredible accident. Now,
there are fower thinges, which
shew the Passion of our Sauiour
Christ to bee exceeding admirable. First, because hee suffered,
whose Maiesty cannot suffer, who
is the glory and ioy of Saintes,
whose dignity is infinite, whose
life is eternall, & whose Power
is incomprehensible. Secondly,
because hee suffered for them, by
whom he was punished, base men
enemyes, and vngratefull persons.
Thirdly, because hee suffered so
many

Admirati-on.

many tormēts, as neuer any mortall man indured, aswell if you consider the torments themselues as also his ignominyes, his irrisions, his pouerty, and other miseryes of his life. Fourthly, because when hee redeemed Man-kinde by his Passion, he vsed admirable meanes for the fulfilling thereof. For first, with the great weakenes of his body hee ioyned great power, wherewith hee beat downe and ouerthrewe the Deuill the Prince of this world. Secondly, hee ioyned perfect Iustice with perfect Mercy: for taking compassion vpon man, hee suffered the rigour of Gods Iustice vpon himselfe. Thirdly, his excellent Wisdome shined foorth in that, which to men seemed exceeding folly: For the Crosse of Christ

to

The Preface.

to the *Iewes* is a scandall, and 1 Cor. 2. to the *Gentiles* folly. Great wisdome also it was ; First, to o-uercome his most subtill enemy by *Art* and *suffering*, and to cast him downe with the same wea-pons, by which he had ouercome. Secondly, to deliuer vs by such a kinde of punishment, in which he might lay vp for vs a medicine for all diseases, and set before our eyes an example of all vertues, and kindle the flames of *Loue* in vs. For nothing doth so much in-cite vs, either to the imitation of *Christ*, or to the loue of *God*, as this bitter *Passion* of our Lord. And thus much shall suffice to haue spoken of affections.

Now that wee may vse these Meditations with fruit & profit for the saluation of our soules, these

The Preface.

these few thinges ought to bee obserued. First, that wee come not vnprepared to meditate, but (as the wise man aduiseth vs) Let vs prepare our soule before prayer. Which preparation consisteth in this, that laying away all will to sinne, wee commit our selues wholy into the handes of God, and put out of our minde all externall cares and cogitations, and pray vnto Christ very earnestly for his grace, that we may obtaine wholsome fruite by this meditation. Secondly, that first of all wee read the Euangelicall text of that Meditation; & then th meditation it selfe either in whole or in part. Thirdly, that we lay aside the booke, and repeat in our memory, what wee haue read; and consider what affections

ons

Eccl. 18.

ons may bee *stirred vp thereby*, and labouring to excite, and moue them in our selues. Fourthly, that we breake forth into some speach and prayer vnto God, through that affection, which is now stirred vp in vs; and that we either praise, or admire God, or pray for the forgiuenes of our sins, or for some other benefite : or (to bee briefe) that we speake those thinges, which our minde so moued shall dictate vnto vs. It will profit vs also to begin first at the beginning of these Meditations; both because we shall better vnderstand the History of the Passion ; and also that by little and little we may proceed from the lesser to the greater.

Also to the end that these Meditations may bee more gratefull and

The Preface.

and profitable, I haue incerted
nothing, which is not sound and
approued, because the vncertain-
ty shall not diminish the authority, nor be a hindrance to deuotiō.
For nothing is affirmed in this
History, but what the Scriptures
say, or the Fathers confirme, or
traditiō vndoubtedly deliuereth.
The documents thē selues, which
are iorned to these meditations,
are for the most part taken out of
the auncient Fathers, or out of
the later Writers, which haue
written best of the māner of meditating vpon the Passion of our
Lord. I haue drawen out some
Meditations of purpose somwhat
long, especially such, as are either
of great force to mooue our affections, or may bee vsed seuerally
for Sermons; as namely, those of
the

The Preface.

the seauen words, which our Lord
spake vpon the Crosse. For I was
desirous in this Booke, not onely
to set foorth the manner of contemplation, but also to helpe the
Preachers themselues, that they
may teach the people profitably,
and stirre vp their mindes with
diuers Meditations.

And I haue thought good to
dedicate this my labour to you,
my best beloued brethren & fel-
lowes, as to those, whose peculiar
institute is to honour and receiue
the blessed body of Christ our
Lord in the most holy Eucharist,
and to defend the honour thereof
against the blasphemyes of wicked Heritikes : that comming to
Christ his most Holy table, you
may (according to the Coman-
dement of our Lord) repeate in
your

The Preface.

*your memory his Passion, Death
and Buriall; and make your bodyes fitt Sepulchers for the body
of our Lord; & with your mindes
render vnto him praise, and
thankesgiuings: and to be short,
being inflamed with the loue of
him, who gaue himselfe wholy for
you, you may likewise imploy your
selues wholy in his seruice, and
the helpe of your neighbours. To
conclude, I pray you that in re-
compence of this my Labour, yee
will vouchsafe to offer vp your
prayers to our Blessed Sauiour
for mee, that by his grace I may
bee partaker of those benefites,
which by his Death and Passion
hee hath purchased for vs.*

Farwell.

Your Seruant in Christ.
Francis Costerus.

✠

IHS.
Of the Passion of our Lord.

The first Meditation of his going out of the house from supper.

The Hymne being said Iesus went foorth beyond the torrent Cedron according to his custome, and his disciples followed him.

Mat. 26.
Mar. 14.
Luc. 22.
Ioan. 18.

CHRIST beganne his passion first from prayer : Secondly from his going out of the place of supper, both because hee would not be apprehended as an eater & drinker, but as one

B   praying

praying vnto God, and the patrone of man-kinde, and also because his Host with whom he supped should sustaine no dammage by his passion, which ought to profite all men and to hurt none. Thirdly, he went beyond the torrent *Cedron*, by which way in old time *Dauid* fled from his sonne *Absolon*: A torrent in the holy Scriptures signifieth the incõmodious things of this life, as in this place, *My soule hath passed the torrent*: all which calamities being very great, our Sauiour ouercame with exceeding constancy of minde. Fourthly, he went into the Mount *Oliuet*: Mount signifieth excellency, and Oliue Charity. Heere do thou

2 Reg. 15.

Psal. 125

thou confider that Chrift beganne his paffion with great,
earneft, and feruent prayer,
with much cõftancy of mind,
and exceeding charitie, in
which vertues he was well ex-
ercifed, as appeareth by thefe
wordes (*according to his cuft-
ome.*) He inuiceth thee likewife to the fame vertues
when he caried his Apoftles
with him : For except thou
beeft diligent in prayer, except thou auoydeft the perils
of euil occafions, except thou
makeft a refolute purpofe, except thou beeft enflamed with
the loue of God, and, to bee
briefe, except thou doeft diligently vfe vertues, thou fhalt
neuer ouercome thy temptations. Follow then our Lord

with his Apoſtles, and pray
him that he neuer leaue nor
forſake thee.

Then he ſaid to his Diſciples

Mat.26.
all yee ſhall ſuffer ſcandall in me
in this night. For it is written,
Mar. 14.
I will ſtrike the Shepheard and
the Sheepe of the flocke ſhalbe
ſcattered : but after I ſhall riſe
againe I will goe before you into
Galilee.

CHriſt in his paſſion tooke
the beginning of his
griefes from his Diſciples,
who ſeeking to ſaue them-
ſelues by flight, did all either
wauer in faith, or openly deny our Lord : Conſider euery
word, (*All*) Firſt not one
ſhall ſtand for me, (*yee*) Secondly, whome I haue be-
ſtowed ſo many benefites vpon,

on, & loued so dearely *(shall suffer scandall)* that is, shall sinne being estranged from me, and none of you in this time of my passion shall bee free from sinne : yee shall suffer scandal, but I will not giue it *(in me)* of whose wordes and deedes after the sight of so many miracles ye can iustly take no manner of offence : *(in this night)* that is, by and by, or in the night of ignorance. Now call thy wits vnto thee, and marke whether these same things may not happen vnto thee, I say, vnto thee, on whome God hath bestow'd so many good things at whose counsailes & deedes neuerthelesse thou takest offence, for that trouble of thy

B 3   vicious

vicious minde in aduersity is
referred vnto Chrift our lord,
who either fendeth them, or
at the leaft permitteth them.
But fuch kinde of fcandall ri-
feth alwaies in the night, that
is, from thy blindneffe; for if
thou wouldeft all at once
looke vpon the benefites re-
ceaued at Gods hands, & the
rewards prepared for thee,
and the euills which thou haft
committed, thou wouldeft
refolue in thy minde neuer to
be moued with any aduerfity.
Confider heere the caufe of
thy offence and fcandall, I fay,
thine owne euil and troubled
will, and pray vnto God, that
he will lighten thy darkneffe,
becaufe thou haft neuer any
iuft caufe of anger & difcon-
tent.

tent : Chriſt promiſeth that he
will goe before them into
Galilee, in which promiſe hee
declareth his owne goodnes,
who neuer foretelleth any
afflictions, without hope of
conſolation. Admire heere
the benignity of Chriſt, and
pray him that he neuer ſuffer
thee to be tempted aboue thy
power, but that he will en-
creaſe his grace in thy temptation, that thou maiſt be able
to ſuſtaine it.

    And Peter *anſwearing ſaid* Mat.26.
vnto him, although all ſhall be Mar.14.
ſcandalized in thee I will neuer
be ſcandalized : Ieſus ſaid vnto
him Amen, I ſay vnto thee, O
Peter, *that in this night before*
the Cocke ſhall twiſe giue foorth
his voyce, thou ſhalt deny me
    B 4   *thriſe :*

thrise : Peter *said vnto him,
although it behoued me to dye
with thee I will not deny thee :
and al the disciples said the like.*

THe Apostles after the
Cómunion of the body
of our Lord had made a firme
resolution to liue well, and
were feruent, and followed
Christ, as thou often times, especially after the receauing
of the holy Euchariſt, doſt se-
riouſly resolue to amend thy
life, but in time of conſolation thou muſt also thinke
of the time of deſolation, and
of the expectation of contrary things, leaſt thou shouldſt
desiſt from prayer through
vain confidence; resolue therfore to doe well, but before
God, & praying for his helpe,
be

be vigilant and obserue all
thine owne actions; be not
rash nor negligent, for if the
prince of the Apostles did slip
being the foundation & rock
of the Church, who spake
confidently out of his loue
and charity, how can he stand
that through pride and ambition, or for some other cause
hath too much confidence in
him selfe, & that doth seldom
resolue to amend his life, nor
set God before his eyes ?
Contemplate heere also that
the sorrow of Christ was not
small, to leaue his Disciples
whome he loued so dearely,
troubled & sorrowfull for his
departure. This place is very
fitte to meditate vpon those
things which a man feeleth in

time of confolation, as quiet-
nes of minde, ioy, illuftration
of the vnderftanding &c. And
contrarywife on fuch things
as he feeleth in time of defo-
lation, as perturbatiõ, fowre-
neffe, and darkneffe of vnderftanding, to the end that he
may in time of profperity propofe vnto him felfe fuch good
things, as in aduerfity he fhall
not change. Pray vnto Chrift
that hee neuer forfake
thee in time of
aduerfity.

The

The second Meditation
of his entrie into the
Garden.

Then came Iesus with them into a village which is called Gethsemani, where was a garden, into which he entered and his disciples.

BEhold the place where Christ began his passion : First neare vnto a village or farme : Secondly, in *Gethsemani,* which signifieth a fatte valley: Thirdly in the Garden: For through sinne we got an vnclean village, that is, worldly and frayle things, which by their own instinct and nature slide down to the earth again, and Christ would begin our redēptiō from thence, whence we were fallen through sinne.

Geth-

Mat. 26.
Mar. 14.
Ioan. 18.

Gethsemani or the fatte valley
as it doth rightly signifie the
valley of mercy, so it doth
plainly declare that the passió
of Christ had neede of great
mercy and clemency, which
changed this world being
full of miseries, into a place
flowing with mercy. Consider then that this world is like
vnto a durty valley, in which
is much durt and filth, with
which men being polluted do
forsake God, but to such men
as follow Christ, this same
world is like a shop of the
mercies of God, & of our merites, in which so long as we
liue mercie is offered aboundantly, and such rewards gotten by good workes as neuer
shall haue end : But it was a
garden,

garden, wherin Chriſt prayed;
r *Adam* ſinned in a garden,
& in a garden wee haue all offended: For what is the world
but a little garden, pleaſant to
behold, wherin diuers herbes
and faire flowers doe delight
the eyes, but not the minde:
All things which the world
admireth are buds & flowers,
which, as they take their beginning from the earth, ſo in
a ſhort time they wither a-
way: to be briefe, Chriſt caried his Diſciples foorth to the
place of his paſſion, being the
laſt place to which he lead his
Apoſtles, that thou maiſt
knowe thereby that Chriſt
doth earneſtly require of thee
that with great diligence and
ſtudy thou ſhouldſt meditate
and

and imitate his paſſion. Pray
vnto thy Lord that thou maiſt
deſpiſe this world, which was
all the cauſe of the paſſion of
Chriſt.

Mat. 26.
Mar. 14.
Luc. 22. *Then he ſaid vnto his Diſci-*
ples, ſit heere, whilſt I goe yon-
der and pray, pray yee leaſt yee
enter into temptation.

COnſider, that if thou wilt
not enter into temptati-
on, that is, if thou wilt not be
ouercome and ſwallowed vp
by temptation, thou muſt ſit
downe and pray; but wee ſit
when we enioy quietneſſe of
minde, and that inward peace
which true humility bringeth,
(for he which ſitteth hum-
bleth his body that he may
reſt in quiet) we muſt pray,
becauſe by prayer victory is
obtained

obtained aginst the Deuill,
and we must pray as long as
Christ prayeth for vs. Heere
againe consider thine owne
slouth and sluggishnes, which
art not touched in conscience
when as Christ is carefull for
thee how thou maist be saued,
and sitting at the right hand
of his Father prayeth still for
thee: To enter into temptation is, to be occupied and
drowned in wickednesse both
inwardly & outwardly; for he
which is ouercome by têptati-
on hath neither inward peace,
nor câ enioy any true outward
comfort, where euery thing
oppresseth the minde, but nothing can satisfie it; whereup-
on also it followeth, that he
which in this world entereth
into

into temptation, shall in the next enter into Hell, euen as hee which in this world is in Gods fauour shall afterwards enter into the ioy of God.

And he tooke Peter, & Iames, and Iohn *with him.*

Mar.14.

COnsider with what great griefe our sorrowful lord left his other sorrowfull Disciples, he tooke these three for his companions with him, that he might open his heauinesse vnto them, who onely amongst all his disciples sawe his glory in the Mount *Thabor,* and who were present at the wonderfull myracle of the daughter of *Iayrus* the Archsynagogue being raysed vnto life, for by how much a man is more perfect, and neerer ioyned

Mat.17. Mar.9.

ioyned vnto God, so much
the more he feeleth the force
of the passion of our Lord in
himselfe,as Saint *Paul* confesseth of himselfe : Consider
therfore what manner of men
these were whome Christ
chose for his companions,
Peter the Pastor of the
Church, *Iohn* a Virgine, who
afterwards should be the keeper of the Virgin his Mother,
and *Iames* the first Martyr of
the Apostles : That heereby
thou maist vnderstand that
nothing doth so much lighten
our cares, ease the labours of
any office, encourage vs to
chastity and to other vertues,
to be briefe, nothing helpeth
man so much in al his labours
vndertaken for Christs sake as
the

the memory of the paſſion of
Chriſt : he tooke vnto him alſo his two Coſins, that thou
maiſt ſee, to what dignities
our Sauiour exalteth his beſt
friends, to wit, to ſuffer innumerable calamities in this life
that hereafter they may haue
the greater rewards in the life,
to come. Doe thou deſire rather to be afflicted in this
world for thy ſinnes, then after thy death to be ſeparated
from Chriſt with euerlaſting
puniſhment.

The third Meditation of
the great perplexitie of
Chriſt in the Garden.

And he began to feare, to
waxe weary, to be ſorrowfull,
and to be ſad.

Mat.26.
Mar.14.

BE-

BEcause that finnes are firft committed in heart before they be done in worke, Chrift would fuffer the forrowes of heart before the paines of body, that thou maift know that he was grieuoufly afflicted not onely in body, but alfo in minde, and there are foure principall kindes of forrowes affigned by the Euangelifts, which Chrift admitted of his owne will in the Garden, and retayned them euen till his death : The firft was a certaine terror and feare of the moft grieuous paines now at hand, and alfo of a moft terrible death, which nature alwaies abhorreth beyond meafure, & alfo of the finnes of all man-kinde which

which he tooke vpon him in
the Garden, and cloathed
himselfe therewith as with a
garment weaued of all kinde
of filthinesse, with which in
the person of all sinners he
must suffer the seuerity of
God. The second griefe was
loathsomnesse, being weary
of all things in this Life, seing
himselfe forsaken not onely
of all men, but also of his heauenly Father. The third was
sorrowfulnesse first , for the
grieuous sins which the *Iewes*
should commit in his death,
and also for the small number
of them which should be per-
takers of this his so great affliction, and likewise for the
vnfaithfulnesse of thee and of
other Christians, who by their
blaf-

blasphemous words and grieuous sinnes should shed and
defile the most precious bloud
which he was now ready to
offer for them. The fourth
was sadnesse, that is, a grieuous trouble or anxiety of
minde, when he sawe there
was no meanes for him to escape : For of the one side the
commaundement of his Fa-
ther, and the great loue of
man-kinde encouraged and
pricked him forward; and on
the other side nature feared
and repugned. These foure
affections Christ tooke vpon
him, that he might prepare a
medicine for sinners who are
troubled with the like passions : For they which are not
content with any estate liue
in

in continuall wearinesse and loathsomnesse; & they which are alwaies pricked in conscience liue in perpetual sorrow; and they which are troubled with the remébrance of death liue in continuall feare; and they passe their life in sadnesse and doubtfulnes which know that their sinnes shall be examined by the strict iudgment of Christ, which happenneth chiefely at the houre of death, when Christ our Iudge standeth at our doores. Doe thou pray vnto our Lord that those his afflictions may bring vnto thee fortitude, ioy, alacrity, and security.

Mat. 26.
Mar. 14.

And he said vnto them, my soule is sorrowfull euen vnto death.

Let

LEt vs weigh euery word wisely: for he doth not say, my soule is fearefull, or I am weary of life, or my soule is doubtfull, least; he should seeme to goe to his passion rather against his will, then willingly: but he saith (*it is sorrowfull*) not onely for the sundry causes of sorrowe , but that therby he might shew that he was very man that suffered. (*my soule*) he doth not say I am sorrowfull, because his wil reioyced and was desirous to dye, but , my soule, that is my nature, which neuer moued his will. Againe, (*my soule*) that is, griefe hath inwardly entered into my soule; least perhappes you might thinke through the continuall contemtemplation of his diuine nature, that he felt no griefe in his foule. (*Euen vnto death*) that is, either becaufe that forrowe continued vntill his death, and no longer, or elfe becaufe it was fo vehement that mans nature could endure no more without perill of death. Pray vnto our Lord that this his forrowe may bring life vnto thy foule.

Mat. 26.
Mar. 14.
Luc. 22.

Stay yee heere and watch with me, and he was drawne away from them, and he went as farre as the caft of a ftone.

Confider firft what euery one muft doe in his troubles, to wit, he muft ftay, that is, expect patiently, and hee muft watch, that is, he muft be carefull that no euill happen vnto

vnto him; for to an vnquiet &
troubled man many vicious
and euil things are suggested.
Consider secondly how vn-
willingly Christ left his disciples. For this worde *(drawne
away)*discribeth a violent pulling, and going,hee went not
farre, but *(as farre as the cast
of a stone)* like as m others are
wont to goe a little way from
their young children , when
they teach them to goe, so as
they may catch them againe,
when they are ready to fall.
All these thinges declare the
loue of Christ,& his greeuous
inward sorrowes , by which
hee was moued to pray vnto
his Father,that he might haue
some comfort from him. Bee
thou moued with the sor-

      C   rowes

rowes of Chriſt thy Lord, who was forſaken of all men, & becauſe he loueth nothing better then to bee with thee, apply all thy endeauours, that he may alwaies remaine with thee.

The fourth Meditation of the firſt prayer of Chriſt.

And kneeling downe hee fell on his face vpon the ground, and prayed, if it might bee, that, that houre might paſſe from him: Saying, O my Father, if it may bee, let this cup paſſe from me: but yet not as I will, but as thou wilt.

Mat. 26.
Mar. 14.
Luc. 22.

COnſider firſt the cere-mony which Chriſt v-ſed in this praier: For he kneeled downe on the ground,

ground, as one guilty of death
for thy ſinnes; hee fell down
vpon the earth, proſtrating
himſelfe to be ſacrificed for
thy ſaluation, & repreſenting
(whoſe perſon hee had now
taken vpon him) the moſt abiect eſtate of ſinners, who as
they are vnworthy to looke
vp to Heauen, ſo lying vpon
the earth with the weight of
their ſinnes, they are worthy
to bee troden & trampled vpon by all men. Conſider ſecondly his wonderfull affection in this prayer, and the
force of euery worde, (*My
Father*) that is, I am thy Son,
that muſt ſuffer moſt bitter
paines for moſt vilde men: O
father, wilt thou not ſpare me
thy only begotten Sonne? (*If*

C 2   *it*

it may bee) hee vnderstandeth
that sauing Gods iustice, there
was no other meanes left for
the redeeming of man-kinde,
but onely by the death of the
sonne of God. Consider heer
in thy minde the loue of God,
who spared not his own Son,
that he might spare thee. *(Let
passe from me)* This prayer was
to escape so cruell a kinde of
death. Yet in these wordes
there lyeth hidden some secret meaning, as if hee should
say, I would not that this affliction should remaine in mee,
but that the fruit thereof may
passe vnto all Christians : I
will drinke, and they shall bee
satisfied: *(This cup)* he calleth
his passió a cup, as that which
containeth the cause of all our
ioy.

ioy. And eeuen as those torments made Christ as it were
drūken with ẏ greatnes of his
loue, so all iust men are made
drunk with ẏ heat of the loue
of God throgh the mediatiō
& merite of ẏ passiō of Christ.
In this place wee may call to
minde the quallities of excellent wine, when men drinke
plentifully therof: for by wine
the inward partes of man are
warmed, it maketh men mer-
ry, it causeth sleep, it lifteth vp
the heart, it maketh men elo-
quēt, & it is drūken with ease
and pleasure: Apply all these
things to ẏ passiō of our Lord,
which Christ begā with great
charity, sustained with cheer-
fulnes, & as one besides himselfe became foolishnes to
C 3   the

the Gentiles, & scandall to the Iewes, and so his charity was not onely diminished by his paines (as in men it often hapneth,) but rather inflamed, euen as stones by rubbing wax hotte : And to be briefe, our Lord was laid asleep in death. If thou, when thou sufferest any thing for Chrifts fake, dost feele the like affections in thy selfe : be thou assured that the passion of Chrift shall bring much profit vnto thee. Consider thirdly the forsaking his owne will in so hard a case, and offer thyselfe ready for all thinges, and defire of God to graunt thee a will indifferent in all occasions.

Mat. 26.
Mar. 14.
Luc. 22.

And when he was risen, from his prayers, hee came to his disciples,

*ciples, and found them sleeping,
and hee said to* Peter, Simon,
*sleepest thou? couldest thou not
watch one houre with mee?*

Consider first : Christ was
troubled, & his disciples
slept, the Church suffereth, and
wee grieue not thereat. Thou
also how slack art thou oftentimes in the seruice of God, &
how earnest in thy priuate busines. Consider secondly that
after a short prayer, our Lord
rose presently vp , as if for
griefe of minde hee could not
stay long in one place, desirous to haue some comfort,
sometimes of his Father, and
sometimes from his disciples.
Euery word spoken vnto *Peter* hath force : (*Simon*) hee
saith not, *Peter*, which newe

name signifieth constancy, but
Simon, his auntient name: So
in euery Christian may bee
found a new name of the sons
of God, with which being
indued they sinne not; and a
name of nature, by which
they are accounted frayle
men, and subiect to many vices. (*Doest thou sleepe?*) *Peter* is reprehended, not for a-
ny great fault, but because he
slept: and belieue thou, that
God valueth much the least
faultes, which thou dost com-
nit. (*Couldest thou not ?*)he
teacheth vs to labour, & be
diligent in doing good works
though they be hard, seeing
that temptations, infirmity of
nature, and such like, which
wee pretend for excuses,
                              shall

shall not excuse vs. (*Our how-er*) he toucheth the short-nesse of time, wherein wee must labour : And where he saith *(watch)*he sheweth the easinesse of the seruice of God, in which is onely re-quired of thee, that thou shalt watch, that is, that thou beest watchfull in all thy actions, to wit, that in all thy sences thou beest carefull, and watch-full, least the Deuill creepe into thy minde: *(with me)*that is, not alone, but hauing me for thy guide. Heere exa-mine thy conscience what he-therto thou hast done for Christ, and what labours thou hast taken for the world, and now at the least referre all things to the glory of God,

C 5   which

which thou doeſt for the world, and pray him that hee will be thy guide in thy ſpirituall warfare.

Why doe you ſleepe ? watch and pray, leaſt ye enter into ṫēptation, the ſpirit truely is ready, but the fleſh is weake.

Mat.26.
Mar.14.
Luc.22.

COnſider firſt the ſharpe reprehenſion of the diſciples after the admonition of *Peter:* for thou ſhalt not therfore be excuſed, becauſe thou doeſt offend in imitatiō of thy Superior. Conſider ſecondly that thou muſt watch & pray, for except thou doeſt worke with God, & God with thee, thou ſhalt doe nothing. Conſider thirdly what that ſp rit is which is ſaid to be ready, and how the fleſh is weake; Firſt, the

the spirite, that is the will of a
good man is ready, & doth often apprehend very notable
thinges. Secondly, ỹ holy Spirit is prompt & ready, but men
being allured by the pleasures
of the flesh doe not alwaies
follow and obey it. Thirdly,
the euill spirit is alwaies busie
and ready to hurt; but we are
weake to make resistance.
These things may worthily
moue thee to watch and pray,
for it is a matter of great moment not to bee deiected in
time of aduersity. Pray vnto
Christ to giue thee not only a
ready and willing desire; but
also power to effect, and to
graunt vnto thee whatsoeuer
he commandeth, & command
what he will.

The

The fift Meditation of the second & third prayer of Christ.

He went away again the second
time, & prayed the same speach,
saying, Abba father all things
are possible vnto thee: if thou wilt,
transferre this cup from me, but
yet not mine, but thy will be done.

CHRIST, acknowledgeth,
that he hath not yet ob-
tained that, which he prayed
for, therefore he prayeth the
second time : becaufe thou
shalt not be grieued, if thou
art not heard by & by, which
art neither so worthy a persō,
nor so earnest a prayer. Marke
euery word of this prayer,
(*Abba pater*)that is, Father, father, which repititiō is a signe
of a moſt vehement calling to
him which is farre off. God
truly

Mat. 26.
Mar 14
Luc 22.

truly is farre off from sinners ;
wherefore wee must say with
Dauid (*Out of the depth I haue
cryed vnto thee O Lord, O lord
heare my voyce :*) And because
Christ in this place did repre-
sent the person of all sinners,
which hee had now taken vpon him, knowe thou that our
heauēly Father is a louing Father of all sinners , that when-
soeuer thou shalt fall into sin,
thou shalt not be dismayed
therewith. And he doth not a
little comfort vs, when he addeth (*all things are possible vnto
thee*) for nothing is impossi-
ble or hard vnto God : & this
word (*if thou wilt*) doth expres
that God can easily helpe vs,
and that he needeth not to
work or labor, because by his
wi!l

will only he can doe al things.
And the reason why he will
not, when we pray vnto him,
is, because through his continuall loue towards vs, he gui-
deth al things to our saluatiō.
Now ioyne these three toge-
ther(*Father*)which word im-
porteth the loue of God:(*All
thinges are possible*) whereby is
declared his omnipotency:(*if
thou wilt*) by which thou seest
the easinesse to performe it, &
thereby thou shalt take great
cōfort of thy sorrowes : It is ŷ
surest way in all prayer to lay
aside our owne will, for God
wil guid thee much better according to his wil, when thou
dost not interpose thine owne
iudgment & sences .Pray therfore vnto God that he will direct

rect thee like vnto a plough
Oxe, without thine own will.

And he came againe & found
them sleeping, for their eyes were
very heauy, and they knewe not
what to answeare him, and lea-
uing them he went away again.

Onsider first how often
Christ doth visite his Disciples, wherby he sheweth the
passing griefe of his minde,
who receiued no comfort by
his prayer, though hee prayed
with great affection, nor yet
could be refreshed by the presence of his Disciples, euen as
sicke folkes are wont to turne
this way, and that way to ease
their wearines. Consider secondly that Christ was neuer
so troubled with any occasions, no not now, whē he was
                            ready

ready to suffer, but that he alwaies thought vpon thy saluatió: Yea & euen now, when
he is in Heauen, hee hath his
eyes alwayes bent fauorably
towards thee. Cósider thirdly
how little man can doe without Christ, how soone he falleth a sleepe, how soone hee
fainteth if Iesus depart neuer
so little from him. Consider
fourthly what it is to haue our
eyes heauy, that is, when wee
are not so apt & ready to meditate on diuine and heauenly
thinges ; by reason of earthly
cares which hinder the mind :
As the immoderate desire of
honor & riches, ambition, the
vanities of this world, & such
like affections of the minde :
Therfore thou must pray vnto
God

God to take from thee that
slouthfulnes & heauines, and
accómodate thee to his owne
will. Cósider siftly how much
ashamed the Apostles were,
who being admonished now
the second time, could not yet
contain themselues fró sleepe;
wherfore amongst themselues
they did carefully both accuse, and excuse their own infirmity : Note also this, *(they
did not knowe, what they should
answere vnto him.)* For if the
Apostles themselues, being
men excelling others in sanc-
tity, &holines of life, in a matter of no great fault, wherein
they might haue aleaged their
owne frailty, were so sorrowfull, & knew not to answere :
what answer wilt thou giue to
                            Al-

Almighty God, when thou
shalt be cyted before him for
matters of great moment, and
many grieuous sinnes shall be
obiected against thee, which
thou hast committed, not only by frailty, but also craftily
& maliciously. Consider sixtly that our Lord did not complaine, that hee was left alone
in prayer and labor : Because
thou shouldest resolue not to
be grieued, if at any time thou
beest inforced to take great
paines, whilst others bee idle.
And pray vnto our Lord, that
hee will stirre thee vp, when
thou art slouthfull.

And hee prayed the third
time, & prayed the same speach,
saying, O my Father, if this
cup cannot passe from me, but
that

Mat. 26.

that I must drinke thereof, thy will be done.

COnsider first that Christ runneth againe to his Father, and crauing still one and the same thing is not heard. This prayer comprehendeth the wonderfull submission of Christ, yeelding himselfe, and all that he had into the hands of his Father, taking it in no euil part, that he was not hard. Learne thou hereby not to be troubled in thy minde, when things succeed not according to thy desire, when thou hast done thy best endeauours. Consider secondly the great necessity that Christ should suffer : For the eternall Father would neuer haue suffered his sonne to haue prayed so often

vnto

vnto him, if thy saluatió might haue been gottē by any other meanes. Consider thirdly this māner of speaking (*if it canuot passe, except I drinke it*) for hee would be vnderstood; that all ỹ benefit of our Lords passió ſhould paſſe vnto vs, who are the mēbers of his body, but as it were drawne through our mouth, that is, through Christ, who is our head. Moreouer as a potió is bitter & vnsauory to the taſt, yet very profitable for the mēbers of ỹ body : So the dolours of Christ were bitter vnto him, and profitable vnto vs. And ỹ passió of Christ paſſeth vnto vs, partly becauſe his merit is cómunicated and imparted vnto vs, and partly becauſe our tribulatiós & labors are sanctified. Therfore so of-

ten as thou shalt suffer any aduersity, so ofte do thou think,
that thou doest participate
with the passio of Christ. And
pray him to mittigate thy miseryes through his dolours,
which hee indured.

The sixt Meditation of his
agony,& bloody sweate.

*And there appeared vnto him an
Angel frō heauen, cōforting him.* Luc.22.

COnsider first, that though
in Christ ỹ diuine nature
was ioyned with humaine nature,into the same person; yet
in this time of his passion hee
tooke no comfort at all from
thence. Consider secondly
how great and grieuous those
torments were, that man was
not sufficient to mittigate
them, but that it was necessary for an Angel to come from

Heauen. Cõsider thirdly what
was ẙ cause why Christ wold
be comforted by an Angell;
to wit, because he wold know
to suffer with vs, when we are
afflicted, and teach vs not to
haue recourse to fraile & vain
delights, such as are cõmonly
drawn from creatures; but vnto spirituall, angelicall, & heauenly things. Cõsider fourthly that God neuer forsaketh
them, that trust in him . For
although he doe not alwaies
free vs from our troubles, yet
he doth euer giue vs his grace
and strength, that we may be
able to beare them. Consider
fiftly that Angells are alwaies
present at our prayers, therefore thou must be carefull
and diligent to worship them
being

being prefent, in a religious
and comely manner, and pray
vnto God according to the
Pfalme *(in the fight of Angells
I will fing vnto thee .)* Confider fixtly how the Angell did
comfort Chrift; for he did it
not by any inward comfort
or grace, (becaufe Chrift admitted no comfort in all the
time of his paffion) but vfed
fome outward wordes, wherin hee propounded vnto him,
both the abfolute neceffity of
fuch bitter paines , and the
great profite, that fhall come
thereby, and alfo the refolute
will of his Father, & the oracles of theProphets,&c.Con-
fider feuenthly whether there
bee any thing, wherein thou
maieft comfort and confirme
Chrift,

Epiph : in
ancorato
& Hærefi
69.

Chrift, and incourage him to doe fomething for thy fake : which will be effected, if he fhall fee thee behaue thy felfe well, & wifely to imploy the tallent, which he hath deliuered vnto thee, and that thou doeft indure thy labours couragioufly : For then hee will behold thee louingly & exalt thee to higher honour. In the meane time do thou pray vnto Chrift, to comfort and inftruct thee, not onely in outward words, but efpecially in inward vertue and wifdome.

Luc.22.   *And being in an agony, hee prayed longer.*

THis agony was a certain inward ftriuing, not of the flefh againft the fpirit, but of nature againft Death : and

in

in all this bitter time Chriſt
was to fight in three ſeuerall
cõflicts, and he was ſuperiour
in euery one. Firſt with nature,
abhorring to dye ſo cruell a
death : Secondly with the iuſtice of his Father, exacting
grieuous puniſhment : Thirdly with the moſt cruell enemy
of man-kinde. But hee began
with the battel againſt nature,
that thou mayeſt knowe how
to behaue thy ſelfe in thy cõ-
flict for thy ſaluation : that is,
that firſt of all thou muſt in-
deauour to ſubdue thy incli-
nation, & to reſtraine thy deſires, which being ouercome,
thou ſhalt finde God pacified,
and the Deuill will flye from
thee. Conſider firſt with
what contention, & with how

vince te-
iſſũ, et
regna.

D   great

great labour Chriſt thy Captaine doth fight; and doeſt
thou hope to bee ſaued without fight? Conſider ſecondly
that in this agony hee prayed
longer, becauſe thou muſt cō-
tinue longeſt in prayer in time
of affliction. Conſider thirdly what that is, which he deſi-
red in his long praier?not that
the cup might be taken from
him (for hee had before vſed
ſhorter wordes to that end)
but, ſince he muſt needes ſuffer, that thou mighteſt obtain
profite by his torments. Admire heere that excellent loue
of Chriſt, who alone is ẙ true
comfort of Angels. Lament
for thy ſinnes which were the
cauſe of his ſuffering, ſtirre vp
alſo in thy ſelfe the other affections

fections of loue, confidence,
& cōmiſeration, whereof this
place adminiſtreth aboūdant
cauſe.

And his ſweat was made like
droppes of bloud, running downe Luc.22.
to the ground.

COnſider firſt by the qua-
lity and quantity of his
ſweate the great griefe, of thy
Spouſe, without which neither the bloud could iſſue
with the ſweate, nor yet ſo
great plenty, as ſhould fall
downe to the ground. Conſider ſecondly that our Lord
both began, & ended his paſſion with a prodigious effuſiō
of bloud & water : That thou
ſhouldeſt knowe, that the diuine nature did bring this
chiefely vnto Chriſt, at that

D 2 time

time, that hee might the longer bee able to suffer those
most bitter torments, which
humane nature al alone could
neuer haue indured. Consider
thirdly that bloud issued out
of euery part, both because
euery member of the Church,
of which number thou art one
should lament the death of
Christ; and also because euery Christian might gather one
drop of his bloud, to wash a-
way their sinnes, and also that
thou mayest know, how liberally he offereth his bloud for
thee, by as many fountaines,
as hee hath members. Consi
der fourthly howe much this
great effusion of bloud and
water did weaken the most
tender body of Christ. Consider

fider fiftly that it ranne down
vpon the earth , to take away
the finnes of men, which are
adicted too much to the plea-
fures of the world.   Confider
fixtly that the droppes ranne
downe vpon the ground, that
thou mayeft vnderftand, that
thou muft make hafte, if thou
wilt bee partaker of this precious bloud, which no fooner
iffueth foorth, but that it runneth away moft fwiftly. Therfore except in this life thou
doeft gather, and lay vp fome
of this bloud, it will all runne
away after thy death, fo
as none will be
left
for thee.

✠

D 3   The

The seauenth Meditation
of the cōming of *Iudas*
with the Soldiours.

Mat. 26.
Mar. 14.

And he came the third time, and said vnto them, sleepe now, and rest, it sufficeth : the houre is come : Behold the Sonne of man shall bee deliuered into the handes of sinners, arise, let vs goe : behold he, that shall betray me, is hard by.

COnsider first that Christ hauing three times visited his Apostles, and found thē sleeping, did the first time reprehend them, the secōd time held his peace, and the third time bad them sleepe on : That thou mayest learne, first to beare with the infirmity of another ; Secōdly to assent presently to diuine inspi-

infpirations; for if Chrift perceiue that thou doft contemn
his admonitions, hee will afterwards holde his peace, and
more fparingly fuggeft thefe
things, which tend to thy fal-
uatiō. Thirdly that when thou
haft begun any good worke,
thou fhouldeft not wauer, nor
change thy minde : for Chrift
after hee had fubdued the in-
clination of nature, & had re-
folued euen againft nature to
dye, did not at any time after,
fhew any figne of forrow, in-
conftancy, or doubt. Confider
fecondly that Chrift framed
himfelfe to take a little reft or
fleepe with his Difciples, but
that could neither bee great,
nor long, efpecially in a man
fo ouerwearied, & fhortly af-

ter to be apprehended. Confider thirdly this word *(It suffereth)* as thogh he taught vs to
vfe a meane or meafure in our
reft and humaine cómodities.
Confider fourthly that this
word*(behold)*is twife repeated
becaufe it was a ftrange thing
that any man could be found,
which would betray the Son
of God & man. Cófider fiftly
(Arife let vs goe,) It is not e-
nough for thee, if thou doeft
not fleep, when Gods glory is
in hand; but thou muft arife,
goe forward,& preuent euils,
& fuffer all aduerfities couragioufly for Gods caufe. Heere
fhake off thy fleepe, and pray
vnto God, to ftirre thee vp
effectually to labour for his
names fake.

As

As hee was yet speaking, be-holde Iudas *one of the twelue* came : *And* Iudas, *which be-trayed him, knewe the place, be-cause* Iesus *had come thither of-ten with his Disciples.*

COnsider first that *Iudas* had no neede to be war-ned to watch; for it hapneth cōmonly, that when mischiefe is to be done, wicked men ne-uer sleepe. Consider secondly (*behold* Iudas *one of the twelue*) It is a strange thinge, that hee, who had receiued so great a benefite at Christ his hand, could euer come to that ma-lice, and ingratitude, that hee would betray his Lord & be-nefactor. Thou mayest learne hereby not to trust in guiftes freely bestowed vppon thee,

D 5   but}

Ma t.26.
Ioan.18

but how much the more God
hath beſtowed vpon thee, ſo
much the more to feare, becauſe God in the houre of
death wil weigh all his guiſts,
as ẙ Scripture here with great
emphaſis ſaith. *(Behold* Iudas
one of the twelue.) Conſider
thirdly that an euill man feareth not to abuſe good things
as *Iudas* came to the place of
the prayer of Chriſt to betray
him : how much better had it
bene for him to haue left his
treaſõ, & to haue ioyned himſelfe with Chriſt & his Apoſtles in prayer: Cõſider fourthly
that ẙ knowledge of many, yea
of diuine things, ſhal not help
a wicked man, but rather ſhall
condemne him, euen as it did
not help *Iudas* to haue known
Chriſt,

Chrift, and the time & place of
the prayer of Chrift, &c. In
this place if thou doeft confider thine owne ingratitude,
who hauing receiued many
good benefites , doeft reftore
nothing but wickednes, thou
wilt admire & deteft thy felfe,
& thou wilt pray vnto Chrift
not to fuffer thee to perifh
with wicked *Iudas.*

*Therfore Iudas, when he had
receiued, his company & the minifters, from the Priefts & Pha-
rifes : hee came thuther with lan-
thornes & torches, with fwordes
and ftaues & armour, fent from
the chiefe Priefts & Seniors of
the people, and hee, which was
called* Iudas, *went before him.*

Onfider firft what a great
company of men affem-
bled

Ioan. 18.
Mat. 26
Mar. 14.
Luc. 22.

bled together to apprehend
Christ: First a cōpany of ỹ *Gentils*, with their tribune, perhaps
fiue hundreth soldiours; then
no small number of the ministers of ỹ *Iewes*, with some of
the chiefe Priests, Seniors, and
Magistrates of the people :
there were therfore two companies, one of the *Gentils*, and
another of the *Iewes*, armed
with sundry weapons, & prepared to hurt : the ring-leader
& captaine of all these was he
(who was called *Iudas*) that is
that famous *Iudas*, who was
knowne to all those *Iewes* and
Gentils. Cōsider secōdly what
they talked among thēselues
as they came, what mindes
they bare towards Christ, &
how they thirsted after his
bloud.   Con-

Conſider thirdly this tytle of
Iudas (who was called Iudas)
that is, he which a little before
was knowne to the Diſciples,
and to good people, when by
the commandement of Chriſt
he diſtributed the almes, whē
he wrought myracles, when
he followed Chriſt, he is now
renowned   amongſt knaues,
and famous amongſt theeues.
Be thou carefull to celebrate
thy name in Heauen, rather
then in the world or in hell.
Cōſider fourthly what a grief
it was to Chriſt, to ſee him,
who was one of the principall
of ÿ Church to become chiefe
amōg knaues : & do thou take
heede, leaſt by the like change
of thy ſelfe, thou giueſt him
cauſe of ſorrowe, by falling
from

from being the sonne of God
to be a slaue vnto the Deuill;
and pray with all thy heart,
that it neuer happē vnto thee.

The eight Meditation of
the falling of the Iewes
to the earth.

*Iesus therefore knowing all
things which should come vpon
him, went forward, and said,
whome seeke yee? they answeared him, Iesus of Nazareth.*

CHRIST went forward to
meet them, that he might
teach thee, first that he was
not ignorant of the practizes
of the wicked : Secondly that
he made hast to die of his own
free wil:Thirdly that he is ready to receiue a sinner,if he wil
reclaime himselfe. Wherefore
stirre

ftirre vp thy felfe to the loue
of Chrift : and offer thy felfe
wholy vnto him, who yeilded
himfelfe cheerefully into his
enemies hands for thy fake.
(*whom feeke yee?*)as if he fhould fay, côfider I pray ye whom
ye feeke, a iuft & innocêt man,
who hath vfed to doe euery
man good, & to hurt no man,
who for your faluation def-
cended down from heauen, &
who at laft fhall come to be
iudge ouer all creatures. Doe
thou confider thefe things,
whenfoeuer thou fhalt be têp-
ted to offend God. For as the   Heb. 10.
blefled Apoftle St. *Paul* faith:
By finning the fon of God is trod-
den vpon, & ignominioufly vfed.
(*Iefus of Nazareth*) they
knew not that he was prefent,
for

for they did not fay we feeke
thee, but *Iefus of Nazareth*.
Note that for thee Iefus is
fought for, to be put to death,
that is,a Sauiour, and, of *Na-*
zareth, that is,flourifhing and
adorned with all vertue, for
none elfe by his death could
deliuer thee from the flames
of hell fire : Therefore in all
thy neceffity thou muft feeke
for him, and pray him that
thou maieft not feeke him to
his fhame and death, but to
thine owne faluation, and in
feeking thou maift finde him,
and hauing found him, thou
maieft alwaies keepe him.

Ioan.18.   *Iefus anfweared them: I am*
he : and Iudas, *who betrayed*
him, ftood with them : Therefore
as he faid vnto them I am he,
                      they

*they went backward, and fell
vpon the ground.*

COnsider first the power
of Christ, ouerthrowing a
whole company by his worde
onely. His wrath therefore is
to bee feared, when hee shall
come to Iudge, which shewed so great power being ready to suffer. Learne hereby to
esteeme much the worde of
God, which bringeth saluatiõ
to the beiieuer, & perditiõ to ỹ
incredulous. Cõsider secondly the miserable change of *Iudas*, who a little before sate at
our Lords table with the Apostles, & is now ouerthrown a-
mongst ỹ wicked: For neither
shall the dignity of thy order,
or religiõ excuse thee, nor the
goodnes of others defẽd thee,
                          nor

nor the piety of thy former
life profite thee, whenfoeuer
thou fhalt forfake Chrift, and
follow his enemies and finne.
Confider thirdly, that one and
the fame word is a comfort to
the good, and a terror to the
wicked : This word (*I am he*)

Mat. 26.
Ioan. 18

did comfort the Apoftles fay-
ling on the fea, prouoked the
Pharifees to watch, and heere
ouerthrewe the armed men.
Thou therefore, if thou beeft
good land, wilt receiue the
word of God with plentifull
fruit; but if thou beeft naught,
thou wilt take hurt by the beft
feede. Confider fourthly, the
difference betweene the ruine
of wicked men, and the fall of
the iuft : the wicked man falleth back, & not vpon his face
becaufe

becaufe when he fuddenly goeth out of this life, he falleth fhamefully vpon thinges which he feeth not ,and vnto punifhments , which he was ignorant of : For to fall vpon the face, is to acknowledge our fins in this life, & by pennance to lament them : The wicked man falleth backward becaufe he becommeth worfe by that, which fhould amend him, that euen againft his will he fhal be compelled to looke vp to heauen. Do thou admire the goodneffe of Chrift, who by fo many meanes fought the faluation of his enemies; and pray him that he will fo ftrike thy heart with his word, that falling vpó thy face thou maieft by humility reconcile the

D. Greg lib. 3 1. Mora, ca: 1 8. & ho. 9. in Eze-chielem.

the Maiesty of God, who is offended with thy sinnes.

Therefore hee asked them a-gaine: whom seeke yee? they say vnto him, Iesus of Nazareth: *he saith vnto them: I haue told you that I am hee: If therefore yee seeke mee, suffer these men to goe away, that the Speech may bee fulfilled, which saide: Because, whome thou gauest vnto mee; I haue not lost any of them.*

COnsider first the malice of the wicked, which is pacified, neither with sweetnes, nor punnishment. For the blindnesse of indurate malice doth increase: as in these men who being taught & admonished who Christ was, did not yet acknowledge him: For they answered not, wee seeke thee,

thee, but, speaking as it were
of another, they saide *Iesus* of
Nazareth. Consider secondly
ỹ great care, which Christ had
of his people, of whome in so
great perils he was more careful, thẽ of himselfe. This is the
perfect loue of our neighbors
to helpe them though it be to
our own losse. Thirdly if in so
great aduersity he had care of
a few Apostles, wil he not now
being free frõ all perils, & quiet, be careful in heauen for his
only beloued spouse ỹ whole
Church? Yes verily he is carefull & desirous to helpe euery
particular mẽber thereof. This
place is full of comfort, to cõsider that our Lord thinketh
on thee. Consider fourthly
how our Lord doth glory in
this, that hee had not lost any

any of his Diſciples. In like
manner how much cauſe of
ioy maieſt thou conçeaue, if
no man be the worſe by thy
words, example, or negli-
gence; but thou haſt rather
gayned, and preſerued many.
Laſtly pray thou vnto Chriſt,
that hee will neuer ceaſe to
haue care ouer thee.

The ninth Meditation of the kiſſe of *Iudas.*

Mat. 26.
Mar. 14.
*And the Traytor had giuen
them a ſigne, ſaying, whome ſoeuer I ſhall kiſſe, that is he, hold
him, and carie him warily.*

THe great name of an A-
poſtle wherewith *Iudas*
was honoured, is now turnẹd
into the name of a Traytor,
and ſo this name, *Iudas,* which
                        amongſt

amongst the ancient *Israelites* was most honourable, is become through detestation of that sinne, almost ignominious amongst Christians. This is the fruite of sinne, that good men auoyd all conuersation with the wicked. Consider the carefull diligence of this traytor, who least he should not haue his money, taught them the way how to apprehend him, and also how to keepe him, and so of a maister of vertue, he became a maister of iniquity : He was before sent, for the conuersion of people, now he teacheth others to destroy the Author of life. Thou doest learne heereby the qualitie of sinne, which resteth not in this, to make a

man

man a sinner, but proceedeth
further, to make him also a
teacher of wickednesse. Pray
thou vnto God, that he neuer
suffer thee to be drawne from
him, least thou fall into sinne
like *Iudas.*

*Iudas went before them, and
drewe neare, that hee might kisse
him, and comming presently hee
said, haile* Rabbi : *& he kissed
him.*

Luc. 2 2.
Mat. 26.
Mar. 14.

Eere admire the good-
nesse of Christ, who ad-
mitted him to kisse him, whō
hee knew to be a traytor. Neither do thou flatter thy selfe,
if thou beest called into Religion, or by Gods permission
exalted to diuine misteryes,
Ecclesiasticall offices, or Holy functions & dignītyes; because

cause Chrift doth fuffer thee,
as hee fuffered the kiffe of *Iudas.* It feemeth that the A-
poftles vfed to kiffe Chrift,
when they came from any
ftrange place : For otherwife
Iudas wold not haue dared to
doe it,& Chrift obiected vnto
the Pharifee,faying *(thou haft
not giuen mee a kiffe.)* Heere Luc.7.
thou mayeft learne the facili-
ty of Chrift in admitting finners, and his great defire to
bee with the fonnes of men.
Come therefore with great
confidence, for hee will neuer
reiect thee , who addmitted
a traytor. Secondly doe all
things fincerely,for he betrai-
eth Chrift with a kiffe, which
vnder pretence of holyneffe
decciueth his neighbours;
             E   and

and hee which receiueth the body of our Lord in the Eucharist, with an vnclean heart, is guilty of the body & bloud of our Lord, which hee putteth into the fowle sinke of his naughty conscience.

And Iesus *saide to him:*
Friend wherfore art thou come?
O Iudas, *doest thou betray the*
Sonne of man with a kisse?

Mat. 26.
Luc. 22.

MArke euery worde, *(Friend.)* First hitherto thou hast beene a friend: Secondly thou commest in the habite of a Friend, offering a kisse, a token of loue: Thirdly I doe not hate thee, but offer thee reconciliatiō, & am ready to shed my bloud & to offer my death also for thy sake, which I must now suffer, if

thou

thou thy selfe wilt. I desire
not that thou shouldst deliuer
me out of the handes of these
Iewes for I am borne to that
end to suffer death , but that
thou shonldest repent thee, of
this thy great sinne, & returne
into grace and fauour. *(Wherfore art thou come.)* First I am
not ignorant with what mind
thou art come hither, I haue
searched already into the bottome of thy heart : returne a-
gaine therfore vnto thy selfe,
for I thy Iudge am not ignorant of thy fraude.   Thou
wretch, whither art thou fallen ? Late an Apostle nowe a
traytor; of late a principal pil-
lar of the Church, now chief-
est amongst Thieues : behold
thine owne basenes, & now at
         E 2   least

least repent thee of thy fault.
(*Iudas*) If thou likest not thy
name of a friend, because thou
wilt not be a friend, yet heare
me calling thee in my accustomed māner. Secondly remēber thy ancient parents, *Iudas*
the Patriarch, and *Iudas Ma-*
chabeus, from whose manners
thou doest degenerate. (*The*
Son of man) him who is admi-
rably the son of man, begottē
in heauen by his only Father,
& borne in earth by his onely
mother, who did neuer any e-
uill vnto thee, but laboured
three & thirty whole yeares
for thy sake, & is now ready to
dye for thee: what cause haue
I giuen thee, that thou shouldest betray mee an innocent?
(*with a kisse*)thou doest abuse
ẏ signe of peace, & turne it to

a marke of treaſon ; as *Ioab* in
times paſt kiſsing *Amaſa*, killed him. Thou knoweſt, that
nothing is more deare to me,
then to be ioined in firme loue
with thee, & doeſt thou conuert this coniunction of loue
to my death?*(doſt thou betray)*
doeſt thou giue me to them,
that hate me deadly, which
will doe me all maner of hurt,
& which will neuer be ſatisfied with my miſeryes? Admire
in al theſe things the benignity of Chriſt & imitate it : ſuffer with thy Lord, who ſuffered ſo many indignities by his
ſeruant, on whō he had beſtowed ſo many benefits, and neuer hurt him in any thing ; &
cōſidering what, & how effectually he ſpake for the cōuer-
E 3   ſion of

2 Reg. 20.

of the wicked traytor, thou
mayſt be aſſured he will neuer
forſake thee, if thou commeſt
vnto him with a contrite hart.
Pray therefore to Chriſt, that
he wil remaine thy friend, and
giue thee grace to ſuffer al iniuryes patiently, and to loue
them, that offer any vnto thee.

The tenth Meditation of the eare of *Malchus* being cut off

Luc. 22.
Mat. 26.
Ioan. 18.

*They which were about him,
seeing what would come, saide
vnto him : Lord if wee strike in
the sword? & behold one of those
standers by, which were with Iesus, Simó Peter, drew his sword,
and striking the seruant of the
chiefe Priest, cut of his right
eare, & the name of the seruant
was* Malchus.   Con-

COnsider first : the feruor
of the Disciples, who be-
ing but a few in number, feared not to oppose themselues
againſt two companyes ; and
to aduenture preſent danger
in defence of their Lord : that
thou ſpare not thy ſelfe when
foeuer Chriſt his cauſe ſhalbe
handling. Secondly:(*And be-*
hold,) a new thing that the A-
poſtle of our Lord ſhould vſe
his ſword:Chriſt taught mild-
neſſe, not fight, which neuer-
theleſſe is to bee vndertaken, when Gods glory is in
danger. Thirdly *Peter* the
chiefe of the Apoſtles drew his
ſworde,whoſe office is to cut
off the rotten mēbers frō the
body of the Church with his
ſpirituall ſword. Fourthly,he

E 4   cut

cut of the right eare, because
all which are excōmunicated
by *Peter*, are excluded frō the
diuine promises of heauenly
things, & they keep ȳ left eare
with which after the pleasures
of this life, they may heare the
maledictiō of ȳ seuere Iudge.
Fiftly : (*Malchus*) (which
name signifieth King) is the
seruant of the wicked Priest :
for they which in this world
are delighted with vain tytles
of honours , are indeede the
bondslaues to vices. Consider
sixtly the power of Christs
word (*suffer these men to goe a-
way:*) For by the power therof
all that great cōpany of men
did his disciples no hurt at all.
Cōsider seauenthly the goodnes of Christ, who would not
suffer *Peter* to doe any more

harm, leaſt by his paſſiõ which
ought to profit all men , hee
ſhold ſeem to haue hurt ſome
mã. Pray thou vnto chriſt neuer to depriue thee frõ ỹ hearing of heauẽly things, nor to
ſhut thy eares againſt good
things, but rather to open the
eares of thy heart, that thou
beng deafe to the babling of
wicked men, maiſt heare what
our Lord ſhal ſay vnto thee.

And Ieſus anſwering ſaid, ſuf-
fer now : Then Ieſus ſaid vnto   Luc 2 2.
Peter , put thy ſword into thy
ſcabbard: For all which take the   Mat. 26.
ſword ſhall periſh with the ſword:
2. *Doeſt thou thinke that I can-*
not aske my Father , and hee will   Ioan. 1 8
giue me more then twelue legions
of Angels ? 3. *The cup which my*
Father hath giuen vnto me , wilt
          E 5   *thou*

Ioan. 18.

thou not that I shall drinke it?
Fourthly, how then shall the
Scriptures be fulfilled? because
so it must be done.

COnsider, first (*suffer now*)
that is, it is enough, proceede no further with thy
sword and defence. He doth
not reprehend the fact of *Pe-*
ter, but he saith it is enough,
that thou in thy defence and
in thy wrath maiest keepe a
meane: according to that, *Bee*
angry, and sinne not: Secondly
consider these foure reasons,
by which he admonished *Pe-*
ter not to goe about to hinder
his passion. Thou maist learne
heereby the willingnesse of
Christ to suffer, who vsed so
many reasons that he might
be permitted to suffer. But
thou

thou doest auoyd all troubles
for Chrilts fake, & feekeft out
all reafons that thou maift fuffer nothing. Thirdly (*which
fhal take the fword*)that is, they
which by their own authority
fhall vfe the fword, not receiuing it from God, deferue by
the law to be put to death;and
although they efcape ẏ fword
of men in this world, yet they
fhall perifh with that fword
which keepeth the entry into
Paradife : Learne to leaue all
reuenge vnto God. Fourthly
confider ẏ great multitude of
Angells, which are alwaies
ready to helpe good men,
that thou maift learne to truft
in God, which hath affigned
fo many Angells to haue care
ouer thee: For *Helizeus* had
experience

experience in him selfe of that
which Christ heere affirmeth
of him selfe : Confider fiftly
(the Cup which my Father hath
giuen vnto me:) He calleth his
paſſion a cup, thereby dimini-
ſhing rather then increaſing
the greatnes therof, that thou
ſhouldeſt not lightly cōplaine
of the grieuouſnes of thy mi-
ſeries : He acknowledgeth that
his father gaue it him; becauſe
thou ſhalt not aſcribe thy afflictions to men or to deuills,
but to God alone, which bleſſed *Iob,* who was vexed both
by deuills & men; *Our Lord*
hath giuen, our Lord hath taken
away, & know that God doth
not leaue to be a father, when
hee doth afflict, but rather
ſheweth himſelfe to be a Father,

4 Reg. 6.

Iob. 1.

ther, when he chastiseth. Sixtly
cōsider that the Scriptures are
fulfilled by ȳ passiō of Christ,
& are likewise fulfilled by thy
passions: For *through many tri-*
bulations we must enter into the
kingdome of God. Giue thankes
to Christ, who with so ready
& so prepared a minde came
to his passiō for thy sake. Stirre
vp his loue in thee, & pray him
that he wil stir vp in thee a desire to suffer for his name, and
that in all things, which shall
happen vnto thee, thou maist
finde out ȳ reasons that it was
iust which thou didst suffer.

And when he had touched Luc. 2 2.
his eare, he healed it.

Onsider first, with what
great benignity Christ
cured the Eare of this
malepert

malepert Soldiour, and cruell
enemy, whome he foresawe
would be neuer the better for
such a benefit, that thou maist
learne to be readier to mercy,
then to seuerity; and to doe
good for euill, though thy
aduersary deserue it not. Secondly the force of the touch
of our Sauiours hand, that
thereby thou maist know the
vertue of the body of Christ:
For if the onely touch of his
hand did restore his enimies
eare, will not his whole body
receiued in the Eucharist cure
both the body & soule of his
friend? Thirdly that Christ being ready to suffer, did heale
the eare; for this is one of the
chiefe fruites of the passion of
our Lord, to make our soules
capeable

capeable of the word of God,
& to cure them through Faith
and Sacraments. Therefore
God would admonish his e-
nemies by this his laſt miracle
before his death to open their
eares to heare the word of
God, and by hearing to lay a-
ſide all malice. To be briefe,
admire the bounty of God, &
pray him that he will ſhewe
thee the like mercy, for thy
innumerable ſinnes.

The eleuenth Meditation
of the captiuity of
onr Lord.

In that howre Ieſus ſaid vnto Mat.26.
the multitude, & to thoſe, which Mar.14.
came to him, the chiefe Prieſts,
the Magiſtrates of the people,
and the elders; yee went forth
                                    as

as to a thiefe with swords and staues to apprehēd me: I was daily with you in the Temple, & I sate teaching, & you did not hold me, nor stretch your hands against me: But this is your houre, & the power of darkenes : And all this was done that the scriptures of the Prophets might be fulfilled.

COnsider first what accoūt was made of thy Lord, to wit, as of a thiefe, for the suppressing of whome there needed so great an army Secondly how he shewed that he was no thiefe, as he which had hurt no man nor lyen hid like a thiefe, but had done good, and had taught nothing in secret, but alwaies publiquely, and called those men for witnesses thereof whome he saw

stand

stand ready to be $ officers for
his death, therfore he admoni-
sheth them to call to remem-
brāce $ doctrine which he had
taught thē, & to change their
mindes; for they should finde
nothing in it but holy, learned, & wholesome counsaile.
Consider thirdly by what
words he gaue his aduersaries
power to rage against him,
without which they could
haue done nothing, and euery
word hath his force: (*this is*) as
if he said, you care onely for
the present, & respect not the
time to come , which is the
property of sinners, not of
iust men : (*houre*) all present
time is short, all the pleasure
of sinners passeth like an
houre, also al $ afflictiō of the
iust passeth away : (*your*) this

this short time is granted vnto you to doe euery thing either for your saluatió or damnation : I say this precious time which afrer this life will not remaine, *(and the power of darknes)* that is to say a darke power, both because they deserue it through the darknesse of their sinnes, & also because they, which vse it, are carryed to the darknes of Hell, & also because darknes remaineth in the power of the wicked, and, to conclude, because power was giuen to the Deuils, the princes of darknesse to doe all mischiefe vnto Christ. Consi der therfore the multitude of the paines of Christ, and their greatnes when it was permitted to wicked Spirits being pract.

practised & most ready in doing hurte, to persecute Christ
by these his most willing ministers. Admire heere also this
most willing permission of
Christ, giue him thanks & offer thy selfe ready to indure al
labours and torments, for his
sake, & pray him that thy power may not bee in darknesse,
but that all thy actions may
be perfected with the light of
faith and of his diuine grace.

Then came the company and
Tribune, & the Ministers of the
Iewes & laid hands vpon Iesus,
and so they held & bound him.

C Onsider first the wonder-
ful insolency of these men
in taking thy Lord, & thinke
of the greatnes of their enuy,
whereby they desired to doe
                              all

Mat.26.
Mar.14.
Luc.22.

all mischiefe vnto Chriſt, and
that our lord had giuen them
power to ſatisfie their deſires.
The Apoſtle *Paul* was taken
with great cruelty, pulled out
of the Téple by force; preſétly
beaten with their fiſtes, & almoſt killed with ſtripes, but it
was nothing to this cruelty,
which ſurpaſſed all cruelty:
Conſider the antient predictions of this his captiuity : *Many clogs compaſſed me about, they
tooke me as a Lyon prepared for
his prey, caſting me downe, they
compaſſed me now about : they
compaſſed me like Bees, and they
burn:d like fire in the thornes :
being puſhed I was ouerthrowne,
that I fell.* Secondly marke the
words of the Euangeliſts : (*a
cōpany, the tribune & the Miniſters*)

Acts.22

Pſal.11
Pſal.16.

sters)not a few, but the whole
army laboured for this captiuity, euery one went about
some thing, (*they came*) they
leaped with great violence as
blessed *Gregory Nazianzene*
affirmeth.(*Laid hands on him*)
not onely apprehending him,
but grieuously beating him.
(*They held him*)as St.*Leo* saith,
they pulled him hither & thither, (*and they bound him*) O
how many cords were pulled,
not by one,but by many,both
because he should not escape,
and also because being seene
in such habit he might be iudged worthy of death by all
men. These bands were due
vnto thee for thy sinnes & except thou beest partaker of
them thou shalt bee bound
with

In Chri-
sto patiē-
te ser.7
de pas do-
mini.

with euerlasting chaynes in
hell. Suffer then with thy lord,
who was so cruelly bound for
thy cause, and endeauour to
be thankefull, and pray him
that by this his captiuity hee
will deliuer thee free frō al the
power of the Deuill, and from
all bonds of euill desires,
which according to the Deuills will might drawe thee
into any sinne, & restore thee
to spirituall liberty, *that being*
deliuered out of the hand of thy
enemie thou maist serue him.

Mat. 26.
Mar. 14.

Then all his Disciples leauing
him fled: but a certaine young
man did followe him, cloathed in
linnen vpon the bare : and they
layd hold of him, but he leauing
his linnen fled away naked from
them.

Consider

COnsider first, that heere are two things declared, whereby thou maist vnderstād the great fury & cruelty which was vsed in taking Christ, and carying him away : One was the flight of his most deare Disciples, who were stroken into so great a feare, that although they burned in loue with him, yet euery one of them fledd away : The other, that a young man in one of the next houses being moued with the tumult, rose out of his bed, couered onely with linnen, came foorth to see what was done in the streete, whome they thinking to bee one of his Disciples, would haue apprehended, but he leauing his linnen, fled away naked.

ked, whereby thou maift gather what a clamor they
made, as if their prey were
now taken; and how much
they raged and defired to hurt
all them, which belonged vnto Chrift: Confider fecondly
that Chrift was forfaken by all
his friends and followers, and
cruelly carryed away by the
hands of the wicked. Learne
heereby not to truft in men
which oftentimes in this life,
and euer in death doe forfake
all men; and pray thy Lord
that he neuer forfake thee; although thou beeft forfaken of
al men, efpecially in the houre
of thy death, when thou muft
goe iuto a ftrange countrye,
without the company of any
man with thee.

The

The twelfe Meditation of the acts in *Annas* house, and his sending to *Caiphas*.

And they brought Iesus first to Annas, *for he was father in law to* Caiphas, *who was the high Priest of that yeare : And* Caiphas *was he, which gaue counsaile to the Iewes: Because it is necessary that one man dye for the people* Io·11·49·

Ioan

COnsider first that Christ was brought to *Annas*, either because he should be caried to his <u>father</u> in law *Caiphas*, an old man, which should succeede ẙ next yeare in the high priesthood, and dwellling in the way to the high Priests house, or else for the traytor, to whome (as

F   Saint

Lib.11. in
Ioan. cap.
37.

Saint *Cyrill* saith) *Annas* was appointed by the Priestes to pay the reward of his treason, for the taking of our Lord. Behold thou the affections of euery man; the cruell ioy of this most wicked *Annas*, tryumphing that at the last his enemy was taken, the flattering congratulations of the Soldiours, the couetousnesse of *Iudas* hauing now receiued his money, the modesty of Christ nad his cheerefull minde to suffer for thee. Consider secondly that mention is here made of the counsaile which *Caiphas* gaue, for the puttiug of Christ to death; that it may be shewed that he persecuted his death who first gaue the counsell of his death.

Secondly

Secondly that thou maist learn
that al things which our Lord
suffered in his passion, did not
happen vnto him so much
by humane counsaile, as by
the will of God. For those
words of the death of our
Lord, although *Caiphas* vttered them out of a wicked
minde, yet he spake them by
the instinct of the holy Ghost,
who vseth to apply the words
of the wicked for the profit of
the iust, & that he might teach
thee, that God the Father in-
ioyned, & God the Son tooke
vpon him this cruell passion,
only for the loue of mākinde,
that thou again mightst be caried into y̆ loue of God with
all thy heart & minde. Thirdly that thou maist know, that

F 2　　　God

God neuer forgetteth finnes paſt, though perhappes they are out of thy minde. For all things are kept in memory, and an account ſhall be demanded at the houre of death.

And Annas *ſent him bound to* Caiphas *the high Prieſt, where the Scribes and Seniours were aſſembled.*

COnfider firſt, that Chriſt ſuffered many wrongs in the houſe of *Annas,* for this word *(hee ſent him)* ſignifieth rhat he did not lightly ſuffer him to goe away, but that he made ſome ſtay: But ſearch out with thy ſelfe what thoſe things were : For bleſſed *Cyrill* ſaith, that the blowe was giuen him in the houſe of *Caiphas,* and many affirme

t hat

that this word *(he sent)* should be taken in ỹ Hebrue for this word *(he had sent.)* Consider secondly what this word signifieth *(bound:)* to wit, that either he was newly bound, or else that his former bõds were not loosed, that he might bee accounted & condemned as guilty & worthy of bonds by ỹ iudgmẽt of this graue mã; But as the wicked Priest did take no compassion vpon him that was bound, so neither doest thou take any pittie vpon thy poore afflicted Neighbour, nor yet vpon thy owne soule, which is grieuously tyed with the bondes of sinnes. Consider thirdly this wearisome iourney, in which thy Lord was cruelly drawne with

F 3   cords,

with cordes, and whipped on
with stripes, whether soeuer
it pleased the wicked people
to carye him. He walked indeede the hard waies, that he
might make the way to Heauē
easie and plaine for thee, and
that thou mightest goe in the
way of ẙ Cōmaundements of
God without trouble. Cōsider
fourthly, and enter with thy
Lord into the counsaile of the
wicked. Behold heere many
Calues and satte Bulls com-
passing ẙ most innocēt Lamb:
(*the Scribes*) the Doctors of
the Lawe : (*the Elders*) the
Magistrates of the people :
(*the Pharises*) the religious
people of the Iewes, being
Gluttons, insolent, and cruell. Consent not thou to their
counsaile,

Psal. 2 1.

counſaile, nor their deedes;
but take the *poore out of the
hand of the mighty;* that God
alſo may haue mercy vpon
thee in the day of thy trouble.

And Simon Peter *followed Ieſus a farre off, and another diſciple : and that diſcip'e was known
to the high Prieſt, & entred with
Ieſus into the high Prieſts court:
but* Peter *ſtood at the gate without : Therefore the other diſciple
who was known to the high Prieſt
went forth, & ſpake to the porter,
& brought in* Peter *euen into the
Court of the high Prieſt, & being
come in, the fire burning in the
mideſt of the Court, and they ſitting round about it,* Peter *was in
the midſt of thẽ, & ſate with the
miniſters at the fire, that he
might ſee the end, and warme
him ſelfe.*   F 4   Con-

Ioan. 18.

Mat. 26.

Mar. 14.

Luc. 22.

Onfider firft whether
thefe flying Apoftles
went, being amazed
with fo great fury of the Soldiours, & now wauering and
doubtfull in their beleefe of
the diuinity of Chrift.   For
who would beleeue, that God
fhould euer fuffer fuch things
efpecially if, according to the
receiued opinion of the *Iewes*,
he thought that vertue fhold
be rewarded with temporall
goods.   Behold *Peter* following a far off, and louing more
then the reft, tooke fome courage vnto him, fo as he doubted not to thruft himfelfe into
the cõpany of the Minifters,
but yet fearefully and incon-
ftantly , hoping that hee
fhould not be knowne. Con-
                                    fider

sider secondly the other Disciple, either Saint *Iohn* as the common opinion is, the vnseperable companion of *Peter*, or else some secret Christian, a rich Citizen, who by reason of some acquaintance with the high Priest, did enter into the house, whilest *Peter*, as a poore and vnknowne man stayed without doores. For poore men are not admitted to come into the houses of great men, and if at any time they are permitted, it is accounted a great fauour to bee placed amongst their slaues. Bee not thou delighted with such a Court, neither thrust thy selfe into the company of wicked men : If necessity enforce thee, depart assoone as

thou canft, leaft thy innocency be defiled with the familiarity of wicked mē. Confider thirdly, that *Peter* came
not in directly, but through
the fauour of a friend ; and
of a woman. Seeke thou
therefore no honour by fauour or by the loue of women, nor yet by any vicious
or fraudulent meanes, leaft,
according to the example of
Peter, thou mayeft expect a
moft certain & affured down-
fall. Alfo if thou chanceft to
get honour lawfully, and art
entred into the Bifhops Pallace the direct way, doe not
ioyne thy felfe with the wicked, nor followe their examples, but enter into thine
owne heart, and fet our Lord
alwaies

alwaies before thine eyes,
who hath called thee to that
estate. Desire these thinges
of Christ, and pray vnto him
to drawe thee after him, and
not to forsake thee for euer.

The 13. Meditation of
the blow in the house
of Chayphas.

Then the high Priest asked *Ioan.18*
Iesus of his Disciples and of his
Doctrine? Iesus said to him: I
haue spoken openly to the world, I
alwaies taught in the Synagogue
and in the Temple, whether all
the Iewes assemble, and in secret
I haue spoken nothing: Why ask
you mee ? Aske them which
heard me, what I haue said vnto
them, behold these know, what I
haue spoken.

Con

Onsider first that when hitherto they had obsercued nothing in all the life of Christ worthy of death, nor yet of bonds, the high Priest began with certaine fraudulent interrogations to draw something out of his answers, which might bee obiected as a crime vnto him. For the ofience of Christ was not the cause of these bondes, but the enuy of the *Iewes*, of which enuy the Scripture in the booke of *Wisdome* numbreth fourteen causes: *Because hee is vnprofitable for vs, &c.* Secondly hee asked him of his Doctrine, whether it differed not from *Moses*, and of his Disciples, with what minde hee had chosen them, what

Doct-

Doctrine he had taught them, and what mindes they carried to the Lawe. Heere inquire thou the Doctrine of Christ, that thou mayst follow it, and of his Disciples that thou mayest immitate their manners. Thirdly Christ answeared boldly, nothing fearing the high Priest, nor that assembly of Noble-men; that thou shouldest not bee afrayd in Gods cause. But hee held his peace concerning his Disciples, both because he could not commend them, (and accuse them hee would not) that thou shouldest neuer hurt any manns fame; praise, if thou canst, but if thou canst not, yet detract not; and also because the question of his Disciples

ciples was mixed with the
question of his Doctrine, the
answeare whereunto satisfied
the high Priest. Consider
fourthly the purity of the doctrine of Christ, which our
Lord propounded to bee examined by his enemies. *(I haue
spoken openly)* Which is a signe
of the purity of his Doctrine :
(To the world) no man is bar-
red from the hearing thereof :
(Nothing in secret) nothing
impure, which neede to hate
or flye the light ; For those
things which I said in priuate:
I would haue published to all
men, & preached in all places.
Consider fiftly that it was accounted a fault in the high
Priest to be ignorant of those
thinges, which Christ had
taught

taught so openly. In the same manner many great and learned men will not goe to Sermons, either because they will not be pricked in conscience, or else because they are so ouerwhelmed with worldly cares, that they esteeme all things cócerning their soules vnnecessary. Doe thou meditate continually vppon the wordes of our Lord, and pray him that hee will alwaies put thee in minde of his wordes.

When hee had spoken this, one of the seruants gaue a blowe to Iesus, saying : doest thou answere the high Priest so? Ioan. 18.

COnsider first that this blowe was giuen, both because these very Seruantes were

were secretly pricked, which being sent to apprehend *Iesus*, returned home saying; *Neuer did man speake so:* And also of flattery, because it seemed not to be reuerently spoken to the high Priest: *(Why doe you aske me)* Proud and high minded men desire to bee dealt honorably withall, and will loose none of their titles; & yet they violate the name of God with many oathes, periuries, & blasphemies. Learne thou hereby that their are many ready to reuenge the wronges of rich and mighty men; but no man wil defend the cause of Christ and of the poore. Consider secondly the iniquity of this Iudgment, where euery one had power to hurt freely with

ap-

Ioan. 18.

applause and allowance of
the Iudges. Thirdly, that this
blowe was of great cruelty,
becaufe particuler mention is
made thereof aboue all other,
being many in number, which
our Lord had already receiued , and fhould afterwards
fuffer. Learne thou to beare
patiently the admonitions of
Chrift, and of other men, and
pray vnto God, that hee will
neuer permit thee to commit
any offence without reproouing thee, either by others or
by thy owne confcience.

Iefus *anfwered vnto him, if
I haue fpoken euill, beare witnes
of the euill : but if well, why
doeft thou ftrike mee.*   Ioan.18.

Onfider firft that Chrift,
who had taught his Dif-
ciples

ciples to turne the other
cheeke to him, that had stricken them, did heere nothing
repugnant to his owne Doctrine; both becauſe he did not
onely offer his cheeke, but his
whole body to bee whipped
and nailed; and alſo becauſe
in this place hee did not complaine, hee offered no iniury
againe, he made not any reſiſtance, but taught him, that
ſtrucke him, and modeſtly referred him to his owne conſcience. Secondly that our
Lord would not altogether
hold his peace, leaſt he might
ſeem to ſuffer ſomething iuſtly for his owne offence, who
ſuffered all thinges for our
our faults and nothing for his
owne. Admire heere and imitate

tate the goodnes of our Lord,
who would not reuenge so
great a wróg, neither in word
nor deed. And pray vnto him
for constancy and meeknes of
minde, that thou mayest bee
milde and humble of heart.

The 14. Meditation of
the denying of
Peter.

And Peter *sate abroade in
the Court below, whom when the
Mayd portresse of the high
Priest saw sitting at the light,
and warming him, & had beheld
him, shee said : And this man
was with him: & the mayd came
vnto him, saying : and art not
thou of the disciples of this man?
he said, I am not : and he denyed
before them all, saying : Woman*

Mat. 26.

Mar. 14.

Luc 22.

Ioan. 18.

I

*I know not the man, neither doe
I know, nor haue knowne, what
thou sayest : And hee went forth
before the court, and the Cocke
crowed.*

Onsider first that whereas
all the Apostles, (as our
Lord had foresaid) had suffered scandall, yet onely *Peters*
deniall is repeated by the E-
uangelists, and by all of them,
both because it seemed so
strange & incredible, that *Peter* could deny Christ, that
this his sinne could not bee
comprehended by the Euan-
gelists themselues ; and also
because many men marke the
faults of their superiours. And
lastly considering that he who
was the foundation of the
Church did sinne, that thou
shoul-

shouldest neither doubt, but
that the other Disciples suffered scandail, nor yet presume
of thine owne strength. For
no man committeth that sinne,
which another would not do;
if the guid be wanting, which
created man. Consider se-
condly when *Peter* denyed
Christ? In the night, & when
it was colde. If thou wilt not
behold the light of truth, and
conuert thy selfe wholy vnto
Christ, in thine owne conscience, and if the loue of God
and thy neighbour wax colde
in thee, doubt not, but thou
shalt fall into errors of faith,
or into more grieuous offences. Consider thirdly, where
he denyed? where Christ was
taken & bound, in the company

pany of wicked men, in spea
king with a woman : auoide
these occasions if thou inten-
dest to be holy. And although
St. *Cyrill* affirmeth that St. *Pe-*
ter denyed not Christ so much
through feare of any hurt,
which might happē vnto him,
as through a kinde of loue,
least hee should be thrust out
of the house, & so depriued of
his presence. Yet it is most
certaine, that he committed a
most grieuous sinne. Beware
thou, least vnder any colour of
deuotion or vertue, thou dost
transgresse the law of God &
of his Church. For euill is not
to bee done that good may
come therof. Cōsider fourthly that Christ is not denyed
by him onely , who saith that
Iesus

Iesus is not Christ, but also
by him, who being christened
denyeth himselfe to bee a
Christian, and the Disciple of
Christ, and this may bee done
not onely in wordes, but also
in deedes, by those which
professe to know God, but in
their deedes doe deny him.
For doest thou thinke (saith
Saint *Bernard*) that any man
thinketh *Iesus* to bee the Son
of God, who neither feareth
his threatnings, nor is moued
by his promises, nor obeyeth
his comaundements, nor al-
loweth his counsells? How
often then hast thou denyed
Christ, and yet hast not done
pennace with *Peter*. Fiftly ŷ
cocke crowed, but hee being
otherwise busied obserued it
not,

not, for our Lord did not yet
looke vpon him. Bee thou at
no time ſo ouerwhelmed with
buſineſſe or ſinnes , but that
thou alwaies attend the voice
of God ſpeaking in thee, and
that thou mayeſt heare thy
neighbour admoniſhing thee.

Mat. 26.
Mar. 14.
Luc. 22.

*But hee going out of the gate,
another Mayd ſaw him, & ſaid
to them, which were there : And
this man was with* Ieſus *of* Nazareth, *and another ſeeing him
ſaid: and thou art of them. But*
Peter *ſaid, O man, I am not,
and hee denyed with an oath, for
I do not knowe the man.*

COnſider firſt how Peter
burning in deſire to ſee
our Lord , who ſtood bound
before the Councell in an inward and higher Chamber,
did

did not goe out of the houfe,
but out of the lower roome, &
began to enquire fomthing of
Chrift: that thou maift deuife
and trie all waies & meanes to
inioy thy Lord in thy meditations, & to obtain him throgh
the workes of vertue. Confider fecondly, that where the
deuill doth once get the victo-
rye, he doth at his returne rage
more cruelly, and wound more
deepely. Firft there came one
maide, and fpake vnto *Peter*
fomewhat modeftly : Then
fome other feruants came to
that Mayde, and at the laft
a great number came together
and did as it were oppreffe
him with their wordes : wherfore *Peter* at the firft did onely
deny : Secondly he added an
G   oath:

oath : Thirdly he beganne to
curſe and blaſpheme. Take
thou heede therefore that the
Deuill neuer ouercome thee;
for he being once ſubdued by
the death of Chriſt, is driuen
away by reſiſtance onely, according to that ſaying, *Reſiſt*
the Deuill, and he will flye from
you. Conſider thirdly the fall
of *Peter :* Firſt he preſumed of
himſelfe : Secondly he ſlept in
the Garden : Thirdly he left
his fellowe Diſciples : Fourthly he thruſt himſelfe into company amongſt wicked men :
Fiftly he denyed. Therefore
the beginning of his fall was
preſumption, and the neglecting of the ſeruice of God.

And

ANd the space as it were of an houre being past, another affirmed, saying : *Verily and this man was with him; for he also is a* Galilæan : *Then they said vnto him : Whether art thou one of his Disciples ?* he denyed and said, *I am not, and they came which stood by, and said : Verily thou also art one of them, for thou also art a* Galilæan, *and thy speach doth make thee manifest : Then said one of the Seruants of the High Priest to him, his cousin whose Eare* Peter *had cut off: Did not I see thee in the Garden with him ? Then hee began to curse, to detest, and sweare, for I knowe not this man of whom yee speake : And foorthwith as hee was yet speaking the*

Luc. 22.

Ioan. 18.

G 2   Cocke

Mat.26.
Mar.14.

Luc.22.

Cocke crowed againe: And our Lord turned, and beheld Peter: And Peter remembred himselfe of the word of our Lord, as hee had said, that before the Cocke crowe twise, thou shalt deny me thrise, and Peter going out of doores wept bitterly.

Consider first, that when *Peter* was come againe to the fire, he beganne to speake more freely with the seruants, to the end that he might take away all suspition from himselfe: For by his speach hee was iudged to bee a *Galilæan*. Thou therefore who art the seruant of Christ take heede of familiarity with the wicked. Let thy communication bee of Heauenly things, as thou maiest perceiue the Apostles
speaches

speaches were in the Acts of
the Apostles, and by their E-
pistles : For he which is delighted with the vaine speaches of secular men, will easily
be drawn to imitate their mā-
ners, and to be warmed with
their fire, and intrapped with
their delights. Secondly, *Peter* was knowne by his speach
to bee the Disciple of Christ,
and a *Galilæan.* Doe thou likewise so gouerne thy selfe, that
all men euen by thy outward
cōuersatiō may know thee to
be the follower of Christ, and
a *Galilæan,* that is, one flying
from the worldly to a spirituall
life, and aspiring to Heauen.
Consider thirdly the benignity
of Christ towards his seruants.
He being opprcssed with so
G 3   many

many miseries, did as it were
forget himselfe, and take care
of his Disciple : He restrayned
him from sinning any deeper,
and caused him after his third
deniall to stay, beholding him,
not with the eyes of his body
(for that he could not doe,
being in an vpper chamber,
and compassed round about
with officers) but turning to
him with the inward beames
of his mercy; with which he
touched his heart, illuminated and mollified it. For the
beholding of Christ doth il-
luminate the Conscience, that
sinnes may be knowne, euen
as the beames of the Sunne
doe lighten a Chamber. Consider fourthly the order of his
Conuersion : First the Cocke
crowed :

crowed : Secondly our Lord
beheld him : Thirdly *Peter* remembred the word of Iefus :
Fourthly he went foorth :
Fiftly he wept bitterly : If
Chrift looke not vpon thee,
the Cocke crowes in vaine.
Doe thou therefore giue eare
vnto the Preachers and Ad-
monifhers, as vnto Cockes;
and pray that our Lord will
turne vnto thee. Obferue the
wordes which thou heareft :
Flye all occafions of euill,
and doe Pennaunce. Heere
thou being a moft grieuous
finner maieft haue greathope
of pardon, feeing that the
mercy of our Lord gaue fo
free pardon for this grieuous finne, that Chrift neuer
obiected it vnto *Peter*. But
G 4   thou

thou who haſt offended with *Peter*, goe not about to excuſe thy ſelfe with *Adam*, but weep with *Peter*, who (as St. *Clement* witneſſeth) did all his whole life time after the firſt crowing of the Cock riſe vp to his prayers, and ſlept no more that night.

The 15. Meditation of the falſe witneſſes in the houſe of Caiphas.

Mat. 26.
Mar. 14.

*B*Vt the chiefe *Prieſts*, and all the counſaile ſought falſe witnes againſt *Ieſus*, that they might put him to death, and they did not finde it, wheras many falſe witneſſes were come in. For many ſpake falſe witneſſe, and their teſtimonies w re not conuenient. But at laſt came two falſe witneſſes,

neſſes, and riſing vp they gaue falſe witneſſe againſt him; for we heard him ſpeaking : I will deſtroy this Temple of God, made with hands, and after three dayes I will build another, not made with hands, and their teſtimony was not conuenient.

COnſider firſt when the high Prieſt could drawe nothing worthy of death from the wordes of Chriſt, then he asked the ſtanders by, who had beene of-ten at his Sermons, and euery one ſpake that, which they thought might helpe to con-demne him, and were very earneſt and deſirous to finde out ſome capitall crime, ac-cording to that ſaying : *They*

G 5 *ſearched*

Pſal.69
Pſal 20.

ſearched for iniquities, ſearch-
ing they fainted ın their ſearch,
they inuented counſailes which
they could not eſtabliſh. Conſider
ſecondly the purity of the life
of thy Lord, which was ſo
great, that it was hard to frame
ſuch a lye of him, as might
carrye any colour of truth,
euen by the teſtimonie of his
aduerſaries themſelues. Learne
thou firſt to accuſe no man
vniuſtly; For a Detractor and
falſe witneſſe are bound to
reſtitution of good name. Secondly to auoyd all lyes : For
a Lyar cannot pleaſe euen the
wicked. Thirdly according
to the example of Chriſt to
liue in ſuch order that the very
enimies of Faith, may finde
nothing in thy life to obiect
                              againſt

againſt thee, but conſidering
thee by thy good workes
may glorifie God our Fa-
ther.

Fourthly neuer to ſeeke
out reaſons againſt thy conſcience to excuſe thy ſinne :
For thoſe teſtimonies are falſe,
and not conuenient, whereby God is not deceiued,
nor thy Conſcience pacified,
Conſider thirdly theſe two
falſe witneſſes ſtanding vp
amongſt the reſt, whoſe teſtimonies are eſpecially rela-
ted, either becauſe they were
of greater moment, that
by them thou mighteſt knowe
the vanities of the others,
or elſe becauſe they con-
tayne the myſterie of the death
of our Lord, which was then
                    in

in handling. But they were not conuenient: First becaufe the witneffes could not agree together, the one faying (*I will deftroy*) and the other (*I can deftroy*) Secondly becaufe our Lord had fpoke no word of deftroying and building againe; but he faid (*diffolue*) and (*I will raife*) fpeaking of his death, and refurrection. Thirdly becaufe he had hurt no man, if he had reftored in three dayes, that, which he had deftroyed. Fourthly becaufe it feemed not to be beyond his power, who had rayfed *Lazarus* from death after he had been dead foure daïes. Fiftly becaufe fuch kinde of braging words feemed rather worthy of laughter and contempt then

Ioan. 12.

then of death. Learn thou firſt
not to wreſt ẙ words of Chriſt
to a contrary ſence: Secondly
not to relate any thing other-
wiſe then it was done : Thirdly
neuer to iudge euill ot ẙ minde
or intention of othĕrs, when
their words or deedes may be
well interpreted. Do thou alſo
ſuffer together with thy Lord
Chriſt, for whoſe death and de-
ſtruction ſo many men tooke
ſo great paines; and pray vnto
him, that thou maieſt be in-
ſtructed in the true vnderſtanding of the Scriptures, and
that hee will neuer ſuffer thee
to fall into hæreſie.

*And the high Prieſt riſing
vp in the middeſt of them, asked
Ieſus ſaying : Doſt thou anſwere nothing to thoſe thinges?
which*

Mat.26.
Mar.14.

which these men obiect against thee, and whereof they beare witnes, against thee? but Iesus *held his peace; and answered nothing. Againe the high Priest said : I adiure thee by the liuing God that thou dost tell vs, if thou art* Christ *the Sonne of our blessed God?*

COnsider first, when nothing was found worthy of accusation, which might seeme as a fault to bee obiected before *Pilate* the Gentile President, the high Priest being angry, inuented certaine questions, to the end that hee might gather some thinges from his answers. His owne conscience informed him, that nothing of any moment was alleaged : Yet he vrged those

thofe things which hee knew
to be falfe. Confider fecondly
that Chrift helde his peace,
both becaufe hee knewe,that
his confcience did anfwer all
thofe things, and alfo becaufe
he would not avoyd death by
his eloquence. Hee teacheth
the firft to contemne all iniuries and lyes, & to fuffer them
patiétly,partly becaufe,thogh
perhaps thou art not guilty of
thofe thinges, which are ob-
ieÖted againft thee, yet thou
haft offended God in many
thinges , whereof no man ac-
cufeth thee ; and partly becaufe thou art neuer ỹ worfe,
becaufe other men thinke
thee to bee euill , For euc-
ry one is fuch as hee appeareth to bee in the fight of
our

our Lord. Secondly not to
thinke them worthy of an anfwer, which do offer wrong;
becaufe their owne confcience doth reproue them. Cōfider thirdly what our Lord
did when hee held his peace.
For this (faith hee) *That they*
Pfal. 108. *fhould loue mee, they did detract*
from mee : but I did pray. Hee
prayed then that the fruite of
his Paffion might paffe vnto
thee : Therfore in euery trouble of thy minde conuert thy
felfe vnto Chrift ; For it cannot bee that hee remembring
this vniuft accufation, can be
vnmercifull vnto thee in thy
troubles, & falfe accufations.
Confider fourthly, that the
high Prieft euill interpreting
this filence of our Lord, did
vfe

vſe adiuration in theſe words *(I adiure thee)* or as the Greek text is *(I coniure thee)* which worde is vſed in the coniuration of Deuils. Marke heere whom thy Lord is accounted to bee, to wit, one obſeſſed of a deuill. And the high Prieſt by his coniuration demanded two things. Firſt whether he bee Chriſt, that is to ſay, the *Meſſias* promiſed in the Law? Secondly, whether hee be the Sonne of God? For therefore was hee put to death becauſe he was Chriſt : and therefore hee redeemed man-kinde by his death, becauſe he was the Sonne of God, that is to ſay, of equall Maieſty with God the Father.

Ieſus ſaid vnto him, thou haſt
ſaid:

Mat. 26.
Mar. 14.

said : I am; but I say vnto you, hereafter yee shall see the Sonne of man sitting at the right hand of the power of God, and cōming in the cloudes of Heauen.

Consider first, that Christ being admired by the name of the liuing God, did holde his peace no longer, both because hee would not seeme to auoide death by holding his peace, and also that thou shouldest alwayes reuerence the name of God. *(Thou hast said,)* That is, so it is, as thou hast spoken, and as thy conscience doth witnes vnto thy selfe. Consider secondly, that hee maketh mention of the Iudgment to come in the wordes of *Daniel.* First that hee might take away the iealousie

Daniel. 7

loufie of his affecting a Kingdome, becaufe hee fought not
an earthly but a heauenly and
eternall Kingdome. Secondly that they fhould abftaine
from this euill iudgement, for
feare of ẏ Iudgment to come.
Learne firft in all thy actions
to remember thy laft end. Secondly in all accufations to
haue patience, becaufe power
fhall be giuen thee to Iudge
thy accufers, and thofe which
haue afflicted thee. Thirdly
alwayes, but efpecially at the
end of thy life, to confeffe a
truth, euen though it be great
loffe both to thy body and
goods. And pray thy Lord,
that hee will ftrike thy flefh
with wholfome feare, and inflame thy hart through ẏ Me-
ditatiõ of his Paffion. The

The 16. Meditation of the
first condemnatiō of Chriſt
and of his mocking.

Then the chiefe Prieſt rent

Mat. 26.
Mar. 14.

his garments; ſaying : Hee hath blaſphemed, what neede wee witneſſes any further ? beholde yee haue now heard the blaſphemy, what thinke yee? they anſwering ſaid, he is guilty of death.

IF in any great matter there happened any grieuous euill, as without doubt blaſphemy is, then the *Iewes* did cut or teare their garments, and by that ſigne did ſhew the grieuouſnes of the matter, which ſhould cut the heart with griefe, and bee reuenged euen with the loſſe of honour and goods. But the high Prieſt was forbidden to cut

his

his garments by this Lawe, *The high Priest shall not vncouer his head, hee, shall not cut his garments.* Neuerthelesse this vnlearned Priest being ignorant of the Lawe, did cut his garment, and by cutting it made an end of the Priesthood of the *Iewes.* Learne thou to be moued with the iniuries offered vnto God, though it bee to thine owne losse & hinderance. Côsider first what opinion the *Iewes* had of thy Lord. He was first accounted an Imposter or Inchanter, wherupon *Iudas* said, *(Carry him warily least in wrapping your eyes with his iugling he slippe from you.)* Secondly iniurious vnto men : *doest thou so, saith hee, answere the high Priest?*

Leuit. 21

Prieſt? Thirdly obſeſſed by a
Deuill, in the exorciſme and
coniuration of ẏ high Prieſt.
Fourthly blaſphemous againſt
God. Fiftly a falſe Prophet,
in the Officers ſcoffing and
mocking him. Behold with
what Titles thy Lord was honoured in this his paſſion.
Conſider ſecondly with what
minde Chriſt heard this gene-
rall voice of the people, *(He is
guilty of death,)* and euen of
that people, whoſe dead hee
had raiſed, whoſe ſicke he had
healed, and whoſe profite hee
had procured. Admire the
malice of wicked men, and
the gentlenes of Chriſt, who
being nothing mooued with
this ſentence of death, offered
himſelf ready to dye for them,
　　　　　　　　　which

which killed him. Pray therfore that by this sentence of
his death, thou mayst be deliuered from the sentence of e-
ternall death.

*And the men, which helde
Iesus, mocked him, beating him,
and they spet in his face, & beate
him with blowes, & they couered
him & struck his face, & asked
him, saying: Prophesie vnto vs,
O Christ, who is hee, that struck
thee.*

Luc.22.
Mat.26.
Mar. 14

COnsider first that Christ in
ỹ counsel was not only tyed with bondes, but also held
by ỹ hands of many, who after
ỹ sentence of death pronounced did handle him most cruelly, as a condemned man, against
whom they could not sinne.
The deuil increased their cruelty, who

who becaufe he had obfer-
ued no finne in him in his
whole life, defired by thefe
tormēts to moue him to fome
impatience. Cōfider fecondly
that then they raged moft a-
gainft Chrift, when hee confeffed himfelfe to be the Son
of God. For then thou muft
expect moft temptations both
by men and deuils, when by
the amendment of their life
and manners thou fhalt fhew
thy felfe to bee the Sonne of
God. Confider thirdly there
were fower kinde of mock-
ings. Firft they beat him with
their fifts and handes about
the head, face, and necke. Secondly they fpit their filthy
fleame in his face. Thirdly
they couered his face, which
by

by the sweet aspect therof seemed to hinder, and stay their
fury and wickednes. Fourthly, they vsed reproachfull
words : (*prophesie*) as if they
should say, thou art not a true,
but a false Prophet. Take thou
heede of these kinde ofillusi-
ons : For first thou doest strike
Christ, when thou hurtest thy
neighbour; & thou dost strike
his head with blowes, when
secretly thou doest hurt thy superiours, & his face, if openly.
Secondly thou spittest vpon
him, when thou pollutest thy
consciēce with euill thoughts.
Thirdly thou couerest his face,
when oppressing thy cōscience
thou perseuerest in sin. Fourthly thou reuilest him, whē thou
dost not belieue his promises,
H   nor

nor threatnings. Looke vnto thy selfe, least by imitating the sinnes of the *Iewes*, thou incurrest the same punishment. For they haue a vayle ouer their heart, so as they cannot knowe Christ : They are in all places derided of all men, and many times they are reuyled and beaten, being hatefull both to God and men. Pray vnto thy Lord, that these his reproaches may free thee from the eternall reproaches of thy soule,

Luc.22.   *And blaspheming, they spake many other things against him.*

ENter thou into the high Priestes Court, and consider what these wicked Officers did all night, and what Christ

Christ suffered. Saint *Theo-philact* saith, that they being drunke at their supper did many thinges very want onely, according to that saying : *They did sing against me which did drinke wine.* And because the Euangelist doth conclude the labour of the whole night in these fewe wordes, looke thou into the writings of the Prophets what they say of these illusions : *Isaias : I gaue my body to the strikers, and my cheekes to the pinchers : I haue not turned my face from them that rebuked and spit vpon me : I haue put my face as a most hard rocke.* Hyeremias : *He shall giue his cheeke to him that will strike him, he shall be satiated with reproches.* Iob: *They opened their*

in Luc. 22

Pfal. 68

Isa. 50.

Hierom. 3

H 2   *mouthes*

Iob.16

mouthes against me, and vpbrayding they stroke my cheeke, they
are satiated with my paynes.
Hereby is signified : Fist that
the whole body of Christ was
stricken most cruelly, beaten
with staues, fistes, and feete;
for these words seeme to signifie so much : *I gaue my body to
them that would strike.* Secondly, that his beard was pulled
off, and his face bloudy. Thirdly that the visage of Christ was
beaten with fistes, and made
blewe : Fourthly, that he suf-
ferd diuers kinds of mockings
and illusions : and to be briefe,
that nothing was omitted that
could be deuised for his paine :
They are satiated (saith he) with
my paines : for thinke, that the
officers vsed our Lord this
night

night by the confēt of the high
Priefts in fuch manner, that although he fhould not be crucified, yet he could not by nature continue long aliue. Therfore it is not to meruailed at,
though he were dead fooner
then *Pilate* expected. Do thou
alfo behold Chrift, marke his
face, (which was expofed to
blowes) fo amiable, his eyes
breathing forth loue, expref-
fing fo much more charity in
them, by how much our Lord
was beaten with ftripes. The
Prieftes departed now to take
their reft, and the officers likewife framed thēfelues to fleep:
onely the Spoufe of thy foule
could take no reft, for he muft
take no other fleepe then in
the bedde of the Croffe.

H 3   Pray

Pray him that his vnquiet rest
may bring euerlasting rest to
thy soule.

The 17 Meditation of the
second condemnation of
Christ in the house
of Cayphas.

Mat.27.
Mar. 15
Luc.22.

*And presently in the morning
as soon as it was day all the chiefe
Priests, and the elders of the people, and the Scribes assembled together against Iesus, that they
might put him to death : and they
brought him into their counsaile,
saying : If thou art Christ, tell vs.*

COnsider first that now the
second time they assem-
ble into councell, both because
more should consent to the
condemnation of Christ (For
perhaps in the night many wer
absent)

abfent)& alfo that they might
confirme in the day time, that
which they had iudged in the
night.There affembled 3.forts
of people,the Priefts, ȳ Elders
of the people, who had the ci-
uil gouernment & the Scribes,
in ẘ fort the Pharifees alfo are
vnderftood,being ȳ Religious
people of ȳ Iewes : that thou
maift vnderftand; 1. That all
men gaue caufe of the death of
our Lord. 2. That Chrift dyed
for all. 3. That all men ought
worthily to acknowledge
themfelues to bee finners, and
to feeke helpe by the death of
Chrift. Cõfider fecondly that
this queftion (*If thou beeft
Chrift*) ẘ was hãdled al night,
was the queftion of the Deuil
tempting Chrift,*If thou art the*

Mat. 4.

H 4   *Sonne*

Luc.13.

Sonne of God, and also of them which mocked our Lord on the Crosse, *If thou beest Christ saue thy selfe*, whereby is signified first that they which doubt of their faith, are the sonnes of the Deuill, and liue in darkenesse : Secondly that this is the fault of all sinners, not to knowe who Christ is : Some will haue him rich, noble, &c. they will not haue him spit vpon, despised, & poore : Others thinke him austere and sowre, and are ignorant how sweete our Lord is : Others contrariwise will haue him so mercifull, that he will not be offended with any sinnes, nor punish any offenders. Doe thou acknowledge in Christ both mercy and iustice, and learne, that

that heerein confifteth the
higheft wifedome, that thou
knoweft the true God,& Iefus
Chrift whome he fent. Then
enter into the counfaile of
thofe wicked men : Behold
thy Spoufe foulely and euilly
vfed by the *Iewes* : Admire firft
& inquire, art not thou Chrift ?
Can it bee, that thou, which
art the Sonne of God, the Author of all Creatures, the glory
of saints, wilt fuffer fuch things
for me, poore and vile worme?
By thefe queftions ftirre vp
thy felfe, that whilft Chrift
fuffereth and is full of confu-
fion, thou in the meane time
feeke not after gaine & worldly honour.

And hee fayde vnto them :
If I fhould tell you, you would
H 5 *not*

Ioan. 17.

not beleeue me : And if I shall aske, yee will not answere me, nor let me goe : But hereafter the Sonne of man shall be sitting at the right hand of the power of God. And they all said : art thou then the Sonne of God ? who answered ; you say, that I am.

Onsider first that our Lord, before hee professed himselfe to bee Chrift, did vse a preface, for whereas hee professed the fame moft plainly in the night and was fo farre from profiting, that thereby a greater accufation was framed againft him ; heere being asked the fecond time , hee feemeth to make fome difficulty in anfwearing : That thou mayft learne

learne that the fuggeftions of
God, being once reiected,
doe hardly returne againe.
Confider fecondly, how often they asked, and neuer beleeued. For there are fome,
which alwayes repeate the
felfe fame queftion, not becaufe they are ignorant, but
becaufe thereby they may
finde out fomething, which
may pleafe their owne will,
and not bee repugnant to
their defire, euer learn-
ing, and neuer comming to
the truth of knowledge. Thou
alfo how many thinges doeft
thou knowe, and how fewe
doeft thou performe? Doubt
not, *But the Seruant, which
knoweth the will of his Lord,
and doeth it not fhall bee
beaten*

2 Tim. 3.

Luc. 12.

beaten with many stripes. Consider thirdly *(if I shall aske, yee will not answere me)* the pride of the wicked, who would not vouchsafe to answere Christ their Lord : What will they doe at the latter iudgement, when they shall haue him for their Iudge, whome they iudged vnworthy of their answer. Thinke thou hereof as often as thou shalt be admonished by God in thy conscience, and thou dost reiect his inspiratiō. Cōsider fourthly that our lord being asked, whether he was Christ, did answere out of *Dauids* Psalme of the sitting of the right hand of his Father, which Psalme he alleaged to them another time, that by that argument (which other-

Psal. 109.

otherwife they could not
folue) they might knowe that
the *Meffias* was the Sonne of
God, which they did eafily   Mat.22.
vnderftand, for they inferred
vpon his anfwere, *Art thou
then the Sonne of God* ? Admire
the goodnes of God which
ceafed not to admonifh, and
to withdrawe them from this
grieuous finne, wherein they
fhould finne not againft man
onely, but againft him, who
was the Sonne of God. Pray
thou vnto Chrift, that the reuerence & refpect of him may
moue thee, that whenfoeuer
thou fhalt finne; thou mayeft
thinke of that faying : *To
thee alone haue I finned, and I   Pfal.50.
haue done euill before thee :* For
it is God, who is offended, &
not man alone.   *But*

Luc. 22.
Mat. 26.
Mar. 14.

But they said, what neede wee testimony any further, for wee our selues haue heard from his owne mouth. And all the multitude of them rising, and binding Iesus, *brought him bound to* Pilate *the President.*

COnsider first from an excellent answeare an euill conclusion ; because hee is Christ, and the Sonne of God, therefore hee must be offered to *Pilate* to dye. Thou oftentimes concludest in like manner : God is mercifull, therefore let vs sinne more freely. Consider secondly out of St. Chrysostome, that the *Iewes* would not put Christ to death secretly, but openly: that the glory, which he had gotten by his miracles, might be

Hom. 85.
in Mat.

be taken away by the pub-
lique shame and ignominy
of his death, and that he might
generally be esteemed a wicked man in all places. But God
permitted it vpon a far different reason : First that hee,
which should dye for all men,
should be put to death not secretly by the *Iewes* onely, but
openly by the *Gentiles* also before all men. Secondly ẏ this
death, which seemed to bee
infamous, and full of ignominy, should sanctifie all Nations, and should bee glorious
for euer throghout the whole
world. Doe thou with ẏ Apostle *Paul Glory in nothing else,*
but in the Crosse of our Lord Ie-
sus Christ. Consider thirdly out
of St. *Leo,* that after Iesus was
offered

Galat.6.

Ser. 8. de
Pasc. Dö.

offered being boūd with hard
knottes, beaten with many
boxes & blowes, defiled with
spittings, condemned before-
hand with clamours : To the
end, that amongst so many
fore-iudgments, wherby euery one desired to haue him dy;
Pilate should not dare to dis-
charge him. Follow thou thy
Lord in this iourney, as neare
as thou canst, and offer him
vp for thy selfe, not to *Pilate*
the President, but to God the
Father, & desire him, that hee
who was once adiudged to
dye for thy sinnes , may by
his death deliuer thee
from all
euils.

***

The

The 18. Meditation of the death of *Iudas.*

Then Iudas, *who had betrayed him, seeing that hee was condemned, repenting himselfe brought againe the thirty peeces of siluer to the high Priestes, and to the Elders, saying : I haue sinned, betraying iust bloud : But they said, what is that to vs? Looke you to it.* Mat. 27.

COnsider first that *Iudas* hearing of the condemnation of Christ by the high Priests, being led by repentance, either good, through the greatnes of his offence, or false; through the shame, whereby hee thought he should neuer be able to indure the reproaches, which would

would infue, brought againe
the money. This alfo was permitted by God, whereby the
innocency of Chrift might be
manifefted to all men, leaft
the *Iewes* by this argument
might confirme the death of
our Lord to be iuft becaufe
his inward difciple, who knew
all fecrets had deliuered him
vp to them to dye. But *Iudas*
betrayed our Lord, not that
Chrift fhold dye, but becaufe
hee would haue the money,
hoping that as at diuers times
before, fo at this time alfo our
Lord might efcape. Learne
firft the innocency of our
Lord, which the Traytor himfelfe confeffed openly, with
moft earneft wordes, and by
throwing downe of ỹ money.
Second-

Secondly the bitter torments
of our Lord, which moued
the very Traytor to repétance.
Thirdly the quallityes of the
Deuill, who bewitcheth our
eyes, before the sinne bee cōmitted, least we should see the
foulnesse thereof; but after
the sinne, hee openeth ỹ same,
that wee should dispaire. Cōsider secondly the answere of
the Priests *(What is that to vs)*
Peter after his sinne cōmitted,
went out from the cōpany of
the wicked, and obtained pardon : *Iudas* contrariwise came
to the wicked, & fell into desperation. Learn hereby ỹ they
which offend the Maiesty of
God because they may haue ỹ
fauour of other men, are after
forsaken by them, & ỹ alwaies
                        after

after this life, when euery one shall beare his owne burthen, and often times also euen in this life. Confider thirdly the grieuous burthen of an euill conscience, w̄ feared neither shame nor death. Doe thou lamenting for thy sinnes, say with *Iudas*, I haue sinned, betraying iuft bloud: ẏ is to say, I haue through my sinnes caft oftentimes from my selfe the paſſion of Chriſt, which was giuē me for my soules health. But trufting in the mercy of Chriſt, difpaire not, but in thy prayer adde this, O Lord reftore it thou vnto me, that it may profite my soule. Confider fourthly, that it is manifeft by the anfwer of ẏ Prieſts, that Chriſt dyed not for any fault.

fault committed by himfelfe,
but ofmeere malice & enuy.
For this *(What is that to vs)* is
as much to fay, it skilleth not,
whether hee dye iuftly or vn-
iuftly, fo hee dye. Confider
fiftly, *(Looke thou to that)* that
euill men giue onely matter
of difpaire : Learne hereby
firft the difpofition of wicked
fuperiours, who care not how
their fubiects liue, fo as they
may inioy their owne profite,
and pleafure. Learne fecondly, to fuffer with the afflicted,
and to comfort them, at leaft
with good wordes, if otherwife thou art not able. Learne
thirdly in thy afflictions, not
to repaire to euery one, but to
feeke out thofe, whome God
hath appointed to be the gui-
ders

ders of thy soule, & are commended for their life and wisdome.

And casting downe the pee-
ces of siluer in the Temple, hee
went aside, and going away, he
hanged himselfe in a halter , &
being hanged, hee brake in the
midst , and all his bowels were
scattered.

Consider first that the fact of *Iudas*, which exceeded all measure of reuenge, deserued no other Iudge, or executioner, then *Iudas* himselfe. For if hee had bin put to death by another, he might haue hoped for pardon : But hanging himselfe, hee cómitted a new sinne of murther, & desperation. Behold how one sinne is increased by another, if thou dost

Mat. 27.
Act. 21.

De Leo
ser. 3. de
Pase. Dó.

doſt not preuēt them in time.
Conſider ſecondly how wickedly ẙ Apoſtataes from faith
and religion doe commonly
periſh. Take thou heede leaſt
thou forſake the Church or thy
vocation : *For thou ſhalt fall
into the ſnare of the Deuill, and
the Deuill will ſtand at thy right
hand,* (ẅ *Dauid* fore-ſpake of
Iudas) *toſſing thee heere accor-* Pſal. 108.
ding to his will, and at laſt caſt-
ing thee downe into Hell. Conſider thirdly, what is the end
of ſinners : Euen this, ẙ hanging in the ayre they ſhal touch
neither Heauen nor Earth, and
poſſeſſe nothing but the rope.
For rhey reiect heauēly things
and are depriued of temporall
goods, ẅ onely they ſought
after , and being inchayned
with

with the chaine of finne, they
are detained and held vp by
the Deuill the Prince of this
ayre. And certainly at ỹ end
of their life, thefe thinges doe
alwayes happen to finners, &
oftentimes euen in this life to
fome, who being defpoyled
of their earthly goods, are ne-
uertheles fo choaked vp with
wicked defires, that they can
hardly lift vp their eyes to
Heauen. Confider fourthly,
that hee cracked in the midft,
and his bowels powred out:
that hee, which had loft the
bowels of charity, might alfo
loofe his owne bowels, & that
hee which imployed all his
care to inioy many thinges,
might loofe alfo his owne en-
trels. Doe thou with *Iudas*
caft

cast away money, riches, and all worldly things, but goe to no other tree, then the Crosse of our Lord, and pray him that he will tye thee fast vnto him, and loosing all the knottes of thy sinnes, binde thee with the chayne of his loue : For if *Iudas* himselfe (as St. *Leo* affirmeth) had obtayned remedy from Christ crucified, if he had not hastened to the halter, thou maiest haue an assured hope to obtayne pardon and grace.   Ser. 11. de Pasc. Dō.

But the chiefe Priests taking the monye said : It is not lawfull to put it into the treasury, because it is the price of bloud : and taking counsell they bought therwith a potters field, for the burial of strangers, and for that cause   Mat. 27.

I   *the*

the field is called Haceldema,
that is, the field of bloud, euen
to this day. Then it was fulfilled
which was spoken by the Prophet
Hieremy: And they tooke thirty
peeces of siluer being the price of
the appriced, whome they priced
of the Sonnes of Israell, and
they gaue them into a potters
field, as our Lord hath appointed me.

Consider first the goodnes
and gentlenesse of God,
who would haue his seruants
so farre from all effusion of
bloud, that in the old lawe he
would not permit them to
haue the money wherewith
the death of any man was
procured. Consider secondly
the preposterous religion of
these

these Priestes, which feared
not to defile their consciences
with innocent bloud, and yet
were affrayd to pollute their
treasury with the price of
bloud. Thou art like vnto
them, so oft as thou makest
great account of small things,
and hast small regard of grieuous sinnes against God, *stray-* Mat.23.
ning a Gnat, and swallowing a
Camell. Consider thirdly the
Iewes conuerted not this money to their own vse, but to ỹ
behoofe of other men : That
by this thou maist learne,
1. That Christ was wholy giuẽ
vnto vs,his very price also being bestowed vpon vs. 2. The
liberality of couetous men,
who giue Almes, not of their
owne, but of other mens
I 2   money.

money. Cõsider fourthly that
with this money a field was
bought for the burial of strangers : that thou mayest learne,
first that not onely our soules,
but our bodies also receiued
great benefite by the death of
Christ : For whatsoeuer good
is bestowed vpon man, wee
ought to acknowledge all to
proceede from the passion of
Christ. Secondly that through
the death of Christ wee haue
true & euerlasting rest. Thirdly according to St. *Ambrose*
and Saint *Hierome*, that this
word (which in another place
is called a field, which God
the workmã made of nothing)
was bought with the price of
the bloud of Christ, not for the
buriall of all men, but only of
                        strangers,

Ser. 51.&
in Luc.
In Mat. 27

Mat. 23.

ftrangers, ỹ therein only they
fhould reft with a quiet côfci-
ence, who making themfelues
ftrangers on earth, looke ftill
to the heauēly country.There-
fore if thou intendeft to bee
partaker of this price,be a ftrã-
ger,fhut thine eyes to worldly
things : defire no earthly
goods, to be briefe, dye vnto
the world, that thou maiſt reft
fweetly in Chriſt. Confider 5.
That this was confirmed vnto
vs, either by the prophefie of
Hieremy, in thofe bookes w̃
came not to vs, or of *Zacha-*
rie (as the common opinion is
the name of *Hieremy being* put
in, not by the Euangeliſt, but
by fome other writer) or of
both, as *Epiphanius* affirmeth.
Thou maiſt learn hereby ỹ the

I 3   price

Hiere. in
Mat.27.
Zach.11
Aug.lib.3
de côfen-
fu Euang.
Hære. 38
Gen.37.

price of Chriſt was not onely
prefigured in the price, for
which *Ioſeph* before time had
beene ſould, but foretold alſo
by the Prophets, with admiration, that for the price of
thirty peeces of ſiluer (whereof euery one is valued at halfe
a Doller) the Meſſias expected
ſo many ages ſhould be bought and ſould. Doeſt not thou
ſell Chriſt, and euerlaſting life
for a baſer price, when thou
refuſeſt and reiecteſt his grace
for a little filthy luſt, for money, or vaine deſire of honor?
Returne then vnto thy ſelfe,
conſider the ineſtimable value of the bloud of Chriſt, and
ſuffer any thing rather then he
ſhall be taken from thee.

The

The 19. Meditation of
the first accusation of
our Lord before
Pilate.

Then they brought Iesus from
Caiphas into the Palace, and it
was morning, and they entered
not into the Palace, because
they would not be defiled, but
that they might eate the Pasch.

Ioan. 18.

COnsider 1. ẏ they made
hast betimes in the mor-
ning to procure the death of
our Lord, leaft perhaps if it
shold be deferred, it might be
hindred throgh the fauour of
the people : for it is the subtil-
ty of the deuill, to carry men
headlong into mischiefe, leaft
by delay they might alter their
purpose. Be ẏ on ẏ cõtrary part
quick to good (for the grace

I 4　　　of

of the holy Ghoſt admitteth no delay) and ſlowe vnto e-uill, for the feete of wicked men are ſwift to do miſchieſe. Take heed therfore that thou omitteſt no occaſion to doe good, and in temptation *reſiſt*, *expecting*, that the Deuill be-ing driuen away, Chriſt may come and helpe. Conſider ſecondly, that Chriſt thy Lord being the louer of purity, was put into the houſe of a Gen-tile, as an vncleane perſon, guilty of many crymes , (which houſe the *Iewes* of Religion refuſed to enter in-to, leaſt they ſhould be defiled with ſome ſpotte wherby they might be forbidden to eate the Paſch)& was thought vnwor-thy to be nūbred amongſt the childen

Pro. 1.

children of God, or to bee
put to death by the hands of
the *Iewes*. If thou beeſt accounted baſe, or a ſinner, imitate this patience of thy Lord,
and let thy chiefeſt care bee
to be better eſteemed of God,
then of men. Conſider thirdly,
that that thing happened to
the *Iewes* which they feared :
For they did not eate the myſticall Paſch, becauſe Chriſt
the true Paſch tooke it a-
way by his death, and that
which they did eate, they celebrated with polluted minds
& hatefull vnto God. Be thou
therefore carefull not ſo much
for ỹ outward beauty & cleannes, as for ỹ inward purity of
thy mind, ỹ thou maiſt receiue
the true Paſch of our Lord in

I 5   the

the Euchariſt; &praying vnto God ẙ thou mayſt be pure in hart, wherby thou maiſt often eate worthily this holy Paſch.

Ioan.18.

Then Pilate *went foorth vnto them,& ſaid,what accuſation do you bring againſt this man ? they ãſwered him if he were not a malefactor we would not haue deliuered him to thee: Then ſaid* Pilate *to them,take ye him and according to your Law iudge him. The* Iewes *ſaid to him : It is not lawfull for vs to kill any men: that the ſpeach of* Ieſus *might be fulfilled, ſignifying what death he ſhould dye.*

Conſider I. The humanity of *Pilate*, who might haue interpreted their refuſing to come into his houſe as to an vnclean perſon, as a contempt
of

of him; yet he yeilded to their religion, being better then thou & many other Christians who being contemned, yeild contempt againe, & by no intreaty will yeild in any poynt or tytle of honour. Consider 2. The proud answere of the *Iewes*, by which they abused the outward face of Religion to the death of an innocent. We (say they) being Priests, making conscience to breake the least commandement of the law, would neuer haue deliuered this man vnto you, except for many causes he had beene most worthy of death. So great was the innocency of our Lord, that without compulsion they would not haue come to accuse him.

Consider

Consider thirdly *Pilates* answere, more wise then the answer of the Priests: For many
times secular men haue more
goodnesse then Priests. The
Gentile seemed to be not a little offended, that hee should
bee required to put him to
death without hearing or có-
uicting him, as if hee should
say, If your Law permit this,
yet the Lawe of the *Romanes*
doth not. But the *Iewes* had
no consideration of this iust
scandall : whome thou doest
immitate, so oft as thou doest
giue cause of scandall, whom
thou doest immitate, so oft as
thou giuest cause of scandall
or reproach to the weake, or
to Heretiques. Remember the
word of our Lord : *It is better*
                              that

that *a mil-ſtone ſhould be hanged about his necke, and he
throwne into the bottome of the
Sea, then one of thoſe little ones
ſhould be ſcandalized.* Conſider fourthly the other anſwere
of the *Iewes,* ſaying : *it is not
lawfull for vs to kill any man;*
that is to ſay, vpon the Croſſe.
For they ſtoned *Stephen,* and
they prepared to ſtone the A-
dultereſſe. For our Lord muſt
be put to death, not with
ſtones, hut vpon the Croſſe,
and not by the *Iewes,* but by
the *Gentiles,* which is ſhewed
by that which followeth, *that
the ſpeach of* Ieſus *might be fulfilled,* who had foretold them
both. Giue thankes therefore
vnto thy Lord, that he paſſed
from the *Iewes* to the *Gentiles,*
                        and

Mat. 18.

Act. 7.
Ioan. 8.

and pray him that he w̄ by the
handes of the *Gentiles* would
vndergoe the Croſſe, & ſuffer
death, will accept for thee the
vnbloudy ſacrifice, which in
remembrance of his Paſſion is
offered in the Church of the
Gentiles world without end.

Luc. 23. ..   *Then they beganne to accuſe*
him, ſaying : We haue found this
man ſubuerting our people, and
forbidding to giue tribute vnto
Cæſar, *and ſaying, that bee is*
Chriſt *our King.*

THey *began* (ſaith hee,) as
the beginning of many
accuſations, w̄ ſhould follow.
(*We haue found*) wee haue not
heard of others, but wee our
ſelues haue ſeene. Conſider 1.
three accuſations, al w̄ depen-
ded vp̄õ one. He doth affirme
(ſay

(fay they) y̌ hee is the *Meſſias,* & King of y̌ *Iewes,* promiſed to our fore-Fathers, and thereby draweth the people vnto him, and he cōmaundeth neither to obey *Ceſar,* nor to pay tribute vnto him. Lying plainly; who knew that our Lord did ſhun a Kingdome, did teach obedience, did pay tribute, and did anſweare, that it ſhould bee payed. Hereby thou mayeſt learn, how enuy makcth a mā blinde , ſo as hee cannot perceiue y̌ ignominy & reproach, that hee doth vnto himſelfe. For by theſe words they proued theſelues lyars beſore *Pilate,* who could not bee ignorant of Chriſt his anſwer to y̌ *Herodyans. Render vnto* Cæſar *thoſe thinges which are* Cæſars.

Auoyd

Ioan. 6.

Mat.27.
Mar.22.

Mat.22

Auoyd thou therefore all perturbation of minde , which
doth both much hinder the
seeing of the truth, & weaken
thy reputation. Confider fecondly wherof Chrift was ac-
cufed. Firft that hee did fub-
uert the people. His office is
to mooue the people, to turne
them vp and down, to fubdue
the flefh, which ruled the fpirit , vnto the fpirit , to place
poore and bafe Fifher-men a-
boue Kinges, and after his life
to throw the proude rich men
downe into Hell, and to lift
poor *Lazarus* into *Abrahams*
bofome. Secondly that hee
forbad to giue tribute vnto
Cæfar. Our Lord doth forbid
to pay tribute vnto the Deuill, who is called Prince of
this

this world ; and requireth no
small tribute of the actions of
men, whome hee would haue
to attempt or execute nothing
without some mixture of sin.
Christ contrariwise commandeth to this tribute vnto God
& that thou shalt refer all thy
actions to his glory. Thirdly
that he is a King & the *Messi-*
as. Thy Lord is truly a King
and the *Messias*, who gouern-
eth and feedeth all his people,
both with his body and holy
spirit. Yeilde thou thy selfe
vnder the gouernment of this
King, fight against his e-
nemies, and follow him
thy Captaine in
all
thinges.
§

The

The 20. Meditation of
the examination of
Pilate.

Ioan.18

Mar.27.

Then Pilate *went againe into the Pallace, and called* Iesus, *and* Iesus *stoode before the President. And* Pilate *asked him: art thou King of the* Iewes? Iesus *answered: doest thou speake this of thy selfe, or haue others tolde it thee of me?* Pilate *answered: am I a* Iew? *thy people, and thy Priests haue deliuered thee to me, what hast thou done?*

COnsider first *Pilate* dealt with Christ, not afore the multitude, but priuately in his house, of Hom. 85. in Ioan. whome (saith St. *Chrysostome*) hee had conceiued a great opinion.

pinion. Thou in like manner,
if thou wilt deale with Chrift,
auoide company & much bu-
fines; enter into the chamber
of thy heart, that thou mayeft
more clearly heare our Lord
fpeaking. Confider fecondly
that the Lord of all creatures
ftandeth as guilty before the
Gentile Prefident, to whom he
muft render account of his
life. Liue thou fo, that thou
needeft not blufh to render
an account of all the actions
before any man. Confider 3.
the queftion of *Pilate.* (*Art
thou King of the* Iewes ?) That
is to fay, can it bee, ẙ thou being fo poore and miferable
and fo many wayes afflicted,
canft call thy felfe King of
the *Iewes ?* Anfwere thou
for

for thy L rd, yea certainly, he
is King of the *Iewes*, whome
the true *Iewes* doe acknowledge, that is, such as knowe
and confesse their sinnes. For
they will obey this King, that
being brought out of sinne,
and deliuered out of the hand
of their enemyes, they may
serue him. Admire thou this
King, whose beauty consisteth not in golde and precious
stones, & outward ornamēts;
but in contempt, disgrace, and
externall ignominy. For these
things haue both made Christ
famous through the whole
world, and also haue beautifi-
ed thy soule. Consider fourthly, the answere of Christ, the
sence whereof is this, did you
euer see, or heare any thing of
mee,

mee, whereby I might be fuf-
pected to feeke for a Kingdome? This queftion fignifieth the abfurdity of the accufation. Ponder heer with thy
felfe, whether thou doft know
thy Lord Chrift, that is, whether thou doeft feele Chrift
raigning in thy minde; or elfe
whether thou art a Chriftian
without any outward fweetnes. Confider fiftly the proud
anfwere of *Pilate*, difdaining,
and taking it in euill part, that
a guilty perfon durft aske him
a queftion. He excufeth himfelfe with ignorance of the
Iewes caufes : I knowe not
(faith hee) what your Nation
dreameth of the cóming of a
Meffias. Thou canft not plead
ignorance in Gods caufe to
whom

whom Chrift hath made ma-
nifeſt euen the ſecrets of God.
And if ignorance did not profite *Pilate,* how can it profite
any Chriſtian, to whom God
hath giuen ſo great know-
ledge? Conſider ſixtly *(what
haſt thou done)* the great innocency of thy Lord, that when
accuſations failed, hee himſelfe muſt be asked. Anſwer
thou what he hath done. Hee
hath made Heauen & Earth,
and all Creatures : hee hath
done all good and no euill.
But for the good done for thy
ſake, which thou doeſt abuſe
vnto ſinne, hee muſt ſuffer the
puniſhment, w̄ thou didſt deſerue. This place is fit to meditate what Chriſt hath done for
thee, and what thou haſt done
againe

againe for him; that admiring
his bounty, thou mayſt giue
him thankes, & deteſting thy
owne ingratitude, thou mayſt
bee confounded with ſhame.

Ieſus *anſwered, my Kingdome
is not of this world: If my Kingdome were of this world, my Soldiours would fight for me, that I
ſhould not be deliuered vp to the
Iewes; but now my Kingdome
is not from hence.* Pilate *ſaid
vnto him; then art thou a King?*
Ieſus *anſwered, thou ſayeſt, that
I am a King.*

Onſider firſt ẙ Chriſt anſwered *Pilate* plainly, who
dealt ſincerely with him; but
to the *Iewes,* who went about
to intrappe him, hee would
not anſwere but adiured.
For our *Lord deteſteth fiction,*
and

and with the simple in his speach.
Consider secondly that hee
applyed himselfe to this *Eth-*
nicke, deriuing his argument
from the vse and custome of
men. You may vnderstand
(saith hee) by this, that I seeke
not a Kingdom of this world,
because I haue no Soldiours,
nor Chāpions for my defence.
But with the *Iewes,* that knew
the Lawe, hee vsed the Scriptures. Thou maist learne hereby that God vseth all waies &
reasons to conuert thee and
others. If thou wouldst consider those meanes, which our
Lord vsed to helpe and cure
thee , thou wouldest admire
Gods prudent loue and charity towards thee. Consider
thirdly(*My Kingdome is not of*
this

this world.) He doth not fay in
this world : For hee raigneth
in his Church, and in thee :
But hee faith, of this world, that
is to fay, It is not like ỹ King-
domes of this world, neither
doth it confift in the multitude of Seruantes and Soldiours, nor in folemnity and
pompe, nor in ryot and brauery of apparrell ; But in the ornament of the foule, in voluntary obedience and multitude
of vertues. And perhaps in
this Kingdome of Chrift there
are more poore, beggerly,
weake, and vnlearned ; then
rich, noble, mighty, and wife
people. Be thou careful therfore that Chrift may rule thee
and thy affections, and raigne
in thee. For if to ferue Chrift

K   is

is to reigne , then Chrift reig-
ning in thee will make thee
a mighty King, ruling ouer
thy felfe,& the whole world.

I was borne in this, and to
this I came into the world, that
I may giue teftimony vnto the
truth: And euery one which is
of the truth, heareth my voyce:
Pilate faith vnto him, what is
the truth ?

Ioan. 18

COnfider firft for what
caufe Chrift came into
the world, to wit, firft that
he might free the world from
the falfenes of Idolatry , and
of diuers errors, and of finne.
Secondly that he might declare the vanity and folly of
thofe things which the world
admireth,& fet before our eies
thofe things as they are indeede,

deede, and not as they seeme
to be. Thirdly ý by this truth
he might rule the mindes of
men. Thou maiſt learn hereby,
Firſt, what thou oughteſt
chiefely to ſeeke for in ý kingdome of Chriſt, to wit to be
deliuered & made free from al
vanity, falſhood, and ſinne.
2. That they are the chiefe ſeruants & inlargers of the Kingdome of Chriſt, ẃ labour in
teaching the truth. 3. That it
appertaineth eſpecially to the
charge of Chriſtian Princes,
and ſuperiours to keepe & increaſe their ſubiects in the
faith of Chriſt. For they are
not ſuperious like *Gentiles*, to
maintain their people only in
a ciuile & peaceable gouerne-
ment, but they are aiſo
    K 2   Chriſtian

Chriſtian Princes ouer Chriſtians, that they may enlarge
the Kingdome of Chriſt. Conſider ſecondly : *I was borne in
this, and to this I came into the
world.* A high ſentence, which
Pilate might haue vnderſtood,
if he had perſiſted in ſimplici-
ty. I am not borne (ſaith hee)
like other men, for I was now,
before I was borne of my mother; I was borne, not thorough the neceſſity of nature,
but of mine owne will, and
for certaine cauſes which moued me to take humane na-
ture vpon me, to wit, that
I might teach men the truth.
If therefore thou wilt liſten
vnto Heauenly Doctrine, and
deale ſincerely with God,
Chriſt will reueale vnto thee
           the

the ſecretes of Heauen. Conſider thirdly *(I was borne)*
and *(I came)* For by his birth
he is our Chriſt, and alſo hath
done all his actions for our
profite; that thou again ſhouldeſt referre all thy time, thy
ſtudies, and thy labours, to
his glory. Conſider fourthly
that Chriſt did anſwere ſecret-
ly to ỹ queſtion propounded
by *Pilate, What haſt thou done ?*
for I haue taught the truth, I
haue reprooued vice : For this
was the onely cauſe that moued the *Iewes* to put him to
death. Doe thou ſeeke out
the truth, and pray vnto God
to lighten thine eyes, ỹ thou
ſleepe not in death, & conſider
earneſtly with thy ſelfe, whether thou be of ỹ truth, that is,

K 3   whether

whether thou beeſt mooued
with the truth, or with pride,
luſt, auarice, and other paſ-
ſions of the minde : *For he*
Ioan. 18. *which is of truth, he is of God,*
but he which followeth lyes is of
the Deuill his Father, whoſe will
he fulfileth.

The 21. Meditation of
the ſecond accuſation
before Pilate.

Pilate went forth againe vnto
Ioan. 18 *the Iewes, ſaying : I finde no*
Luc 23. *cauſe in this man : But the high*
Mar. 27. *Prieſtes accuſed him in many*
things ; and Ieſus *anſwered no-*
thing : Then Pilate *asked him,*
ſaying to him : Doſt thou not
heare howe great teſtimonies
they ſpeake againſt thee? doſt thou
not anſwere any thing ? behold in
how great things they acuſe thee ?
                                But

But Ieſus *anſwered not him to* | Mar. 15
any word, ſo as the Preſident
wondred greatly.

COnſider firſt, that *Pilate*
expecting no anſwere to
this queſtion*(what is the truth)*
went foorth, either becauſe he
thought that queſtion apper-
tained not to him, or elſe ẏ it
was not conuenient at ẏ time.
To whom thou maieſt knowe
thy ſelfe to be like, ſo oft as
thou paſſeſt ouer lightly heauenly things; or as oft as thou
ſhalt thinke, that thoſe things
which are ſpoken of euerlaſting life, of perfection, or of
chriſtiã life, appertain not vnto
thee; or as often as thou doſt
lightly leaue ẏ which before
thy God thou hadſt iuſtly
　　K 4　　　purpoſed.

purpofed. Thinke no time vnfitt for diuine inftructions. Confider fecondly that *Pilate* found no caufe of death in Chrift; the *Iewes* a falfe caufe; and God the Father a true caufe, to wit, the purging of thy finnes for the faluation of thy foule. Ponder earneftly with thy felfe vpon this caufe. For the reafon why thou louest not Chrift fo well as thou oughteft, nor art fo thankfull as thou fhouldeft be; nor art fufficiently moued with this his fo great and bitter paine, is, becaufe thou doeft not earneftly acknowledge, nor re-uolue in thy minde, that thou wert the caufe of thefe his bitter paines. Confider third-ly the great and manifould crimes

crimes obiected againſt thy
Lord in the ſight and hearing
of all the people, who wondred exceedingly at ſuch new
and ſtrange things. Doe thou
patiently ſuffer for thy Lords
ſake all ſlanders, iniuries, and
reproches. Conſider fourthly
the deepe ſilence of our Lord,
wherein *Pilate* the *Gentile* admired the wiſedom of Chriſt,
and the *Iewes* were made more
audacious to adde more and
more grieuous accuſations.
Admire thou the patience of
God, who beeing hetherto
offended with ſo many and
ſo grieuous ſinnes, both of
thee, and of other men,
doth not onely ſtill holde his
peace, winke at them & pardō
them, but alſo doth beſtowe

K 5   many

many benefites vpon thee;
that thou being moued with
his bountifull liberality, maift
at laft remember thy felfe.

But they were more earneft,
faying : He moued the people,
teaching through all Iurie, be-
ginning frō Galilee *euen hither*:
Confider firft the clamors
of the *Iewes*, who hauing
no hope to effect any thing
by truth, raifed vp troubles,
tumults, and clamours, like
thofe which defēd an ill caufe
wherein they imitate the Deuill, who when he can doe nothing by his owne fuggeftions, thē he ftirreth vp friends,
parents, and companions; he
moueth the inward concupifcence; he hindereth and dark-
neth the vnderftanding. Doe
thou

Luc. 23.

thou nothing impatiently, i-
mitating our Lord, who was
not prouoked nor moued by
any iniuries, except to loue the
more dearly. Confider 2. that
Chrift was heere reputed captaine of the fedicious : Thou
knoweft (fay they) O *Pilate*,
the *Galilæans* to be factious
people, whofe bloud thou
didft lately mingle with their
facrifice : behold hee *is* the
head and Ring-leader of all
mifchiefe, borne to raife fedition among the people,
Verily O Lord, thou doeft
moue the people, but not to
fedition, treafon, robberies,
and man-flaughters, which is
the property of Heretiques,
which ftirre vp fuch motions
in their Sermons; but to the
change

change of their life and manners, that forsaking their pleasures and sinnes, they may all
giue themselues to the exercise of vertue. Thou fillest the
Monasteries with religious
people; the Deserts with An-
chorites, the Prisons with
Confessors, and the gallowes
with Martyrs. Through thy
motion Virgins cast away
their braue artyre, Rich men
choose pouerty, Noble men
submit themselues to the wills
of others, and young men by
a vowe of religion offer themselues as a Holocaust vnto
thee. Pray thou also that our
Lord may mooue thee. Con-
sider thirdly whome he is said
to teach, to wit, the *Galilæans*, that is, Passengers;
and

and *Iewes*, that is, Confef-
fors, and praifers of God.
But hee began from *Galilee:*
For the beginning of Chriftian doctrine is, to paffe from
finne; the middle is, to confeffe our dayly defects, with
forrowe of heart, and purpofe
of amendment, and to praife
God in true obedience; and
the end is, to behold the face
of God in Ierufalem in the vi-
fion of peace. Pray our Lord
to bring thee to the perfection of this wifedome.

And Pilate *hearing* Galilee,
asked if the mā wer a Galilæan,
& as foon as he knew that he was
vnder the iurifdiction of Herod,
he fent him to Herod,*who alfo in*
thofe dayes was in Hierufalem.
                    Galilæan,

Luc. 23.

GAlilæan, is heere to bee seperated from *the man*, in this sence, whether this mã be a *Galilæan*. Consider first, that either *Pilate* did not knowe the name of *Iesus*, or else that he disdained to name him. Wicked men knowe not *Iesus*, suffering, mocked and bound ; they knowe the honours of the world, but not the ignominy of the Crosse: Therefore they shall not bee knowne of *Iesus*, that is, their Saviour, and they shall neuer reape the fruite of saluation, which reiect the Passion, being the instrument of saluation. Consider secondly, that *Herode* the Iewe came to *Hierusalem* against the feast of Pasch. For sinners vse to cele-

celebrate the Feaftes of the
Faithfull with outward ceremonies onely, in brauer Apparrell, with daintyer Difhes
&c. But they doe not receiue
the inward fruit of the Feafts,
neither doe they labour fo
much for the inward orna-
ment of their Soule, to the
which they ought to bee caried from the outward ceremonyes. Confider thirdly, thy
Lord is faide to bee vnder the
iurifdiction of *Herode*, a wicked man, Inceftuous, Adul-
terous, and a Murtherer:
that thou mayeft willingly o-
bey thy Superiours, though
they bee not very good, hauing refpect not to their vices but to the vertue of o-
bedience. Confider fourthly
the

the fower Iudges of Chriſt,
two Prieſts *Annas* & *Cayphas*,
and two ſecular men *Herode*
the Iewe, and *Pilate* the Gentile. For Chriſt was adiudged
to death by all ſtates of men ;
hee was ſlaine for the ſinnes
of all men : hee ſuffered and
dyed for the ſaluation of all
men. Therefore doe thou
confidently lay all thy ſinnes
vpon him, that being free'd
from them, thou mayeſt receiue eternall ſaluation prepared by him.

The 22. Meditation of
the acts in the houſe
of Herode.

Luc 23.

Herode, *when he ſaw* Ieſus,
reioyced much, for hee was deſi-
rous a long time to ſee him, be-
cauſe

cause he had heard many thinges
of him, and hee hopea to see some
signe done by him : And he exa-
mined him with mary questions:
but hee answered nothing vnto
him.

COnsider first, that this
Herode neuer came vn-
to Christ, neuer heard
his wordes, nor neuer saw his
miracles ; but yet hee knewe
many things of him by the report of others. Wherefore he
was glad, that hee had occasion to see and behold him ; but
he was not moued with hope
or desire of saluation , but
with a desire to see some sign.
Thou mayest learne first, what
this King thought our Lord
to bee ; an Inchaunter, a Iug-
ler, a Foole. Secondly, that
the

the cuſtome of worldly men,
is , more willingly to heare
newe thinges, ẇ may delight,
then good things,ẇ may profite. Cõſider 2. that Chriſt admireth not ỹ outward pompe
and royall dignity,but beholdeth the beauty & foulnes of
the heart ; neither would hee
vouchſafe to ſpeak vnto him,
ſeeing hee expected no profit
therby. Learne thou 1. not to
eſteeme too much theſe outward ſhewes: for in the future
examination of the Iudge the
humble poor man ſhalbe better eſteemed, then the proude
rich man. 2.Not to vtter thy
wordes in vaine, but to direct
thy ſpeaches alwayes to ſome
good purpoſe,remembring, ỹ
in the day of Iudgement thou
ſhalt

shalt render an account of e-
uery idle worde. 3. To flatter
none, to auoyd oftentatió, not
to expose Religious and Holy
things to be laughed at, not to
abuse the Scriptures or diuine
ceremonyes to Iefts and prophane matters. Confider 3.
what queftions were propou-
ded to Chrift by *Herode*, to
wit, vnprofitable & curious :
Perhaps , whether hee were
Iohn Baptift; whether he could
deftroy & reftore the Temple;
& whether his Father in times
paft killed the Infants for his
caufe. Do thou ask profitable
things of our LORD, & pray him
to anfwer to thy queftiós for ƴ
profit & faluatió of thy foule.

*And the chiefe Priefts and
the Scribes ftood conftantly ac-
cufing*

Luc. 23.

cusing him; but Herode *despised him with his Army, and mocked him, cloathing him in a white garment, and sent him backe to* Pilate.

Consider first, that Christ suffered 4. thinges in this Kings Pallace. For 1. hee was grieuously & constantly accused by the Priests. Secondly he was despised and mocked by *Herode*. Thirdly hee was euil intreated by the malepert Soldiours, no lesse then by the Seruants in the house of *Cayphas*. Fourthly, hee was cloathed in a white or Λαμπρα, that is, a bright garment, in signe of an affected Kingdom, or of folly, as one that was able to say nothing before the King in his owne defence.

Con-

Consider secondly that *Herode* was offended at the silence of Christ, lesse then the Priests, who pronounced him guilty of death, but more then *Pilate*, who by his silence admired the prudent grauity of our Lord. Thou mayst learne that by the same causes some fall more grieuously then others, & those most grieuously, which are in highest estate and calling. *Pilate* was a lay Gentile ; *Herode* a laye man, but a Iewe ; *Cayphas*, the high Priest of the Iewes. Consider thirdly, that Christ is a King, but such a one, as the world knoweth not, but doth accuse laugh at, and dispise. By these irrisions our Lord deserued for himselfe to bee exalted aboue

aboue all Kinges, and for vs,
that wee fhould bee indued
with true wifdome, bee made
immortall Kings in tne Kingdome of Heauen, & bee cloathed with the white garments
of immortality. Reioyce therfore, if thou doft fuffer irrifion
and perfecution with Chrift
ror iuftice, becaufe thine is the
Kingdome of Heauen : And
beware, leaft Chrift be mocked
by thee, if thou doft contemn
the poore, and his Seruants, &
neglect his Sacraméts, words,
& Cómandements. Laftly do
thou accópany ŷ fpoufe of thy
Soule, cloathed in this fcorn-
full garment, in his iourney to
Pilates houfe : marke what
fcoffings hee heard ; obferue
his eyes, & what countenance
he

hee shewed; & pray vnto him
with thy whole heart, ỹ thou
maist be a foole vnto ỹ world,
so thou bee accounted wise
vnto Christ.

And Herode *and* Pilate,
were made friends in that day :
for they were enemyes before,
one to another.   Luc.23.

COnsider first a double mi-
stery. 1. That wicked men
agree together against Christ
and his followers : Heritiques
oppugning the Church ; and
the Deuills vexing the iust
man.   The other , that the
death of Christ made peace
betweene the *Iewes* and the
Gentiles; and so ỹ the first and
principall Office of the passion of our Lord was to
bring and maintaine Peace.
                              There-

Therefore presently after his Resurrection, in his first & second meeting, hee said to his Disciples, *Peace bee vnto you.* Hee would, that wee should haue peace with God, to whō hee payed the price of our sinnes; with our own conscience, which he deliuered from sinne, and filled with inward grace ; and with our neighbours, whome hee commaundeth vs to loue , hauing infused his diuine loue into our hearts. As often therefore as thou feelest inward war within thy self; as oftē as thou seeest ẙ thou hast lost peace with God; as often as thou shalt perceiue thy neighbour angry at thee, or dost experience his hatred against thee : Presently

fently turne thy felfe to the
Croffe of Chrift, as to him,
which is thy onely true Mediator, and will reftore thee vnto peace with all men.   Confider fecondly, *(In that day)*
that is, the very fame day :
That thou mayeft learne how
eafie it is for our Lord to make
peace, and to pacifie mindes,
that are moft incenfed, and to
helpe thee in thy greateft afflictions, although there bee
no humane meanes.   Pray
therefore vnto God, that hee
will bring tranquillitie vnto
the Chriftian cómon wealth,
ceafe the troubles of warre,
and giue a conftant
Peace vnto
his
Church.
L   The

The 23. Meditation of
the requiring of
Barrabas.

But Pilate *calling the chiefe*
Priests, *and the* Magistrates,
and the people, sayd vnto them :
yee haue offered vnto me this mã,
as auerting the people; and be-
hold I examining him before you,
finde no cause in this man of
these things in which yee accuse
him, no nor Herod *neither, For*
I haue sent yee vnto him, and
behold nothing worthy of death
is done vnto him : therefore I
will dismisse him, being correct-
ed: And on the solemne day, the
President *had a custome, and*
must of necessity dismisse one of
the prisoners, whom soeuer they
should require. And he had thẽ a
notable prisoner called Barrabas,
who

Luc. 23.

Mar. 27.

Mar. 15

who was take with the seditious,
who in the sedition had commit-
ted murther: Then Pilate *said:*
yee haue a custome, that I dis-
misse one in the Pasch: whome
will yee that I dismisse vnto you?
Barrabas, *or* Iesus, *who is called*
Christ? *for he knew, that the high*
priests had deliuerd him by enuy.

COnsider first, that *Herod*
though he sawe nothing
worthy of death in Christ, yet
he did not deliuer the innocent out of the handes of
the *Iewes*; but to gratifie the Priests, and the President, hee referred the know-
ledge of the cause to *Pilate.* In
like manner euery one desireth to please man, but none
to please Christ. Consider secondly, that so many Iudges

L 2   sought

fought the life of Chrift, and nothing was found worthy of death, or of imprifonment. Doe thou fo order thy life like vnto Chrift, that the Deuills at the houre of death may finde nothing of their owne on thee. Purge thy foule with daily examination of thy confcience, and often confeffion of thy finnes; fo as nothing paffe out of this world with thee, but that which is holy. Confider thirdly (*corrected or chaftifed I will let him goe*) *Pilate* thought to deliuer our Lord, but corrected : not becaufe he deferued it, but in fauour of the raging people, that they might be fatiffied with his ftripes. Thou feeft firft , that the people could

could not be ſatisfied, but
with the bloud of Chriſt: both
becauſe euill men are delighted onely in ſinnes, which
drawe bloud from our Sauiour; and alſo becauſe iuſt men
haue no ſweetnes but through
the bloud of our Lord ; nor
any reioycing, but in the Galat. 6.
Croſſe of our Lord Ieſus
Chriſt. Conſider fourthly, that
Pilate intended a good work,
when he purpoſed to ſet
Chriſt free, but not puie, but
mingled with much euill, to
wit, with beating and whipping Chriſt. And thou do-
eſt imitate him, as oft as thou
attempteſt any good thing,
mixed with ſinne ; when
thou giueſt almes out of
money euill gotten ; or goeſt

L 3   to

to the Church, that thou
mayeſt ſeeme religious, or
doeſt any other thing not
with a true intention. Conſider fiftly, when *Pilate* thoght
of the deliuering of our Lord
after this manner, then hee
remembred a more milde
way. For he ſawe the peo-
ple aſſembled together, that
according to their cuſtome
one of the priſoners ſhould
be giuen vnto them, whome
they ſhould chooſe out of
many, which the Preſident
ſhould propound vnto them,
of what crime ſoeuer they
were accuſed, and that in re
membrance of the people
of Iſraell, which about that
time of Paſch were deliuered

red out of the bondage of
Egypt : When he remem-
bred this Custome, he resolued to name Christ alone,
(whome he knewe to be well
liked of many for his noble
acts, and hated onely of the
Priestes and *Pharisees*) with a
Murderer, a Captayne of the
seditious, and a hatefull man,
making no doubt, but that
they would choose Christ before that most wicked man.
Thou seest first, that the Author of life is compared with
a turbulent murtherer :& thou
art angry if neuer so little be
detracted from thy honor and
tytles. Thou seest secondly
the holy custome of deliuering
a prisoner in remembrance
and

and fauour of the benefite of
their deliuerie out of the bondage of Ægipt. Thou being
so often deliuered from the
snares of the Deuill, and from
the bonds of sinne; succour
and helpe also thy neighbours
in memorie of this benefite,
that by thy labour and help,
they may be freed from the
bonds of their debtes, sinnes,
miseries , and of all other
euils.

Mat. 27.

*And as he was sitting in place
of iudgement, his wife sent vnto him, saying : haue thou nothing to doe with that iust man:
for I haue suffered many things
this day in my sleepe for him.*

COnsider first when the
people were sent away to
deliberate whom they would
choose,

choofe, *Plate* fate in iudgement, and receiued this mef-
fage from his wife, admoni-
fhed either by her good Angell according to the opinion
of *Hilarius*, *Chrifoftome*, *Am-
brofe*, *Hierome*, *Auguftine*,
and *Origen*; or elfe by a wicked fpirit, who perceiuing his
owne power by little and little to be weakened, and that
his iudgement was at hand,
and that the holy Fathers in
Lymbo did exult for their
fpeedy deliuerance, indeuo-
red to hinder the death of
Chrift, according to the doctrine of *Ignatius*, *Ciprian*, *Gre-
gorie*, *Rabanus*, and *Bernard*.
Thou learneft here the innocency of Chrift, witneffed by
the very Angels, either good

Hil.cã.33
In Mat.
Chr. ho.8
in Mat
Am. lib.1
in Luc.
Hierõ. in
Mat.
Augu.fer.
121.de.tē.
Ori.tract.
35.inMat
Au. Epiſt.
ad Philip.
Cip.fe. de
Pafc. Dõ.
Gre.li.33
Mor.c.21
Rab.cita-
tur inCa-
thena di-
ui Thom.
Ber.fer.1.
de Paſc.

or bad. And if this vision came by the helpe of the deuill, thou maist see the malice of men; whome when the Deuill hath once incited to euil, he cannot call backe from sinne: For the malice of concupiscence, and the force of sinne is so great, that it cannot be taken away, but by the help of God alone. Therefore the Priestes which were prouoked by enuy, were not warned; but *Pilate*, whom the disease of concupiscence had not yet stirred vp Labour thou with all thy strength to subdue the force of thy concupiscence. Consider secondly the Epithetó of Christ (*that iust man*) for he is truely our Iustice, perfectly iust in himselfe, without sinne, & alwaies
doing

doing moſt iuſt workes, by
which he ſatiſffied his Fathers
wrath for vs, and left an example for vs to imitate. Conſider thirdly *(haue thou nothing
to doe with that iuſt man)* that
is, meddle not with his buſineſſe, let there be no dealings
betweene thee and that iuſt
man. Learne, ẏ this iuſt man
doth not appertain to wicked
men, and that onely good men
are partakers of his iuſtice.
Doe thou pray this iuſt man
to vouchſafe to admitte thee
into his commerce and ſocie-
ty, that thy wares from his
wares, that is, thy good
workes from his merites may
bring much profite to the
ſaluation of thy ſoule.

But

But the chiefe priests & elders stirred vp the multitude, & perswaded the people that they shold demaund Barrabas *and destroy* Iesus : *and when the multitude were come vp, they began to pray* Pilate, *that hee would doe as he did alwaies vnto them. And the President answering said to thē : which of the two will ye haue dismissed ? They all cryed out together, not him, but* Barrabas *take away him and dismisse vnto vs* Barabas : *And* Pilate *answering againe said to them : What then shal I do with* Iesus, *who is called* Chrst? *but they cryed out againe, let him be crucified, crucifie him crucifie him: but* Pilate *said vnto them the third time : for what euill hath this man done ? I finde no cause of death in him : therefor I*

Mat. 27.

Mar. 15

Luc. 23.

Ioan. 18.

fore I will correct him, & difmiffe
him : but they vrged with many
cryes, defiring, that he fhould be
crucified, and their voyces in-
creafed, and they cryed more, let
him be crucified.

Onfider firft, that ỹ people inclyning to Chrift,
were ledd by the Priefts to
demaund *Barabbas*, and to
deftroy Chrift : That thou
maift knowe fuft, that one
fpeach of wicked men doth
more hurt, then many exhor-
tations of Saints can profite.
For that which Chrift had
builded with great labour in
three yeares, is heere ouerthrown in a moment. Beware
therfore of the fpeach of euill
men, efpecially of hereciques,
whofe words creepe like a
canker.

canker. Thou feeft fecondly,
that the authority of Superiours is of great force, either
to good or euill. If therefore
thou haft any of Chrifts fheep
vnder thy charge, vfe thy authority to the glory of God.
Confider 2. the ingratitude of
ẙ people, which efteemed fo
great a Benefactor leffe then
a Theefe, and chofe him to the
Croffe. Thou learneft firft to
contemne the applaufe of the
world, which hath fo cruell an
end. They cryed a little before
Bleffed is hee, which commeth in
the name of our Lord: and now
in other words *(Not this man)*
but *(Let him be crucified.)* Secondly thou feeft the blinde
iudgment of the world, which
contemning the higheft good
                          choofeth

chooseth the worst things, ha-
teth a benefactor, and imbra-
ceth an enemy. Take thou
heed, least for a small gaine or
humane fauour, thou dost betray Christ against thine own
cóscience, least the same happen to thee, which fell vnto
the *Iewes*, to whom in stead of
the Messias which they expected so many yeares, & at last
reiected & condemned) came
Barrabas (which signifieth the
sonne of the Father) a Murtherer, a Rayser of sedition, a
Deuill, by whose will they are
ruled: that they ẘ refused to
heare Christ comming in the
name of his Father, might
heare Antechrist speaking in ẙ
name of his Father the Deuill.
Consider 3. the fearfull speach
of

of *Pilate*, (*What shall I doe with
Iesus*) : the wicked Iudge seeketh the allowance of ẙ people. Bende thou thy minde in
all thy iudgments and actions
not to the will or manners of
the people, but to the Commaundements of God. Con-
sider fourthly (*For, what euill
hath bee done*) the innocency
of Christ, so often repeated :
That thou mayst euer remember, that Christ dyed, not for
his owne sinnes, but for thine;
this worde shall condemne all
sinners at the last Iudgement.
Why (will our Lord say) haue
yee forsaken mee, and fled vnto the Deuill ? For, what euill
haue I done ? What haue you
found in my manners & Do-
ctrine, that is not pure, and a-
greeable

greeable to reason? What e-
uill haue yee had from me, or
what good haue you found in
the seruice of the Deuill? Doe
thou now meditate vpō these
thinges, and perseuere in the
faith of Christ. Consider lastly, howe these clamours did
wound the heart of Christ,
and how hee was more grieued for this so great and hey-
nous a sinne of his beloued
people, then for the torment
of the Crosse. Doe thou comfort him with thy deuoute
prayer, and forsaking the Deuill and his pompes, yeild thy
selfe wholy a slaue and
seruant vnto
Christ.

⋆§⋆
⋆ ⋆
⋆

The

The 24. Meditation of the whipping of our Lord.

Then Pilate *apprehended him and whipped him. Then the Soldiours of the President taking* Iesus, *carryed him into the Pretors court, and they gathered together all the company vnto him.*

Onsider first, that the spouse of thy soule, that hee might betroth himselfe vnto thee, was diuers waies mocked, spit vpon, pulled, and beaten : but nowe hee is come to woundes and bloud ; that hee, which gaue vnto thee his honors, liberty, and other corporall goods, and suffered himselfe to bee spoyled of all these for thy sake,

sake, might now in like manner plentifully shed his bloud,
and powre out his bowels,
that hee might see, what liberality thou wilt vse towards
him againe. Consider secondly two causes, why *Pilate* v-
sed this whipping. The one
was, that by the sight of the
body of Christ torne with so
many stripes, hee might some-
what pacifie the fury of the
Iewes, and stay them, from the
desire of the Crosse. The o-
ther was, that if neuerthelesse
they persisted in their fury,
this whipping should goe before his crucifying. For by the
lawes of the *Romanes,* such as
were to be crucified were first
whipped But ỹ true cause of ỹ
whipping of Christ according
to

to the will of his Father, was firſt that thou, which wert ſicke in euery part of thy body, mighteſt bee wholy cured by the woundes of his whole body. Secondly that he might receiue thee wholy, who gaue himſelfe wholy for thee. Thirdly, that thou ſhouldeſt open the bowels of thy loue towards him, who by theſe ſtripes opened his body to thee. Conſider thirdly, that *Pilate* deliuered Chriſt to the *Pretorian* Soldiours, who aſſembled their whole band, which was the tenth part of a Legion, to wit; Sixe hundred ſixty ſixe Soldiours)by whom hee was carried into the court of the Pretor, that is, into a more ſpacious roome, & forſaken

faken of all friends was expofed vnto ỹ prey, like a Lambe
in the midſt of Wolues. Enter thou into this Court; mark
attentiuely the cruell wantonnes of the Soldiours, and the
modeſty of Chriſt in all theſe
miſeryes, his cleare and amiable countenance, and his incredible patience. Firſt they
deſpoyled him of all his cloathes, & ſet him naked amõgſt
them. Conſider the ſhame-
faſtnes of thy moſt chaſt Lord
ſet naked before ſo great a
company of men, and keepe
the clothes, which hee put off,
to couer thy nakednes. Then
they tyed his holy body to a
piller, with his armes ſtretch-
ed vp, that his whole body
might bee ſubiect to ſtripes.
Then

Then euery one made a whip,
either with roddes brought
thither of purpofe, or elfe of
cordes, (for this word φλαγελ-
λιον, which wee call a whip, as
Euthemius noteth, is a fcourge
wouen with little cordes or
leather thongs) and euery one
fell to worke. Pray thou thy
Lord, that this his nakedneffe
may couer thy foule with his
heauenly grace and vertues;
and thefe his bonds free thee
from finnes; and this his being
alone amongft his cruell enemyes, may deliuer thee from
the handes of thy enemyes.

*Secondly, of the whipping it
felfe.*

Onfider firft how cruell
it was. By the auncient
Law the *Iewes* were forbidden
to

to giue any man aboue forty
ſtripes, this being added for
the cauſe of the Commaundement, *Leaſt thy brother ſhould*
depart before thine eyes fowly Deut. 25.
torne with ſo many ſtripes. But
the *Gentiles* who were neither
tyed by the *Iewes* Law, nor
moued with any commiſera-
tion, exceeded this number
ſo farre, as it was reuealed vn- St. Gert.
to ſome Saints, that hee recei- lib. 4 diui-
ued to the number of 5. thou- nam inſu-
ſand 4. hundred ſtripes: w̃ will mationū,
not ſeem improbable, if theſe Cap. 35.
few things be diligently cõſi-
dered 1. The Law of beating,
by which it was decreed that
the guilty perſon, ſhould bee
ſtricken by euery one of the
Soldiours, a Free-man with
ſtaues, and a Bond-man
with

with whippes. By which Law
thou doſt learn, that thy Lord
Chriſt was beaten with whips
like a Bond-ſlaue , that hee
might reſtore thee to liberty,
and that hee was beaten by
Sixe hundred and threeſcore
Soldiours , according to the
will of euery one. Secondly,
the cauſe of the Lawe of this
whipping of thē, which were
cōdemned to the puniſhment
of the Croſſe, to wit ; that the
body of him , that was to bee
crucified, ſhould bee ſo disfi-
gured, ẙ the nakednes ſhould
not moue the beholders to a-
ny diſhoneſt thoughtes, when
they ſhould ſee nothing plea-
ſing or beautiful, but al things
torne and full of commiſeration. Thirdly the purpoſe, of

Pilate,

Pilate, who hoped to spare his life by this so great cruelty vsed against him. Hee would therefore, that this correction should bee most sharpe, by which hee might pacifie the desire of reuenge in his most cruell and inhumane enemies. Fourthly, the hatred of the Priestes, whome to please, the Soldiours vsed all extremityes against Christ. Fiftly, the great care and hast, which thePriests vsed in the carrying of the Crosse of Christ, least Christ should dye before hee was crucified : Which doth plainly shew, that he was beaten with so many stripes, that hee could not long continue. Consider secondly the mãner obserued in this whipping.

M   For

For firſt his breaſt was faſt tyed to a piller, and they cruelly
rent his backe, according to
that : *Vpon my backe haue ſin-*
ners builded : or according to
the Hebrues : *Haue Plough-*
men ploughed : that is to ſay,
haue moſt cruelly torne it.
And when that part was cut
with ſtripes, then our Lord
was vntyed, that the fore-part
of his body, his breaſt, his belly, his thighes, might bee as
cruelly vſed, according to the
Prophet : *From the ſole of his*
foote, to the crowne of his head
there was no wholenes in him.
And ẏ this was ſo, thou mayſt
knowe by this, when *Pilate*
ſhortly after bringing foorth
Chriſt vnto the people ſaide :
Behold the man. Hee did not
ſhew

.Pſal. 128

shew his backe couered with Purple, but his breast and his fore-part for them to behold. Doe thou with the eies of thy soule beholde the cruelty of the Soldiours, and the amiable patience of Christ. Listen with thy eares to the wordes, laughters, and scoffings of these deryding Soldiours, w they vttered blasphemously, whilest they were whipping, tormenting, and binding the body of Christ. Admire the deepe silence of Christ in all these stripes, who complained of no paines, neither in crye, nor sighe. To bee briefe, doe thou inwardly feele the paynes of these stripes, which peirced euen to the very bones and bowels.

M 2 Ga-

Gather vp the bloud, which dropped downe vpon the ground; apply it to thy sinnes and wounds; & pray thy Lord, that he will not suffer it to be shedd so plentifully for thee in vaine.

Thirdly after his whipping.

COnsider first, the tormentors were wearyed; the whippes and rodds fayled; and Christ, being spent with paines and losse of bloud, was scāt able to stand vpō his feet. Spare not thou thy selfe, but spend thy youthfull yeares and strength iṅ the seruice of thy Lord. Consider secondly how thy Lord crept vp and downe to gather vp his scattered cloathes, and put them on, not without great paine, which

which cleaued to his wounds,
and were spotted with bloud,
and hurt his soares. Doe thou
gather together the Church,
being the vestment of Christ :
and spare no labour to gayne
soules which are washed with
that bloud. Wash the wounded body of Christ with thy
teares, and anoynt it with the
oyle of Charity and Deuotion, and omitt nothing which
thou thinkest may helpe towards the cure of this body,
and of the members thereof.
Consider thirdly, that Christ
our Lord did drinke his bloud
thus plentifully vnto thee in
this his whipping, & in his coronation following in ỹ third
houre, in which same houre
after his ascensiõ into Heauen,

M 3   he

he sent downe the holy Ghost
into the hearts of his Apostles
& of his whole Church. That
thou mayest learne, first that
the bloud of Christ was plentifully shed, that the grace of
the holy Ghost might plentifully bee communicated vnto
thee. Secondly that at the
same time, when the effusion
of this bloud is remembred, &
renewed in the Church by the
Sacrifice of the Masse , thou
being present shouldest with
open heart plentifully receiue
the fruit of this bloud, ẏ grace
of the holy Ghost, and diuers
other guiftes. The Meditation
hereof stirreth vp admiration,
increaseth confidence, inkind-
leth loue , mooueth compassion , bringeth sorrowe for
                         sinnes,

sinnes, exhorteth to labour,
and melteth the soule in gi-
uing thankes.

The 25. Meditation of
the Crowning of
our Lord.

Then they vncloathing him,
put a scarlet Garment about   Mat. 27
him, and weauing a Crowne of   Mar. 15
thornes, they put it vpon his head   Ioan. 19
and a Reede in his right hand.

COnsider first, that those
Torturers deuised a new
kinde of torment, which
might both afflicte, and
also make him to be mocked :
That hee, which called himselfe King of the *Iewes*, might
bee cloathed in royall ornaments.   Consider secondly,
in this place foure kindes of
         M 4   mock-

mockings. Firſt, they pull off al his clothes, w̄ a little before he had put on, renewing the griefe of his wounds, to w̄ the cloath cleaued, and ſtripping his holy and virginall body naked, not without ſhame and confuſion. Secondly, they put on a ſcarlet garment, that his purple bloud ſhed all ouer his body, and the purple garment put vpon him might ſhewe foorth a royall ornament. Thirdly, in ſtead of a Dyademe they ſet vpon his head a Crowne, wouen of many buſhie thorns, which (ſaith *Tertullian*) did teare & deface the Temples of our Lord. Fourthly, they gaue him a Reede in his hand, in ſtead of a Scepter. O thou Chriſtian, behold

Li. de corona militis.

behold thy King, behold the
tryumph of his coronation.
Consider thirdly, that ȳ great
benefites which our Lord prepared for vs, are signified by
these illusions. For first the taking off of his garments,
whereby our Lords body deformed with so many woūds,
spotted with bloud, spittle, &
dirt, & loathsome to behold,
was vncouered; signifieth the
foulenesse of thy soule, defiled
with the spottes of so many
sinnes; which foule spottes
Christ by his passion remoued
from thee vpon himselfe, that
he might cleanse thee from all
filth. Secondly, by the scarlet Garment is signified our
nature, which is bloudy and
guilty of death, which Christ
M 5   assuming

affuming to the vnity of his
perfon, did Sanctifie ; and alfo
thy finnes, being as redde as a
Worme, which Chrift tooke
away by his Paffion ; and alfo
the members of the Church
the body of Chrift, which being in this world diuerfly afflicted , are couered with this
garment of Chrift, that they
fhall not faint, but increafe in
merites. For nothing doth fo
much comfort the afflictions
of a Chriftian man , nothing
doth fo much aduance piety,
as the earneft meditation of
Chrift. Thirdly his Crowne
of thornes is thy barren and
fharpe pricking finnes, fprung
through concupifcence out of
the curfed earth of thy body.
Fourthly our *Lord* holdeth a
Reede

Reede in his hand, whereby is signified, that by thinges accounted base in the world, as his Crosse, Passion, and Humility, hee winneth the Kingdome of the whole world, and vpholdeth all fraile, vaine, and scrupulous men by his Passion, and right hand. Doe thou pray our Lord to make thee partaker of all these thinges, and remember that it is vndecent for dainty and delicate members to lye vnder a head full of thornes.

And they came vnto him, and bending their knee, they adored, and mocked him, and they began to salute him, saying : Haile King of the Iewes.

Mat. 27.
Mar 15.
Ioan. 19

Consider first foure other kinde of irrisions :
First

First (*They came vnto him*) as seruants vse to come vnto their King, asking him in mockage, if he wanted any thing. Whome thou doest imitate, being a Christian onely in name, and indeede a bond-slaue vnto the Deuill, confessing Christ in wordes, but in thy deedes denying him. Secondly they adored (*bending their knee*) or as Saint *Marke* saith (*their knees*) none of them bending both their knees, but euery man one. His adoration is fraudulent that kneeleth on the ground with one knee, and holds the other vpright, vpon which his body may rest. Whó th. u dost imitate, when in thy outward gesture thou adorest God,

God, & in thy minde thou fol-
lowest pride, lust, and other vices. 3. (*They mocked him*) diuers waies, as their wanton
wickednes did prouoke them.
He is mocked vpon earth,
whose Maiestie the Angells in
heauen adore. But yet, because
God cannot be mocked, doe
thou shew thy selfe before
him with all submission & purity of heart. 4. (*They saluted
him, saying, haile King of the
Iewes*) an excellent speach,
wherewith thou also maist salute the King of those *Iewes*, w
acknowledg their sins, & sing
praises vnto God. Blessed art
thou if thou hast a King, by
whome thou maist be sweetly
gouernd in this world, & after
this life be made partaker of
his

his Kingdome. Cõsider 2. that Chriſt by ſeeing and hearing thoſe ignominies, did cure all poſterity frõ the Serpents hiſſing into the eares of *Eue*, and from the vanity of her eyes, through the curioſity wherof ſhee infected our eyes. Pray our Lord to conuert all theſe to the profite of thy ſoule.

And they ſpit vpon him, and they tooke a reede, and ſtrooke his head with the reede, and they gaue him blowes.

Mat. 27.
Mar. 15.
Ioan. 19.

COnſider firſt, 4. other kinds of mockings. 1. *(They ſpit vpon him)* defiling in ſo vnworthy & ſcurrile manner, not only his face, but his breaſt alſo, & his whole body: Yea the body of him, *Who is the brightnes of glory, and the ſubſtance of the*

the Father, whome the Angels
desire to behold. 2. (They take
a reede) faining to doe him
seruice, as though they would
ease him, being weary of the
burthē of his Scepter. 3. (They
strike his head with the reede)
that the Thornes might bee
deeper fastened into his head.
Marke how by these blowes
the thornes pierced to ỹ very
Scull of his head, & fasined in
the ioining of ỹ bones, & were
there brokē. 4 (They gaue him
blowes) not with their bare
hand, but being armed against
the pricking of ỹ thorns. Heer
do thou admire together with
his other vertues, our Lords
Charity, Patience, Meeknes,
Benignity, & aboue al, his hū-
ble obediēce, by w̄ he yeilded
him-

Heb. 1.
1 Pet.1

himselfe to the will of his tormentors, and being commanded to fit downe, to lift vp
his head to the Thornes, to
holde the Reede in his hand,
to expofe his Face to blowes,
hee obeyed without delay.
Confider fecondly, that thefe
Ethnicks, though they offered
many iniuryes to our Lord;
yet they neuer couered his
face; that Chrift with the eies
of his mercy might behold vs
louingly, and forfaking the
Iewes might of *Gentiles* make
vs Chriftians. Thou learneft
firft, not to couer the truth
with new opinions, nor to de-
cline to Hærefie; but openly
to profeffe the true Faith, how
great a finner foeuer thou beeft. Thou learneft fecondly,
                              not

not to neglect thy cõscience,
when it pricketh and warneth
thee of thy sinnes : For the
beginning of thy conuersion
is, when thy conscience re-
prooueth thee. Pray vnto thy
Lord, that he neuer turne his
face from thee, that hee preserue thee in the true Faith,
and adorne thee with true
vertues, especially with humble and willing obedience,
that thou mayest faithfully o-
bey thy betters , not onely in
light and easie thinges, but
also in great, sharpe,
and difficult
matters.

The

The 26. Meditation of *Pilate* his bringing foorth of our Lord to the People.

Pilate went foorth agaíne, and said vnto them: Behold I bring him forth vnto you, that yee may know, that I find no cause in him.

COnsider firft, that when *Pilate* thoght our Lord had beene fo cruelly vfed, that it would haue moued a ftony heart to compaffion, then hee brought him foorth. yet going himfelfe a little before, to prepare the hearts of the *Iewes* to pitty. The wicked Iudge doth herein condemne himfelfe, when hee côfeffeth him to bee innocent, whome hee had handled fo cruelly, to pleafe other men.

Confi-

Confider fecondly (*Behold I bring*) for it is a wonderfull thing, that God, who hath beftowed vpon men fo many & fo great benefits, fhould fuffer fo many wronges and wounds by mē. Admire thine owne ingratitude. God hath brought thee into this world, adorned with all goodnes : & thou bringeft him foorth, and cafteft him out of thy heart, fhamefully mifufed with thy grieuous finnes, & doeft not fuffer him to reft in thy houfe, which thou haft filled with theft and other finnes. Doe thou rather bring him foorth to bee prayfed and adored by the people. Firft by preaching him, & his will to the people, and then by thy good works,

expref-

expressing his holy life : That
thou mayest say with the A-
postles *(And now I doe not liue,
but Christ liueth in mee.)* And
bringing him foorth let all
men vnderstand , that there is
no cause to bee found in him,
why he should not be admitted by all men, when as thou
canst see nothing in him , but
signes of loue, bloud shed for
thee, stripes, and wounds, so as
it may be truly said of him :

*Cernitur in toto corpore sculp-
tus amor.*

In all his members Loue ingrauen is.

Then Iesus *went forth, carrying his thorny Crowne, & purple garment.*

COnsider first , howe thy
Lord came forth amógst
the people. Beholde a high
place,

Galat. 6.

Ioan. 19.

place, to which they ascended
by twenty three marble steps,
(which are kept till this day at
Rome with great reuerence,)
and before that a most spaci-
ous Court, filled with many
thousands of people, who had
assembled themselues out of
all *Iudæa* against the feast of
Pasch.   All these so soone as
they espied our Lord cóming
forth with Pilate, came prea-
sing nearer, that they might
better beholde this sadde and
horrible spectacle. *Goe forth
also, yee Daughters of* Ierusa-
lem, *and behold King* Salomon   Cant.3.
*in the diademe, wherewith his
Mother the Synagogue of the
Iewes h ith crowned him.* Goe
thē also forth, O my Soule, &
behold the Diademe, and the
royall

royall otnamenis, which thy
finnes haue fet vpon thy God.
Marke attentiuely the whole
body of thy peaceable King,
cruelly torn with his enemyes
handes : that he might gaine a
moft affured peace with God
for thee,& for thy confcience.
Behold his Crowne wouen of
boughes,decked with thorns,
and droppes of bloud in liew
of precious ftones : His hands
and armes carry cords in ftead
of bracelets: His necke and all
his body, is tyed with a rope,
in ftead of a belt,& Chaine of
gold:The works of his apparrell is fcars & wounds :His diuine Coũtenance with fleame,
fpittings,bloud,& filth,is as it
were painted,or masked, and
difguifed. Let thefe thinges
moue

moue horror in others, & cō-
paffion in thee. Maik ẙ words
of *Iſaias.* *Hee hath no beauty*
nor comelines ; wee ſaw him, and Iſi.33
he had no countenance : That is,
hee looked not like a man, *and*
his countenance was as it were
hidden, & looking downe ; & wee
eſteemed him, as a Leaper. Doe
thou reuerence this attire of
thy Lord with the inward affection of thy heart, in ẘ hee
fought againſt thy enemies, &
got victory & glory for thee.
For euen as thou eſteemeſt
thoſe thinges, & keepeſt them
carefully, by which thy friend
hath gotten riches, & honour
for thee ; ſo thou oughteſt re-
ligiouſly to meditate , worſhip, and imbrace thoſe ſpit-
tings, whips & reproaches, ẘ
haue

haue brought aboundance of
so great goods vnto thee. For
our Lord knoweth his owne
attyre, and he will more easily
receiue thee comming in such
garments , then in worldly
pompe and brauery: And hee
had rather haue thee to pray,
and worship him in this poor
array, then in all thy braue attyre. Consider secondly, that
Ioan. 1   this sack of the body of Christ
which came down from Hea-
uen, full of grace and truth, is
now opened, and torne in all
partes , breathing out of his
holy bowels a wonderfull sa-
uour, so sharpe, that it driueth
Mat.24.   away Deuils; so peircing, that
it entreth into stony hearts,
and so sweete, that it draweth
the Eagles from all partes of
the

the world. For *whe*‒*e the body shall bee, thither also will the Eagles be gathered.* Purge thou the noſtrils of thy heart, purge thou the filth of thy vices; that being ſtirred vp with ẙ ſweetnes of the ſauour of God, *Thou mayſt runne into the ſweet ſauour of theſe oyntments.* And pray vnto our Lord to drawe thee after him with his ſweetnes, & to inſtill into thy heart the loue of his Paſſion, that thou mayeſt contemne the world in reſpect therof. *(And he ſaid, behold the man)* by this worde, *Pilate* endeauoured to mooue ſome commiſeration, ſhewing firſt the bitternes of his punniſhment, as if hee had ſaid, knowe that hee is a man and not a beaſt; if hee haue

Mat. 24.

Cant. 1

N   com-

committed any fault, he hath
paid wel for it : therfore ô mē,
take pitty vpon a man, it is the
part of beasts not to spare the
conquered. And again, behold
he is a man, & a most miserable man, whom ye haue accused as King of the *Iewes*; there
is no cause, why yee should be
afraid of this King, whome
through the great deformity
of his body, & cruell tormēts,
yee can scarce knowe to be a
man. Doe thou apply these
words profitably vnto thy
selfe in this māner. I. (*Behold
the man*) he is set before thee
to imitate, in this habite, in
these gestures, and in this
shape of body, and minde.
Abraham was proposed to
our Aunceſtours for an example

ample of life. *Marke the Rock* (*saith* Isaias) *out of which yee were cut,* Heere a man is proposed vnto thee, of whom our Heauenly Father saith : *Heare him :* and the Sonne of God : *Learne yee of mee, for I am meeke and humble of heart.* Looke therefore not vpon other mens manners, but vpon this mans, vpon this face of Christ : who although hee be God, whose vertues and deedes thou canst not attayne vnto, yet he is true man, indued with the same frayle and humane nature like thee and other men. Thy first Father *Adam* made thee of a man like to foolish Beastes : If thou wilt returne to the auncient dignity of

Isa.51

Mat. 27.

Psal. 84.

N 2   humane)

humane nature, ioyne thy-
felfe with this man. Secondly
(*beholde the man*) to whome
thou maift flye in all thy ne-
ceffities : thefe fpittings are
fuffered for thee; this bloud
is fhedd for thee; and all thefe
euills are indured for thy fake:
both that thou fhouldeft take
away thy finnes, and cure thy
wounds by thefe medicines,
and alfo that thou fhouldeft
pay them to the eternall Father for thy infinite depts.
Thirdly (*behold the man*)
marke what thy finnes haue
brought vnto this man : thy
pride hath caufed thefe irri-
fions and this contempt; thy
couetoufneffe, this nakednes;
thy drunkenneffe, this effufi-
on of bloud; thy luft, thefe
thornes;

thornes; and thy sloath, these
bonds. O man, behold this
man: but who art thou, and
what is he? thou a man like a
worme, he a man and God.
Oh how great glory is due vnto him, and how much shame
vnto thee? yet what is he become for thy sake? and what
sufferest, or doest thou for
him? *he is made a worme and no* Psal. 21
man, a scorne of men, and an ab-
iect of the people. And this, because he would carry thee vp
to God. But thou being carefull of nothing lesse, then of
exalting his glory, apply-
est thy selfe about thine
own honor, wealth,
and
commoditie.

**

N 3   The

The 27. Meditation of the third accusation of our Lord before Pilate.

Ioan. 16

Then whē the high Priests and the Ministers sawe him, they cryed, saying, crucifie him, crucifie him.

COnsider first, the people holding their peace, and inclyning to cōmiseration, the Priestes and their ministers, and flatterers were not pacified. That thou maist knowe first, ẙ no man is moued more hardly to repent his sinnes, then he, which sinneth of set purpose and malice. For they, which fall thorough weakenesse and ignorance, are sooner recalled, and deserue pardon ; but they, which

which wittingly and willingly
are euill, are rather hardned &
indurate, thē any way amēded
by admonitions. 2. That the
enimies of Chriſt and of his
Church, are neuer ỹ better for
being vſed gētly & curteouſly.
For theſe kind of mē are to be
ſubdued by thretnings, terrors
& conſtancy, & not by ſuffer-
ance. Conſider 2. That euen as
theſe wicked men did vpon
the ſight of the bloud of
Chriſt thirſt after his death,
like dogges vpon the ſight of
the bloud of a wilde Beaſt :
So thou oughteſt to be inflamed with the loue of the
paſſion of our Lord by the
contemplation of his paines,   Pſal. 38.
that the fire of Deuotion
may be inkindled in thy
N 4   medi-

meditations. Confider thirdly how the words of thefe wicked people did pierce the bowells of thy Lord (*crucifie him, crucifie him*)of which he foretold in the Prophet : *I haue left my houfe : I haue put away my inheritance : I haue giuen my beloued foule into the hands of her enemies : my inheritance is made vnto me like a Lyon in the word.* Suffer with thy Lord, and lament thy finnes, which continually fend foorth the fame cryes, and are bloud-fuckers, inftantly crying, *Bring, Bring.*

Hiere 12

Iro.30

Ioan. 19.

Pilate *faid vnto them, take yee him and crucifie him : for I finde no caufe in him.*

Onfider firft that *Pilate* being moued with difdaine , anfwered fomewhat fharply sharply vnto the *Iewes*. Admire thou thy own coldnesse, who art a Christian, & knowest the dignity of Christ, and the greatnesse of his paines, and doest confesse, that thou wert the cause thereof, and yet art not moued, neither with commiseration towards Christ, nor with disdaine against thy selfe. Learne iustly to be angry at them, which goe about to incite thee, and others vnto sinne : that is to say, at the Deuill, and his ministers. Say vnto him, if thou wilt offend the goodnesse of God, I finde no cause in him, but of loue, reuerence, and thankesgiuing. Consider 2. Though *Pilate* was loath to pronounce ỹ sentēce of death

N 5   against

againſt our Lord; yet he did not hinder his death, but wold put it ouer to other mē. Whō thou doeſt imitate, as often as thou leaueſt to the will of others that miſchife, ẅ thou thy ſelfe dareſt not cōmit. Conſider 3. That this wicked Preſidēt, after all this grieuous puniſhment, found no cauſe in him, either of death, or ſtripes. Doe thou inquire the cauſe in the opened bowells of Chriſt, to wit, his burning loue, ẅ cutt & brake aſunder this ſacke of his body, & poured foorth his bloud ſo plētifully. What will the holy Angels do ẅ were aſtoniſhed in ẙ natiuity of this Lord, at the wonderfull loue which cauſed almighty God to take vpon him a frayle and infants

infants body. How will they
be amazed both at this loue
of God, w for man was cótent
to be esteemed a worm, rather
then a man, & to be the scorn
of men, and the outcast of the
people,& the scum and laugh-
ing stocke of all men; & also
at the raging malice of the
Iewes, who would neuer bee
satisfied with the paines and
punishment of their *Messias*,
which so many ages before
was expected,& promised vnto them; and likewise at the
hardnes of thine owne heart,
which is not softened and
melted with this burning charity of thy Creator. Admire
thou these thinges, and pray
thy Lord to inflame thy heart
with the loue of him.

      The

Ioan. 19

The Iewes answered him: we haue a Lawe, and according to the lawe he ought to dye, because hee made himselfe the Sonne of God.

Onsider firſt, the proud anſwere of the Iewes *(we haue a Lawe.)* They belieued in the lawe, which they had in writing; and did not fulfill it in worke. Thoſe men doe imitate them firſt, which boaſt of the word of God, and continually obiect the ſame, and are wholy in the commendation of faith : when in the mean time they do nothing worthy neither of faith, nor of the holy Scriptures, nor yet of a Chriſtian man. Secondly, they which place all pisty in outward ceremonies onely, and

not

not in ẏ worſhip of God, & in
brotherly charity. Conſider 2.
That according to the Lawe
Chriſt ought to dye. For the
whole lawe of *Moſes*, and of
the Prophets, foreſhewed the
death of Chriſt; for all the ſacrifices of the old Law, were
ſhadowes of the ſacrifice of
the Croſſe : and all the Prophets referred their propheſies
to the death of the Meſſias.
Therefore the *Iewes* ſaid true,
but not according to their
owne intention, whoſe meaning was, that the ſinne and
blaſphemy of Chriſt deſerued
death by the Lawe, that thou
maieſt learne, that God
turneth to thy good thoſe
things, which are badly ſpoken or done by the wicked :
and

and also that thou shouldest
drawe goodnes euen out of
wicked men. Consider third-
the cause of his death (*Because
hee made himselfe the Sonne of
God.*)   A most true cause of
death : First if thou doest consider, God the Father ; for the
Son of God, being made man,
made man the Sonne of God,
assuming humane nature into
one person of the Sonne of
God. For wee should neuer
haue come into grace with
the eternall Father, but by the
death of that man, who was
the true and very Sonne of
God Secondly, if thou consider the *Iewes* ; because hee
liued the life of the Sonne of
God.   For therefore their
enuy was exasperated to the
death

death of Christ, because his most Holy life reprehended their wicked behauiours. Take thou heede, that neuer any other fault bee noted in thee, but onely that thou art the sonne of God. For if thou doest suffer for that cause, thou art happy, and the faithfull Disciple of Christ. And because the Sonne of God did vndergoe this death to make thee the Sonne of God, pray him that hee will lighten thy soule with his Grace, and exalt thee to bee the Sonne of God, and after this life by communicating his Diuinity vnto thee, he will number thee amongst the Sonnes of God, and graunt thee thy portion among his

Saints

Saints, which shall bee called the sonnes of God.

The 28. Meditation of
the second examination
of Christ made by
Pilate.

When Pilate *heard that speach bee feared more, and entred againe into the Pallace, and said vnto him, whence art thou? but* Iesus *gaue him no answere.*

Ioan. 19

COnsider first, that *Pilate* being an Ethnicke, and possessed with the error of the *Gentiles*, feared least Christ was ẙ Son of some God, as perhaps of *Iupiter*, or *Mars*. For so the Poets faine of *Romulus*, and *Remus*, and of diuers others : and Christ his modesty in answering, and his graui-

grauity of manners confirmed
this opinion. Hee feared therfore the indignation of the
God his Father, whose Sonne
hee had so vniustly whipped.
The *Gentile* feared the vaine
wrath of the *Gentile* God, and
feared not the grieuousnes of
his sin : neither did the *Iewes*
feare the most iust wrath of
the true God. Thou likewise
doest feare sometimes shadowes, dreames, and childish
fancies ; and art not affraid of
the Deuill, who is alwayes
at thine elbowe, when thou
sinnest ; nor the district iudgment of Christ, whome thou
doest offend ; nor Hell mouth
gaping for thee. Consider secondly *(Whence art thou.)* E-
uill men neither knowe God
the

the giuer of all good thinges, nor from whence any good commeth to them. *The Oxe knoweth his Keeper, and the Asse, the manger of his Lord.* Hennes, Cattes, and Hogges when meat is cast vnto them, lift vp their heades, and looke vpon them, that cast the same : And man, who hath receiued so many benefites frō God, doth neither thanke, nor knowe God. Consider thirdly, that Christ made no answere. First, because it was not necessary seeing hee had manifested his innocency before ; and also satisfied this question, saying : *My Kingdome is not of this world: I was borne for this, and for this I came into the World, &c.*

For

For our Lord spake but sel-
dome, and neceſſary thinges,
and (as St. *Chryſoſtome* ſaith)
leaſt hee might ſeeme proude
by his continuall ſilence. Secondly, leaſt by his anſweares
hee might bee thought deſirous to eſcape, and to auoyde
death . which he might eaſily
haue done, if either hee himſelfe, or any other for him had
ſeriouſly defended his cauſe.
Thirdly leaſt hee ſhould giue
holy thinges vnto Dogs. For
at this time *Pilate* by his great
ſinne of whipping him , had
made himſelfe vnworthy of
an anſwere at Gods handes.
Fourthly, becauſe an Heathen
man could not vnderſtand
the anſwere of that , which
the Angells cannot conceiue.
                         For

Hom. 87.
in Mat.

Isa 53

For from whence is that Person, which with his Maiesty filleth both Heauen & Earth; which alwayes springing in the bosome of the Father, is alwayes borne and perfect; whose generation noe man can declare . Thou therefore pondering in thy minde the Maiesty of thy Lord, and seeing him before this wicked President thus fowly torn, deformed, with so many stripes, and couered with so many spittings, filth, and torments, admire and aske him, whence art thou ? Art thou hee, whose Father is God, whose Seruants are the Angels , and whose Kingdome is Heauen ? For if wee may Iudge of a man according to his habite , thou seemest

seemest to bee a Worme, rather then a Man, brought forth of the durte, rather then comming from Heauen.

Then Pilate *said vnto him : Doest thou not speake vnto mee ? doest thou not knowe, that I haue power to crucifie thee, and power to dismisse thee ?*

Ioan. 19

Consider first, the pride of *Pilate.* First because hee thought he was contemned by this silence of Christ, hee threatneth him with his power and authority. For a proud man is soone angry, and will not suffer indignity at anothers hand, and yet careth not what iniury hee offereth to them himselfe. Secondly, that hee attributeth to himselfe the power, which hee hath receiued

ued from another : that thou
mayest learne, first to referre
all thy good things vnto God
from whome thou hast receiued them, least hee take them
from thee for thy ingratitude.
Secondly to acknowledge
those guiftes, and to vse them
to the honour of thy Lord,
least by abusing thē thou beest grieuously punished. Consider therefore earnestly with
thy selfe thine owne wealth,
authority, learning, strength
of body, and thy other guifts;
and howe much good thou
mayest doe thereby, either for
the increasing of Gods glory,
or the saluation of thy neighbours ; and how much good
thou hast done : and labour
instantly to doe as much

as

as thou art able ; for neither
worke, nor reason, nor wisdome, nor knowledge shall
bee in Hell, to which place
thou makest hast. Consider **Eccle.9.**
secondly, that *Pilate* acknowledgeth free power in himselfe to crucifie our Lord, and
to dismisse him : That thou
mayest learne, first, that thou
doest not want free will to
doe well, or ill; and that thou
mayest vse it to the exercise
of vertue, and not to commit sinnes. Secondly, that it
is an euill freedome, whereby
wee may doe euill ; and an **Au. Epist**
excellent necessitie, which **45.**
bringeth vs to better thinges.
Doe thou then ioyne thy selfe
so vnto Christ, that it shall not
bee in thy power to doe ill,
but

but that thou mayest will and doe onely good and vertuous thinges. For that is true Christian liberty, so to bee able to worke through vertue, and to effect those things, which reason & faith doth dictate; that wee would not sinne, though it were lawfull, the will being so confirmed in good, that it cannot bee diuerted by any impediments, either of concupiscence, or any other thing.

Iesus *answered, thou couldest haue no power against mee, except it were giuen thee from aboue. Wherefore hee, which hath deliuered mee to thee, hath the greater sinne.*

Ioan.19

COnsider first, that by these wordes Christ abated the pride of *Pilate,* teaching him, that

that hee had of himſelfe no
power, but that, which was
either giuen him from aboue
by *Cæſar*, whoſe Vicegerent
hee was (as St. *Auguſtine* in-
terpreteth this place,) or granted him from God in Heauen,
without whoſe ſpeciall permiſſion no man could doe a-
ny thing againſt Chriſt the
Sonne of God. *Pilate* recci-
ued this power with the enemyes of our Lord, when hee
gaue them lycence in the garden to rage againſt him, by
theſe wordes : *This is your
hower, and the power of darknes.*
And although it was neceſſary to haue a more peculiar
permiſſion to rage againſt
Chriſt, then againſt any other
Chriſtian. Yet thou mayeſt
        O   learne

Tract. in
Ioan 116.

Luc. 22.

learne truely with Saint *Cyprian,* that the Deuill can doe
nothing againſt man, except
God perinitt him. Conſider
ſecondly, (*he which deliuered
me to thee, hath the greater ſin*)
to wit, then if he had offered
any other man to be put to
death by thee : or greater ſin
then thou; partly becauſe thou
maiſt be much moued there-
vnto by reaſon of thy authority, and by the people, and
the chiefe men, whereas hee
did it of himſelfe by priuate
hate, and ſetled malice ; partly becauſe thou knoweſt not
the dignity of my perſon, and
office, w̄ the *Iewes* muſt needs
knowe by the propheſies of ẙ
Prophets, hauing ſeene ſo many myracles, w̄ could not happen,

pen, but by the *Messias*, so as
they had no excute of their sin
Thou seest first that al sins are
not alike (as some men fayne)
but that those sinnes are more
grieuous, which come of deliberate malice, then those w̄
are cõmitted through weakenes or ignorance: and they sin
more which mocke and persecute the godly, then they
which deride wicked men:and
they offend more which induce men to sinne, then they
which are induced ; for the
sinne of such redoundeth also to the inducers.   Secondly, thou learnest to ab-
staine from all sinnes, but e-
specially frõ those w̄ are committed againstGod; as Here-
sie,blasphemy,periury,irrision

Ioan.15

O 2   and

and prophanation of holy and
diuine things. For althogh in
the blinde iudgement of men
(which thinke nothing to bee
a fault, but that, which tendeth to the hurt of our neighbour) thofe thinges feeme
fmall : yet God will reuenge
more fharply the wrong done
vnto him felfe, then to any
other creature. Admire thou
the bounty of Chrift, who fo
louingly taught the wic-
ked Iudge : & pray
him, that he will
neuer giue
thee
libertie
to
finne.

*
* *
*

The

The 29. Meditation of
the fourth accusation
of Christ before
Pilate.

From thence foorth Pilate *sought to dismisse him : but the* Iewes *cryed, saying : if thou dost dismisse him, thou art not friend to* Cæsar: *for euery one that maketh himselfe King, contradicteth* Cæsar : *but when* Pilate *heard these speaches, he brought* Iesus *foorth, and sate in the iudgement seate, in the place called* Lithostrotos, *but in* hebrewe Gabbata; *and it was the* parasecue, *about the sixt houre.*

Io n.19

Onsider first, that *Pilate*, when he heard mentio of sinne thoght earnestly of the dismissing of Christ, for feare of cómiting a

O 3   greater

greater offence : that thou
maift learne hereafter to ab-
fteyne from finne for the loue
of Chrift; for thou haft offended God long enough, and
defiled thy confcience with
the filth of finne : but be thou
more conftant then *Pilate*, v-
pon whom God hath beftow-
ed more grace. Confider fecondly, the burning hate of
the *Iewes*, who wanting matter of accufation, terrifyed
the Iudge with threatnings,
and as it were inforced him to
do wickedly: as if they fhould
fay : Wee will complaine of
thee to *Cæfar*, whofe enemie
and competitor of the kingdome thou haft fauoured.
Wicked men vfe to threaten,
when they cannot preuaile by
truth.

truth. If thou fearest none
but God, thou shalt ouercome
all thy enemies. Confider
thirdly, that *Pilate* hitherto
played the man, fo long as it
concerned not himfelfe : but
when he thought his owne
honour and reputation was
called in queftion, he yeelded
to their threatnings, and was
quite difcouraged : like to
thofe, who defend the truth,
as long as they fhall fuffer
no inconuenience thereby :
but if they perceiue any
ftorme, they prefently turne
fayle, and yeeld vnto the
tempeft, and will not fuffer any kinde of trouble.
Doe thou flie the world,
leaft it carry thee away
from the affaires of Chrift

to some vniust action. For he
which maketh himselfe a king
and ruleth ouer himselfe, and
ouer his desires, is not a friend
to *Cæsar*, the deuill (I meane)
ẙ prince of this world, whose
friendship if thou seekest, and
dost feare his wrath, thou shalt
get that, which happened to
Pilate, who by the complaint
of the *Iewes* in another cause,
lost *Cæsars* friendship, & dyed
miserably in exile. The Deuill
followeth those that feare
him; and flyeth and forsaketh
them, that hate him. Consider fourthly, that the place,
day, and houre of the condemning of Christ is distinct-
ly noted : first, to declare the
greatnesse of the sinne, when
the onely begotten Sonne
of

of the true God was condemned to dye on the Croſſe.
Secondly, to ſignifie the my-
ſterye which is contayned in
the ſame. *It was the day of
the* Paraſceue, that is, the ſixt
day, in which man was created, in which man was to bee
redeemed, in which the true
Lamb was to be immolated,
and in which the typicall
Lamb was ſlaine. (*About the
ſixt houre*) that is, a little before noone, in which houre
the typicall Lambe was prepared to be ſacrificed, and
men doe commonly pamper
and cheriſh their bodies. The
place λιθόϛρωτος, ẙ is, ſtrowed
with ſtones : and במה, that
is, high, becauſe Chriſt was
condēned by men more hard,

and more proud then the very stones; and did receiue this sentence of death for thy pride, and for the hardnes and blindenes of thy heart. Pray vnto thy Lord to lighten thy blindenes, to mollifie thy hardnes, and to suppresse thy pride.

And Pilate *said to them, behold your king : and they cryed, away with him, away with him, crucifie him.*

COnsider first, that *Pilate* preuailing nothing by other reasons, began to prouoke them to mercy by laughter, as if he should say : behold your great King, who yee accuse of aspiring : for he which scarce looketh like a man, how can he hope to be a King ?

King? or elfe that he fpake thefe words, to make them deny their *Meffias*, and to fubmit themfelues to the bódage of the *Romanes,* which was hatefull vnto them. For yet there remained a little fparke of pietye in his minde : that thou mayft learne how hardly our Lord forfaketh vs. Confider fecondly, the three names giuen to Chrift in this time of his paffion by *Pilate* and the *Iewes, A man, a king, the fonne of God :* which three names the Sages acknowledged by their offerings. For faluation could not be giuen vnto vs, except God and man fhould fuffer, who by his Paffion tooke away the kingdome of the world from the

Mat. **2.**

the deuill. Confider thirdly, the word full of comfort, (*behold your king*)by which word the conditions of our King are shewed vnto vs, who is not a sowre, hard, and importunate exactor, oppressing vs with labours, and leading vs with great burthens, and imposing a grieuous yoake vpon vs; but louing and gentle, bestowing on vs through his aboundant charity, his owne labours, dolours, bloud, and life, and that bloud by which alone all the filth of our sinnes is ...thed away: who caryeth also our sinnes & beareth our burthens : briefely, who refresheth vs with his body and bloud,and lifteth vp his sweet

Osea. 11 yoake vpon our shoulders.To this

this King thou haſt giuen thy
name in baptiſme : thou haſt
begun to fight vnder his banner ; behold therefore diligēt-
ly his armour, and obſerue the
manner of his fighting with
his enemy. For thou muſt vſe
ỹ ſame weapons, & fight in the
ſame māner : and if thou doſt
deſire to be rewarded with
the like Honours, thou muſt
ſtriue for the victory, by humility, contempt, Charity, and
other vertues. Cōſider fourthly, the vnbridled rage of the
Iewes, who reiected the King
of iglory, together with his
Kingdome. (*Away with him,*   Luc. 19.
away with him) (ſay they) we
will not haue him reigne ouer
vs. But do thou take this king
of the *Iewes*, reiected by the
                         Iewes,

Iewes, and giuen to the *Gentiles*; and bring him into the house of thy Mother, and into the chamber of her, that bare thee. Make him thy King, and not the World, nor the Deuill, nor thy Belly, nor Mammon. And say not now, *Behold your King;* but beholde, our King, yea, my King, who hath loued me, and giuen himselfe for me. And beware, that thou doest not againe by any sinne crucifie this King, whome thou hast once admitted, least hee complain of thee, saying: *Yee, all yee people, doe nayle me :* But rather being fastened thy selfe vnto the Crosse with Christ, pray him, that hee will fasten thy flesh with his feare.

Cant.3

Mala. 3
Galat. 2.
Psal. 118.

Pilate

Pilate *ſaid vnto them, ſhall I* | Ioan. 19.
crucifie your King? The Prieſts
anſwered, wee haue no King,
but Cæſar.

COnſider firſt, in this queſtion of *Pilate,* howe vnworthy a thing it was , that
the *Meſſias,* who was promiſed to Man-kinde from the
beginning of the world, and
expected ſo many ages, and
at laſt, thorough the mercy of
the eternall Father , ſent for
the ſaluation of the *Iewes* ;
ſhould come to ſuch and ſo
miſerable a death , and as an
vnworthy & accurſed perſon
ſhould bee demaunded to the
horrible puniſhment of the
Croſſe. Do thou look vpó thy
ſelfe,& mark whether perhaps
thou art not in the ſame error.
                    Thou

Thou knoweſt that thou wert borne into this world to this end, ẙ at the laſt thou ſhouldeſt enioy God in euerlaſting and heauenly felicitie. Thou knoweſt that all the whole world was made and framed by God for thy ſake, and that for the ſame cauſe the very Son of God diſcended down from Heauen, was borne of the Virgin *Mary*, and conſecrated all his labours, yea his Paſſion and Death vnto thee. But thou hauing no conſideration of all this, doeſt by thy ſinnes driue away God from thee, when thou oughteſt to imbrace him; thou ſhutteſt vp heauen, & neglecteſt wholy thy ſaluation. Conſider ſecondly the franticke choiſe of
the

the Priests. They refuse the
Messias sent by God, as if it
were in them to choose a
Messias according to their
owne will and pleasure, & not
rather to receiue the *Messias*,
whome God gaue vnto them.
O intollerable madnes of mē !
who will make to themselues
a God according to their
owne will ; or deuise a newe
Religion ; or frame the manner of seruing God out of the
holy Scriptures, wrested and
interpreted according to their
owne fantasies. Wherefore
they are truely called Hære-
tiques, that is, choosers. It is
Gods office to appoint Religion, and the manner how to
serue him ; and not ours, to
choose. Consider thirdly the
nature

nature of enuy, which seeketh
the hurt of another, though it
bee to his owne losse. The
Romane gouernment was very grieuous and hatefull vnto
them, and yet the Priests, both
for themselues, and for the
whole people, preferred it before ỹ sweete yoake of Christ.
Learne first to lay aside all e-
uill affections of thy minde,
least thou fall into more grieuous sinnes. Secondly, not
to esteeme so much of outward Nobility, or power, that
thou shalt therefore breake
the least Commaundement of
God, or swarue one iote from
truth and iustice. For Nobility, power, and authority, are
of no estimation, except the
same be vnder Christ, and for
Christ,

Chriſt, from whom all power
proceedeth, both in Heauen
and Earth, and vnto whom all
Honour and power is due.
Conſider fourthly, that this
fooliſh election of the *Iewes*
is côfirmed by God : for they
haue beene both depriued of
their *Meſſias* nowe ſo many
yeares ; and alſo giuen into
bondage to ſtrange Kinges,
who burned their Citty, and
ouerthrew their Temple, leauing not one ſtone vpon another, *Did eate* Iacob, *& made
his place deſolate, diſperced them
amongſt the* Gentiles, *oppreſſed
them with grieuous ſeruitude,
that they ſhould bee a reproach
to their neighbours, a mocking
ſtocke, & illuſion to them which
were round about them.* Doe
thou

Mat. 22
Mat. 24.
Pſal. 78

thou defire nothing of God. but to bee guided by him, and to take from thee the grie-uous yoake of that tyrant the Deuill.

The 30. Meditation of the condemnation of Chrift.

Mat. 27.

And Pilate *feeing, that he profited nothing, but that the tumult was made greater, taking water, wafhed his handes before the people, faying : I am innocent of the bloud of this iuft man; Looke yee to it.*

PIlate who was a Heathẽ, being mooued with the touch of confcience and reafon, and defirous to difmiffe Chrift vncõdemned ;
the

the *Iewes* beginne to mutiny.
Confider therefore, firft, how
much that afflicted the minde
of Chrift, that a Heathen, being a ftranger frō the knowledge of God, and from the
Sacraments, fhould bee carefull for his deliuery ; and they,
vpon whome God had befto-
wed the knowledge of him-
felfe, and honored them with
many Sacraments, fhould fo
tumultuoufly labour to haue
the fentence of death pronoū-
ced againft him. Learne, not
to maruaile, if fome thinges
happen vnto thee, contrary to
equity and reafon. Confider
fecondly, that the wicked doe
mutiny. For euen as Hell is
replenifhed with tumult and
horror : fo all thinges, which
are

are suggested by the Deuill,
are referred to tumulte and
perturbation,either outwardly amongst the Citizens, or
else inwardly in mens minds.
Consider thirdly the ceremo-
ny of *Pilate*, who washed his
hands with water, but did not
wash away the guilt of conscience,for sinnes are not purged with outward water, but
with teares. Doe thou apply
this water of teares to thy
sinnes already past ; but doe
not vse them, to the end thou
mayest sinne more freely.
For as all sinnes committed
may bee cleansed by teares
and pennaunce : so there is
nothing , which can giue libertie to sinne. Consider
fourthly the wordes of *Pilate*:
I am

(*I am innocent.*) Hee thinketh himselfe innocent , because hee condemned him a-
gainst his will. But he cannot
bee innocent, which sendeth
Iesus to the Crosse, with the
same lippes, by which hee had
pronounced him innocent
before. Thou learnest also,
that they are like vnto those
Iewes, which will neuer take
any warnings, nor bee mooued with any reasons. And
they immitate the sinne of
Pilate : First, which sinne a-
gainst their owne conscience
at the request of others. Secondly , which vnder any
pretence excuse themselues,
and lay the blame vpó others.
Thirdly, which couer the wickednes of their minde with
any

L. ib. 3. ad
A uari. ca.
80

any colour of good. But see that thou doest vse this word of *Pilate* more warily to thine owne benefite : *O Lord, let me bee innocent by the bloud of this iust man.* For seeing hee only is iust, and our true Iustice, nothing can bring mee innocency of my soule, but by the bloud of this iust man, shed for iustice, for the remission of sinnes.

And the whole people answered, saying : His bloud bee vpon vs, and vpon our Children.

Mat. 27

Consider first the blinde fury of enuy : They doe not deny him to bee iust, but whatsoeuer hee bee, they demaund him to be crucified : and ẏ they may giue courage
to

to the fearefull Prefident, and
haften the death of this iuft
man,they binde themfelues &
their pofterity to moft grei-
uous miferies. This worde
wounded the heart of Chrift
our Lord, by which the people of God, who fhould haue
been deliuered by this bloud,
defired the reuenge thereof to
light vpon themfelues. Confider fecondly, how great folly it is, to wifh for that euill,
wherof thou knoweft not the
greatnes. For if euery finne
deferueth a great & grieuous
punifhment, for the efchew-
ing whereof this bloud was
fhed ; oh what a Hell is due
for that finne, by which this
bloud was fhed ? They are
like vnto thefe bloudy *Iewes*,

P   Firft,

firſt, who nothing eſteeming the future paines of hell (the greatnes whereof they knowe not)cõtinue in offendiug God with their ſins. 2. Which vndertake difficult matters without conſideration. 3. Which load theſelues with other mẽs ſins, not weighing what will follow. Conſider 3. The boũty & goodnes of God,who as according to ỹ deſire and requeſt of *Pilate* he ſpared the *Gentiles*,ſo he deait leſſe ſeuearely with ỹ *Iewes*, thẽ they required: for he receiued euen many of them into fauour and grace, & brought many thouſads of ther poſterity into faith & ſaluatiõ.Do thou take heed, leaſt thou through thy ſinnes be guilty of the body,& bloud
of

of our Lord : but pray, that his bloud may be vpon thee and thy children, for thy saluation, and the remiffion of thy finnes.

Then Pilate *willing to satif-fie the peop'e, adiudged, that their petition should be done : and he dismissed vnto them him, which was sent to prison for murther and sedition,* Barrabas, *whome they demaunded : but* Iefus *being whipped he deliuered to their will, that hee should bee crucified.*

Mar. 1 5
Luc. 23
Mar. 27.
Ioan. 19

COnfider firſt, that the Prieſtes finned in the death of Chriſt of enuy ; the people, through the perſwa-fion of the Elders ; *Pilate,* to fatisfie the people. None was free from finne : for the

P 2   firſt

first sinned of malice, the second of ignorance, the third
of fraylty. For Christ vnder-
went the punishment of the
Crosse for all sortes of sinners
whatsoeuer. Consider secondly the manner of his codemn-
nation, neuer vsed before : for
First, omitting all crimes, for
which he ought to be codem-
ned, he was pronounced, iust,
by the iudge himselfe : *I am
innocent* (saith he) *from the
bloud of this iust man :* as if hee
should say, who is not codem-
ned for his faultes, but for his
iustice. Secondly, a guilty
person, loaden with most
grieuous crimes, is let goe,
that the iust man may be condemned : for our Lord dyed to
this end, that he might by his
death

death deliuer all sinners from eternall death. Thirdly, hee was not onely adiudged after the accustomed manner to the Crosse, but also to be tortured vpon the Crosse, according to the will of the *Iewes.* For these are the words: *he deliuered him to their will, that he should bee crucified.* For he would be deliuered wholly to the will of the wicked, that thou shouldst yeild thy selfe entyrely to his will. Pray therefore vnto thy Lord, not to deliuer thee to the will of thy enemies, but that through this most vniust sétence of his death he will deliuer thee frõ the iust iudgement of euerlasting death.

P 3 The

The 31. Meditation of the carrying of the Croße.

*And the Soldiours tooke Ie-
sus, & pulling off his scarlet gar-
mēt, they cloathed him in his own
vestments, & brought him foorth
that they might crucifie him.*

Consider first, ẏ thy Lord,
whome *Pilate* seemed hi-
therto a little to fauour, is now
destitute of al humane ayde, &
deliuered vp to the executioners ; least thou shouldest bee
forsaken of God, & deliuered
vp to the Deuill. Behold his
tender body, wounded in euery part, & rubbed with their
cruell hands. Thou canst not
indure to be touched vpō any
light hurt : what paine then
doest thou thinke our Lord
indured

indured by the rude & barbarous pullings of the ſoldiers ? Conſider ſecondly, how the ſoldiours pulled off his garment, making his moſt chaſt heart aſhamed to be ſeene naked afore all ẙ people. Behold how his purple garment cleauing to the congealed bloud, being violently pulled off, did renue the wounds, make them bleed afreſh, & plucke away the torne skin together with the fleſh. But Chriſt put off this garment, ẙ he might with more alacrity take vp ẙ wood of the Croſſe. For euen as worke men, when they goe about any great labour, put off their cloathes, that they may worke the more nimbly; ſo it is written of Chriſt,

P 4　　　　that

that in this his paſſion he did
foure times put off his clothes
when he was to effect any
great worke. That thou ſhouldeſt not be ignorant with how
great deſire he wrought thy
ſaluation, Firſt, when by his
whipping he was to ſhedd his
bloud for thee ouer his whole
body. Secondly, when he was
to receiue a crowne of thorns
vpon his head, to prepare an
aſſured Kingdome for thee in
Heauen. Thirdly, when he was
to lay this wood of the Croſſe
vpon his ſhoulders, as the
Scepter, or Soueraignty of the
Kingdome, or as the Key of
Dauid, with which he ſhould
open heauen for thee. Fourthly when he was to aſcend that
tree of the Croſſe, as the thron
of

of *Salomon.* Confider thirdly,
that his owne cloathes were
giuen him againe, that his face
being all polluted, and as it
were difguifed with fpittings,
bloud, and filth, yet he might
be knowne by his accuftomed
apparrell. But our Lord put
on thofe veftments, that hee
might both confecrate vnto
God his veftment, ẏ Church,
and euery member thereof,
with his Croffe, and his frefh
bleeding Wounds ; and alfo
that he might teach vs to indure the Croffe and all afflictions. It is not read, that the
Crowne of Thornes was ta-
ken from his head ; that according to the olde Prophefie of *Dauid,* (which Saint
Iuſtine cõplaineth was razed

Colloq cũ
Triphone
Pfal 98.

P 5   out

out by the *Iewes*) our Lord *might raigne frō the wood.*Con-sider 4. That our Lord was brought foorth out of the cit-tie, ȳ as one vnworthy to dye in the holy Citty, hee might be put to death amongſt the wicked. But our Lord went foorth, 1. To teach, that hee offered this ſacrifice for the whole world, and not for the *Iewes* onely, for whom the ſa-crifice was offred in the Tem-ple ; yea rather that this ſacri-fice ſhould not be profitable to the *Iewes* ſo long as they truſted in their auncient rytes & ceremonies ; according to that ſaying : *we haue an altar, of which they haue no power to eat, who ſerue the Tabernacle.* Ther-fore he went foorth carrying
                                 his

his Croſſe; ẏ hee might as i^t
were with his ſheep-hook inforce thee, a ſtray ſheepe, to
come home vnto his fold. 2.
That thou ſhouldſt not thinke
that Chriſt is found amongſt
the cares of the world, the
troubles of the Cittye, and
multitude of buſineſſe. Hee is
abroad in quiet of conſcience, in contempt and naked-
neſſe, and want of all things.
*Let vs then goe foorth vnto
him* (ſaith the Apoſtle)
*without the Tents, carrying
his reproach.* Flye the world,
that thou maiſt finde Chriſt.

   *And carrying his Croſſe,
hee went foorth into that place
which is called* Caluaria, *and
in the* Hebrue, Golgotha :
There were alſo carryed two
            wicked

Ioan. 19.
Luc. 23.

*wicked m n with him, that they
should be put to death.*

COnsider first, that in the
whole City there was no
man found to carry ỹ Crosse
of our Lord to the place of pu-
nishmēt. The soldiers would
not,& the *Iewes* esteemed the
very touching of it an execra-
ble thing, because the Scripture saith, ỹ *accursed was euery*
one, which should hang on the
wood : therfore our Lord must
needes take the wood of his
punishment vpon his owne
shoulders. Consider & weigh
with thy selfe, whether thou
doest not imitate them, when
it is grieuous vnto thee to
haue one thought of the passion of our Lord, and a most
hard thing, to suffer any little
affliction

Deut. 21.

affliction for the loue of thy
fpoufe. Confider fecondly,
with what infolency they lay d
that wood vpon his tender
fhoulders, beeing wounded
with many ftripes. The world
giueth this grieuous and troublefome Croffe, which thou
muft beare alone, without the
helpe of any other but Chrift:
*who impofeth a fweete yoake and
a light burthen, and he himfelfe
lifteth it vp with his grace, and
exalteth it ouer the iawe bones.*
Pray our Lord to lay thy fins
vpon this Croffe, carrying
them from thee to his owne
body, and wafhing them a-
way with his bloud & death:
For *he is the Lambe of God,
which taketh away the finnes of
the world.* Confider thirdly,
whither

Mat. I I.
Ofea. I I.

Ioan 3.

Hom. 84.
in Ioan.
In ca.5 ad
Ephe.
In Epiſ.ad
Paulā ad
Marcel.
Orig.tra.
35. in
Mat.
Cip in ſer
de reſur.
domini.
Athā. de
paſ. dom
Ep.p.hær.
40
Amb.epiſ.
19.
Aug ſer.7
de Temp
Theop.&
&thy in
Ioan.19
ña.3.

whither our Lord went:to wit
to a hil neer ỹ citty, called *Golgotha*, ỹ is, *Caluaria*, either by
reaſon of the ſepulture of our
firſt parent *Adā*, & of his ſcull
there found, (of ẃ opinion St.
Chryſoſtome , and St *Hierome*
report ſome to haue been) or
elſe of the ſculls of dead perſons, which had ſuffered death
in this hill, being the place of
execution The place was filthy and infamous : but Chriſt
ſanctified it by his death, and
with his bloud waſhed away
the ſinne of *Adam.* Conſider
fourthly,that 2.Theeues were
carryed to execution with
Chriſt : that according to the
propheſie of *Iſaias, Hee might
be reputed with the wicked,*and a
rumour be ſpred abroad, ỹ 3.
                 Theeues

Theeues the ſame day were
iudged to dye. For it is likely,
that about the moſt famous
Feaſts, whē the whole people
vſe to aſſemble themſelues together, their cuſtome was, to
condemne and execute ſome
guilty malefactors, for exāple
to the reſt : and now at the requeſt of the *Iewes* (whoſe will
Pilate intēded to ſatisfie)there
were certaine of the moſt notorious malefactors choſen, of
whō thy Lord ſhould bee ac-
coūted y̆ captain & leader. So
great was the deſire of y̆ *Iewes*
to obſcure the name of Chriſt.
But our Lord choſe to be crucified with thoſe theeues and
malefactors to another purpoſe and intent. Firſt, that
thou ſhouldeſt know that hee
dyed

dyed for sinners, & that there is no offence so great, but it may bee purged by the death of Christ. Secondly, that by this his disgrace and ignominy hee might obtaine eternall glory for thee, make thee of a theefe to bee a Iudge in the world to come. Pray then thy Lord to drawe thee to the hill with him, and to cõmunicate vnto thee the merites of his Crosse.

Mat. 27.
Mar. 15.
Luc. 13.

And going forth they found a certaine man of Cyrene, *called* Simon, *comming from the countrey, the Father of* Alexander *and* Rufus : *him they compelled to take vp his Crosse, and they inforced him to carry the Crosse after* Iesus.

Consider

Onſider firſt, y̓ the *Iewes* perceiuing the weaknes of Chriſt, being ſpent with labours & paines, and with the loſſe of ſo much bloud; and fearing, leaſt he might dye before he ſuffered the moſt grieuous torments of the Croſſe; being moued, not with pitty, but with cruelty, cauſed this Gentile to carry the Croſſe after *Ieſus*. But God directed this acte of theirs to another end. For he ſignified hereby; Firſt, that the Croſſe, being conſecrated with the bloud of our Lord, was giuen to Chriſtians, conuerted from Gentiliſme, who followed Chriſt going before them loaden with his Croſſe, being themſelues alſo loaden with their croſſes

crosses in sundry manners, as
some by Martyrdome, some
by fastinges, some by watch-
inges, and by other voluntary
afflictions, some by conque-
ring themselues, and subduing
the wicked motions of the
minde. Secondly that it is not
enough that Christ carry his
owne Crosse, and that wee
onely beholde it by faith and
contemplation. But it behoo-
ueth vs to set our hand to it,
and in holy workes to follow
Christ, which saith : *Hee which*
will come after mee, let him deny
himselfe, and take vp his crosse
daily, and follow mee. Consider
secondly, who hee is, which
doth profitably carry the
Crosse of Christ. First, *Symon,*
that is to say, obedient to the
Com-

Commaundements and sug-
geftions of God. Secondly,
Comming from the Countrey:
who putting off the rudenes
of finnes, forfaketh his vnci-
uill manners. Thirdly, of *Cyrene of Pentapolis,* that thou
fhouldeft carry the Croffe of
Chrift in thy fiue fences. Confider 3. that this *Symon,* was
conftrained euen againft his
wil, to lay this croffe vpon his
fhoulders : to teach thee, Firft
to offer violence to nature,
which abhorreth fuch a croffe
and the change of manners,
and mortifying of thy fences.
Secondly, not to thruft thy
felfe rafhly into perils, but patiently to fuffer the euills, w
others doe vnto thee. The
Soldiours lay the Croffe vpon
him ;

him ; for wicked men by their
vexations and torments giue
occasion to the iust to suffer
with Christ. Consider fourthly the profite, which this *Symon* had, as a reward of his labour, though hee carryed the
Crosse euen against his will.
First his name, by the diuul-
ging of the Gospell through
the world, is consecrated to
eternall memory. Secondly
his Citty & Country is made
knowne to all Christians.
Thirdly his children were not
onely Christians, but also famous amongst Christians. Do
not thou therefore feare the
Crosse, & troubles for Christ
his name , for the Crosse of
Christ maketh men glorious,
and bringeth many commo-
dities

Chrif hō.
1.ad Pop.
Antio.

dities with it. But thou muft follow after, not runne before *Iefus*; nor choofe what croffe thou likeft, but accept of that, which hee fendeth : And pray him to lighten thy burthen with his grace, & to ftrengthen thy fhoulders.

The 32. Meditation of the Women following Chrift.

And there followed a great troope of people, and of women, which mourned, and lamented him : and Iefus turning vnto them faid : O Daughters of Hierufalem, *weepe not ouer mee, but weepe ouer your felues, and ouer your Children.* Luc. 23.

Onfider firft, that an innumerable multitude of people

people flocked together to
this sorrowfull spectacle, to
whō perhaps (as the custome
is in some places at this day)
there was some signe giuen of
the future execution. And because the womē only are said
to lament & weepe, it is an argument, ў there were many
mockers, & curious spectators
according to ў saying : *They
spake against mee, which sate in
the gate.* But with what affection wilt thou follow thy
Lord ? With what minde wilt
thou suffer with him ? With
what eyes wilt thou beholde
him? Doest thou want occasion of sorrow & teares in this
spectacle, since our Lord goeth tnus loaden and deformed
for thy sake, and not for himselfe?

Psal. 68

selfe? Thou didst play abroad
in the streete, and in the Kings
priuy chamber, ℈ sentence of
death was giuen against thee.
The onely begotten Sonne
of God heard it, and hee went
forth, putting off his Diadem,
cloathed in sackcloath, wea-
ring a Crowne of thornes vpon his head, barefooted, bleeding, weeping, & crying out
that his poore seruant was
condemned. Thou seest him
come foorth, thou askest the
cause, & hearest it. What wilt
thou doe? wilt thou still play,
and contemne his teares? or
rather wilt thou not follow
him, and weepe with him, and
esteeme the greatnes of thy
danger by the cōsideration of
the remedy? Cōsider secondly
that

Beat. Ber.
ser. 3. in
nat. Dom.

that the teares of these women were gratefull vnto our
Lord, who in signe of loue
turned himselfe towards them
in the midst of his torments.
Yet hee prooued them, be-
cause out of a wrong cóceipt
of humane pitty they lamented his death, as the greatest
euill, and extreamest misery,
without any benefite at all.
Do thou mourne, lament, and
weepe, First, because thou
wert the cause of all these so
great paines. Secondly because thou hast hitherto born
an vnthankefull minde. Thirdly, because perhaps this death
of thy Lord will not bee the
cause of thy saluation & glory, but of thy greater damnation. Consider thirdly, the
               difficulty

difficultie of this thy Lords
iourney, which caufed the
women to follow him with
teares. Remember thou the
feauen hard wayes, which thy
Lord walked for thee in this
his Paffion, that hee might
ftop vp the feaué wayes of the
feauen deadly finnes, which
lead thee vnto Hell, & might
open the way to euerlafting
life, by the feauen guifts of the
holy Ghoft. For hee went,
Firft, from the houfe where
he fupped, to the Garden. Secondly from thence to *Annas.*
Thirdly to *Cayphas* his houfe.
Fourthly to *Pilate.* Fiftly to
Herod. Sixtly again to *Pilate*,
& feauéthly to the Croffe. Do
thou in all thy trauailes meditate vpon thefe wayes, and
Q   for

and for the loue of thy Lord
runne in the way of his Commaundements.

For behold the daies shall come,
in which they shall say, blessed are
the barren, & the wombes, which
haue not brought foorth, & the
breasts, which haue not giuen
sucke: then they shall begin to
say to the Mountaines, fall vpon
vs, and to the Hills, couer vs.

Consider 1. the goodnesse
of thy Lord, who in the
middest of his paines, seeketh
by his admonitió our saluatió,
and by the terror of future
miseries endeauoreth to moue
vs to pennance. He speaketh
also to women, not to men;
1. least because he was punished by men, he should seeme
to threaten reuenge. Secondly
that

Luc. 23

that by thefe euills, foretold
vnto women, who had offended leffe, men might vnderftand, that the like at the leaft
fhould happen vnto them. 3.
By this prediction to comfort
thofe women, which lamen-
ted fo much the death & paffi-
ons of our Lord; fignifying
thereby, both that he did vn-
iuftly fuffer this death, which
in a fewe yeares fhould bee fo
deepely reuenged; and alfo
that they might efcape this
reuenge, which would leaue
to bee the children of this
earthly Hierufalem,& conuert
themfelues to the faith of
Chrift. Confider fecondly,
whereas in former times the
barren were accurfed, now
the barren in Chrift are
Q 2   bleffed.

blessed. For there is giuen to
Eunuches : that is, to them,

Isa. 56.

which liue chaste and single in
the Church, a name better then
from sonnes and daughters.
Consider thirdly, that in all
troubles of this life wee must
say vnto the mountaines, fall
vppon vs, and to the hills, couer vs : that is to say, we must
haue recourse to the helpe of
Saints, who in the Scriptures
are called by the names of
mountaines and hilles ; as in

Isa. 2.

*Isaias : the house of our Lord
shall be a prepared mountaine :*
that is to say, Christ the head
of the Church, *in the toppe of
the mountaines, and he shall be
eleuated aboue the hills,* exceeding in dignitie and worthy-
nes, all Saints, great and lesse.
                 Consider

Consider fourthly, although these predictions of our Lord pertaine cheifly to the ouer-throwing of Hierusalem: yet they may and ought to be referred also to all sinners, who by their sinnes were cause of the death of our Lord, and yet are not made partakers of his merits, nor returned into Gods fauour by his death. For they which now liue securely, and whome no danger will make to refraine from sinnes, shall then *runne into the dennes and Caues of the earth*, (as the Prophets haue fore-spoken) *From the face of God, sitting on the throne, and from the wrath of the Lambe.* For there shall come

Iſa. 2.
Oſea. 11.
Apoc, 6.

Q 3   a great

a great day of wrath on them: and who shall be able to stand? The countenance of the Iudge shall be terrible to the wicked, and his sentence intollerable. Then *the barren shall bee called blessed*, that is, they whome the world accounted vnprofitable; and *the wombes which haue not brought foorth*, that is, which haue not followed the concupiscence of the flesh, but haue subdued the vices of their belly and throat; & *the pappes which haue not giuen sucke*, that is, the humble, and such as are not high minded. Pray thou thy Lord, that thou maiest not feare the face of his fury in the day of wrath, and last reuenge, & whilst time serueth

bee

bee reconcyled vnto Chriſt :
For if they doe theſe thinges Luc. 23
*in greene wood, what ſhall bee
done in the drye ?* Conſider
firſt , Chriſt is the wood ,
euer greene and flouriſhing,
delectable to behold, mo-
derating the great heate with
the ſhadowe of his thicke
leaues, bringing foorth fruit,
pleaſant both to the taſte
and ſmell, delighting the
earth with the ſinging of
birds. For by his diuine nature, and by the inward
grace of the Holy Ghoſt,
hee doth not onely exceede
all beauty, but alſo preſerue,
cheariſh, and comfort all
creatures. Thou alſo art wood,
but dead without the ſappe
of Grace, barren without
Q 4   the

the fruite of charitie; naked and vnprofitable, without the leaues of good workes. Confider fecondly, who they are which doe thefe things in the greene Wood: that is, which gaue thefe tormets and death vnto Chrift thy Lord. Firft, God the Father, who fpared not his owne fonne, but deliuered him vp for vs al. Secondly, the Deuill, who prouoked his fernants to put Chrift to death. Thirdly, the *Iewes*, and other minifters of his death But all thefe did not concord in the paffion of Chrift to one end. For God the Father punifhed his Sonne for the loue of thy faluation, and like *Abraham*, carrying the fword of iuftice in

Rom. 8

Gen. 22

in his hand againſt his ſonne,
and the fire of Charitie to-
wardes thee, hee layed the
wood vpon his ſonnes ſhoulders, to be carryed by him,
for the burning of the holo-
cauſte. The Deuill greiuing
at the conuerſion of many,
indeauored to hinder the
courſe of his preaching, to intangle the *Iewes* in the moſt
grieuous ſinne of innocent
death, and to ouercome the
patience of Chriſt by his torments. And the *Iewes* being
moued by enuie, could not
indure to be admoniſhed to
amend their liues by the
wordes and example of
Chriſt. Conſider thirdly, the
argument of our Lord : *If*
they doe theſe things in greene
Q 5 *wood,*

wood, what shall be done in the drye? First, if I suffer this for other mens sins, what shalt thou suffer for thine owne? Secondly, if the Father doe so grieuously afflict his innocent and obedient Son, what will he do against his wicked and disobedient seruāt? Thirdly, if the deuills could by their officers doe these things in another kingdom against the sonne of God, what will they bee able to doe in hell in their owne kingdome against their owne bond-slaues? Fourthly, if by the permissiō of God wicked men raged thus against the onely begotten Sonne of God for the sinnes of men, why shall any man meruaile that God will permit men to

vexe

vexe and moleſt men, when
their ſinnes deſerue it? Pray
thou thy Lord to ingraft thee
into himſelfe being the green
wood, and that neuer more
puniſhment bee exacted of
thee, then that which he himſelfe ſuffered for thee.

The 33. Meditation of
the crucifying of
our Lord.

And they came into the
place, which is called Golgotha,
which is a place of Caluaria:
and they gaue him wine to drinke
mixt with gall: and when he had
taſted, hee would not drinke: and
it was the third houre.

Luc. 23.
Mat. 27.
Mar. 15.

COnſider firſt, the aſcen-
ding of this hill, howe
painfull it was vnto thy Lord,
how hee inforced his tender
and

and confumed body, that it
fhould not faile to procure
thy faluation, but that in the
mountaine nearer vnto heauen he might ftande before
God the Father, and offer Ho-
locauft as a fauor of fweetnes
for thy finnes. Follow thou
the Lord afcending his hill as
neare as thou canft, and ftand
by him in this hill euen vntill
death. Confider fecondly,
how the executioners made
ready the Croffe : how they
bored the holes for the nailes,
and prepared nayles, ham-
mers, and ropes; thy Lord
behoulding them with his
eyes. Doe thou alfo behold
them, and lament, and be-
ware; becaufe thou doeft prepare a Croffe for thy Lord,
as

as often as by thy ſinnes thou
deſerueſt a place in hel for thy
ſoule, which is created to his
owne likenes. Conſider thirdly, that according to the cuſtome of ſuch as were put to
death, they offered a cup to
Chriſt , but much differing
from that was vſed to be giuen to others.   The drinke
was mixed with wine, Myrre,
gall, and vineger (for *St. Ma-*
thew vſeth in ſtead of wine
this word ὄξος : Vineger) that
none of his ſences ſhould
want his paine and puniſhment. His cruell enemies compaſſe him round about, troubled his ſight ; their cruell
wordes , vpbraydings, and
blaſphemies tormented his
hearing ; the ſtench of the
place,

of the place, and of the filth,
which couered his face, offended his smelling ; his touching suffered most grieuous
paines all ouer his body ; and
because no sence should bee
without his tormēt, this most
bitter drinke was giuen him
to afflict his taft. Is it not reason then (thinkeft thou,) that
thou shouldeft suffer some affliction or trouble for thy
Lord, which for thy fake had
no part of his body free from
paine ? But Christ tasted this
sowre potion for thee , to
drawe from thy soule to his
owne body all the sharpnes
and bitternes of thy sinnes ;
and left for thee sweete wine,
mixt with no sowernes, that
is to say, the grace of God,
and

and a pure and quiet confcience. Confider fourthly, *When
he had tafted , hee would not
drinke :* for Chrift tooke vpon him thy finnes in his body
as in his mouth, but hee polluted not his foule with the
filth of finne : that thou alfo
fhouldeft as it were tafte the
malice of finne with the
fowernes of pennaunce, but
by no meanes fuffer it to
enter into thy foule. Confider fiftly, that the houre of
his execution is noted , to
wit, the third houre , which
in the Equinoctiall is from
Nine of the clocke in the
morning till twelue at noone:
whereby thou mayeft note
the great haft , which they
made, partly leaft *Pilate* fhold
change

change his minde, and partly leaft Chriſt ſhould dye before he was crucified. Saint *Iohn* writeth, that the ſentence was pronounced almoſt at the ſixt houre, that is a little before noone : And *Marke* affirmeth that Chriſt was crucified the third houre, that is, before the clocke had ſtrucke 12. Conſider thē what haſt was made, how cruelly thy Lord was pulled, drawn with ropes, and whipped forward. Take heed, leaſt thy feete run vnto ſinne, but runne chearfully this way of our Lord, and caſting away all impediments, flye vnto the Croſſe of Chriſt, and pray him to remoue all ſowernes & difficulties from the exerciſe of vertues.

And

And there they crucified him.

COnfider firft, that the Apoftles did not expreffe fo great an action in many wordes, which thou mayft eafily vnderftand, both by the accuftomed punifhmēt of the Croffe, and by the hatred of the *Iewes*, and by the auncient oracles of the Prophets. For firft they pulled off his garment with great infolency, & renued the woundes, fticking vnto it, making his facred body bleede, and appeare all naked. Secondly, they outragioufly threw him downe vpon the Croffe, which lay on the ground, thinking it fufficient if hee were nayled aliue on the Croffe. Thirdly, they pulled one

one hand to the hole, which they had boared , and draue a naile through it with a hammer ; and the bloud issued foorth aboundantly , according to the olde figure : *They stroke the Rocke, and the waters flowed out, and the Riuers swelled vp.* Fourthly, when one hand was fastned, they tooke the other, and stretched it to the other hole, which being farre distant , they pulled it, either with their handes , or with cordes , with all their force; and that being also fast nailed, they came to the holes for his feete , and with great violēce they brought his holy feete vnto it, and (as St. *Cyprian* saith) fastened them with nailes. *Dauid* did plainly foreshewe

Psal. 77

Ser. de Pasc. Dō. Psal. 21.

shew this stretching foorth of
our Lord in these words; *I am
spred abroad like water* : I am
wasted and decayed with the
extremity of paines, and destitute of all strength, like water
powred out, hauing no power
to stay in any place. *All my
bones are dispersed*, that is,
are loosened, & pulled out of
their places, the colde, drynes,
and extensiō vpon the Crosse
dissoluing all the ioynts of my
members. *They haue digged my
handes and my feete, they haue
numbred all my bones* : so cruel
was this extension of his mēbers, ŷ euery bone, being pulled from another, might easily
be seen. Thirdly, they lift vp on
high the tree of ŷ Crosse, cloathed with this solemne hoast ;
and

Num. 2 1.
Exod. 29.

Leuit. 23

and let it fall down with great violence into the hole, which they had digged for it : For so was the brasen Serpent lift vp in the wildernes, & the hoasts of the Sacrifices were wont to be offred vnto God by lifting them vp on high. In all these thinges doe thou ponder and thinke vpon the most bitter torments of thy Lord ; behold the banner of the Crosse lift vp ; look vpon the streams of bloud running down from his hands & feete ; goe quickly and draw whilst the springs are flowing, and before their veynes be dried vp. Consider secondly, why thy Lord chose this death of the Crosse for thy saluation, and no other death. There are many causes thereof.

thereof. Firſt, becauſe there
was no death more long,
more grieuous, more ignominious, nor more proper and fit
for the procuring of thy ſaluation. For hee would not haue
his body deuided ; that the
Church his myſticall body
might bee preſerued whole :
He would not be burnt, with
any other fire, then the fire of
charity : Hee would not bee
ſtrangled with a halter, drowned with water, or ſmothered
with earth, leaſt hee might
ſeeme to haue retained ſomething to himſelfe, and not to
haue ſhed all his bloud moſt
liberally for thy ſake. Secondly, that being lift vp on high,
like an hoaſt, hee might place
himſelfe, as a Mediator, betweene

tweene God the Father and mankinde, *Being the only Mediator of God and men, reconciling the lowest thinges to the highest.* Thirdly, to throw downe the Deuils, the Princes of the ayre, quite out of the ayre into Hell; or at the least to subdue their forces. Fourthly, that he might see thee with his eyes a farre off, drawe thee vnto him with the chaines of his bloud, receiue thee at thy cōming with his armes spred, shewe thee his inward partes, and hide thee in his woundes, binde thee vnto him with the linkes of charity, haue thee, ingrauen in his handes; alwayes before his eyes, keepe thee imprinted in his heart, and with his feete fastened to
seeke

1 Tim.2

seeke nothing but thy saluation. Fiftly, that thou shouldest no more fasten thine eyes vpon the ground, but lift them vp on high, beholde him a farre off, runne vnto him, require of him thy saluation, and all good thinges, thinke vpon him alwayes in all thy busines, followe his life, and fulfill his Commaundements. Heere doe thou speake, whatsoeuer thy spirit shall put into thy mouth.

And they crucified with him two Theeues, one on the right hand, and the other on the left, and Iesus in the middest : And the Scripture was fulfilled, which saith : and hee was reputed with the wicked.

Mat. 27.
Mar. 15.
Ioan. 19
Isa. 53.

Consider

Onsider firſt, the malice of the *Iewes*, who by this ignominy endeauoured to deface the name of Chriſt, & in ſtead of the *Meſſias*, to make him reputed a notorious theefe. But Chriſt vſed this their ſinne to ſhewe forth his owne glory, to prepare our ſaluation, and to giue hope to all ſinners. For firſt, wheras there were three nayled on the Croſſe, & hee placed in the midſt, as the chiefe offender : yet hee alone with his Croſſe is glorious vnto the whole world. Secondly, dying betweene two ſinners, hee payed the ranſome for all ſinnes. Thirdly, hee gaue hope of pardon to all ſinners, and did fore-ſhewe that hereafter he

hee would be conuersant a-
mongst sinners,& be alwayes
ready to assist them, whē they
call for helpe, and neuer forsake them as long as they liue.
Consider secondly, that hee
chose to dy amongst theeues,
rather thē amongst other sinners. First,that whereas theft
is a most grieuous sin, which
both offendeth God, whose
image it taketh away,and also
hurteth our neighbour,whom
it depriueth both of goods
and life, he might signifie that
there is no offence so great,
which is not cleansed by this
his death,nor any man so wicked, which may not obtaine
remission of sinnes. Secondly
because euery sinner is a thiefe
and a robber, which by his
      R   sinne

finne killeth his owne foule,
taketh away honour frō God,
defileth his creatures, and depriueth the Church of a liuely
member, that is, of himfelfe,
whome hee hath bereaued of
fpiritual life. Confider 3. that ẙ
good theefe, as well as ẙ bad,
fuffered the punifhment and
death of ẙ croffe with Chrift :
but the one turned his punifhment to the benefit of his own
faluation, and the other, to
the hurt and loffe of his foule.
That thou fhouldeft vnderftand, that Chrift is alwayes
prefent, both to good & bad
in their afflictions, and doth
fend them troubles and miferies, to this end, ẙ they fhould
remember themfelues, and lift
vp their eyes and hearts vnto
him.

him. Doe thou then pray vnto God, that in all thy tribulations thou mayeſt haue re-
courſe only to his diuine help,
and not bee ouer carefull to
vſe other meanes.

The 34. Meditation of
the Title of the
Croſſe.

And Pilate *wrote the title*
of his cauſe vpon his Croſſe, and
the ſuperſcription was ouer his
head, and it was written in Hebrue, Greeke, *&* Latine.

C Onſider firſt, that *Pilate*
ſet vp the Title óf the
cauſe of his death, and
vſed the words follow-
ing. Firſt, that thy Lord might
bee thought worthy of this
death, as a traytor, arrogating

Mat. 27.
Mar. 15.
Luc. 23.
Ioan. 19

R 2   the

the name of a King vnto himfelfe; and that *Pilate* might be
cleared before *Cæfar* of the
cryme of not condemning his
competitor of the kingdome.
Secondly to bee reuenged of
the *Iewes*, who had threatned
to complaine of him : for hee
mocked them, ẏ hee had crucified their king, and that king
alfo, whome their aunceſtors
had fore-tolde, fo many ages
before, and had expected with
fo great affection and defire.
Thefe were the caufes, that
mooued *Pilate* to make that
tytle.   And Chriſt alfo our
Lord ordained this tytle for
himfelfe ; but for farre other
reafon, drawne from the myſterie of our faluation. Firſt,
that thou fhouldeſt knowe,
                                    that

that hee suffered this death of
the Crosse, not as a guilty person, but as a Sauiour, adorned
with all vertues, that he might
rule thy soule, and that thou
shouldest submit thy selfe to
be wholy gouerned by him,
who being nayled both hand
and foote, cannot hurt his beloued people, but offereth the
all saluation from his open
woundes. Secondly, to let
thee vnderstand, what mer-
chandize are offered to thee
to be solde out of this shop of
his Crosse. For all houses and
shops haue commonly their
signes. Heere then thou mayst
finde all saluation in *Iesus*, all
flowers of vertue in *Naza-*
reth, and all security in the
King. Runne thou hither in all
R 3   thy

Isa. 55.

thy neceffityes, and buy, and take what thou lift, without money, or any other excháge, for this marchant requireth nothing of thee, but thy company, and thy loue. Thirdly, that thou mayeft know by the Table fet before the houfe, what doctrine and Artes are read & taught in this fchoole. For Schoole maifters vfe to write before their gates, what things are taught within their houfes. Heere thou mayeft learne to bee faued, to follow all vertues, to rule thy felfe, to conquer thy enemyes, to gouerne wifely others, that be vnder thy charge. Our Mr. Chrift doth now teach from the chayre of his Croffe, euen as hee taught being an Infant

in

in the manger of the Stable.
But thou perhaps defireft an
eafier chaire. But fuch doctrine is not taught, but out of
fuch a chaire : for there is no
way to faluation , but by the
croffe and by many tribulations ; and the habits of vertues
are obtained by painfull actions. If thou wilt rule thy felfe
perfectly and fubdue thy enemies, the world, the flefh, and
the Deuill ; thou fhalt not
feeke after the eafe of thy body ; but thou fhalt bee feuere
againft thy body, and pull it
out of the power of the Deuill
by fafting, watching, workes
of humility, contempt, & tribulations , according to the
example of this Maifter. Neither fhalt thou bee able to

R 4   gouern

gouern others rightly, if thou
relyest onely vpon thy power
and authority ; except according to this lesson of Christ
thy teacher, thou doest out of
the very bowels of thy charitie, apply thy selfe wholy and
all thinges in thee to the profite and good of thy subiects.
Fourthly, that by this tytle
thou mayest feele, of what
force the sign of the Crosse is,
which thou makest with thy
handes. For it is not a iugling
tricke, or a flye flappe, as the
blaspheming enemies of the
crosse doe tearme it : But it is
the vertue & power of Christ,
for the safety of all beleeuers;
that thou being signed therewith, mayst be knowne by thy
badge to bee the seruant of
                                    the

the *Messias* thy King ; and be
a terror to the Deuil; and haue
entraunce into the house of
Christ,and that all thy actions
may tend to the glory of God
and to thy owne saluation.
Consider secondly, that this
Tytle was written in diuers
languages. Firft , because it
concernes all men to knowe
this King ; and therefore it
was set in a high place , that
thou mayest beholde it a farre
off,stand still,read,vnderstand
and follow this King, forsaking all other maisters,whom
thou hast hitherto serued. Secondly, because the crucified
Messias is to bee knowne and
praised in all Languages. Cōsider thirdly, the māner of the
writing. A part of this Tytle
R 5   being

being preferued with great
deuotió of Chriſtians at *Rome*
in the Church of the Holy
Croſſe in *Hieruſalem* doth declare vnto vs : Firſt, that the
Title was of wood ; Secondly
not written with a pen , but
grauen with iron ; Thirdly, y̓
the *Hebrue* was firſt, then the
Greeke, and laſtly the *Latine* ;
Fourthly, that the Greeke and
Latine was written like the
Hebrue from the right hand
to the left.

SVNERAZANEI

ALL which thinges are
not without their my-
ſteries. For firſt theſe
three languages onely
were ſet vpon y̓ Croſſe, which
were

were moſt vſuall at that time,
and ſo continue vntill this
day : the *Hebrue* for the *Iewes*,
the *Greek* for the *Eaſt* Church,
and the *Latine* for the *Weſt*.
For ſeeing that all Learning is
written in theſe tongues, the
Scriptures in *Hebrue*, Philo-
ſophie,& Rethoricke in *Greek*
and *Latine*; Chriſt taught vs
hereby, ẙ there is neither any
diuine knowledge, nor hu-
mane learning and eloquence
of any force,except it bee ſanctified by the bloud of Chriſt,
and referred to the glory of
him crucified. And therefore
the holy Church vſeth theſe
languages onely in her diuine
ſeruice, as the moſt common,
and thoſe that are conſecrated
with the bloud of our Lord
Secondly,

Secondly, the tytle was ingrauen, becaufe it fhould laft for euer ; and in wood, becaufe by the wood he fhall alwayes raigne ouer them, whome the wood had ouerthrown. Thirdly, the Hebrue was firft in order, which the reft doe imitate : For our faluation is from the *Iewes* , to whofe diuine Scriptures all humane wifdome is to bee directed. Fourthly, they are written from the left hand to ȳ right, to fignifie, that if thou defireft to be exalted by wifdom with Chrift, thou muft humble thy felfe, and not be proud in thy owne conceipt. *For knowledge puffeth vp*, & wifedome without Chrift is earthly, carnall, and diabolicall. Fiftly, the Greeke

1 Corr. Iac. 3.8.

Greeke is before the Latine :
for firft the Grecians, and then
the Latines were conuerted
to the faith, and leauing the
manners and cuftoms of their
fore-fathers, followed that
doctrine, which God gaue to
the *Iewes* in the *Hebrewe* language, : that thou fhouldeft
not rely vpon thine owne wifdome, but follow them with
thy whole heart, whome thou
knoweft to be the feruants of
God. Pray our Lord to in-
graue this tytle in thy heart.

Iefus of Nazareth King of
the Iewes.

Ioan. 19

Onfider firft, and marke
euery word of this tytle,
(*Iefus*) a Sauiour : which name
our Lord receiued, when hee
firft fhedd his bloud for thee.
For

For then feeking thy faluation, he gaue part of his bloud
as a pledge, that he would
aftewrards giue it all for thee.
He then receiued at thy hands
circumcifion, which was the
figne of a finner, (euen as it is
the figne of a theefe to bee
boared through the eares:)
that the eternall Father omitting thee a finner might fatif-
fie his wrath vpon his fonne.
This name vntill that day was
obfcure, and of fmall reputation; but being faftened to the
Croffe it became fo glorious,
that *In the name of* Iefus *euery
knee is bowed* (*Of* Nazareth)
not of Bethlehem, although he
were borne in Bethlehem. Firft,
becaufe there was a greater
myracle and benefite wrought
              in

Phil.2.

in *Nazareth* by the incarnati-
on and conception of our
Lord, then by his Natiuity in
Bethlehem. Secondly, becaufe
Nazareth fignifieth flourifhing and Chrift is an oderife-
rous flower hanging on the
Croffe, which rendreth vnto
vs the wholefome fruite of
grace and glory. *(King)* who
being crowned with a Dia-
dem cloathed with bloud like
a purple roabe, raigneth vpright, and faft tyed by the
feete, ready to help thee; with
his hands boared through becaufe he would not keepe his
guiftes, but beftowe them
plentifully vppon thee; and
with his armes fpread, that he
may imbrace thee, when thou
commeft. He did not write
Bifhop,

Bifhop, or Prieft, although
he did the office of a Prieft,
but, King : both becaufe hee
once by himfelfe immolated
the bloudy facrifice ; *by which*
he did confummate the fanctifi-
ed, and raigneth for euer and
euer ; and alfo becaufe it is a
prieftly kingdome, & a king-
ly priefthood, where Chrift
being God is king, doing all
things in power ; and Chrift
being man is Prieft, obtaining
all things by facrifice. *(Of the*
Iewes) fent firft to the *Iewes,*
not to the gentiles. *For I am*
not fent (faith our Lord) *but*
to the fheepe which perifhed of
the houfe of Ifrael ; *and the gen-*
tiles doe honour God for his mer-
cie : that thou maift thanke
God, that the *Meffias* was taken

Heb.10
Ezo 19
1 Pet. 2

Mat. 15
Rom.15.

ken from the *Iewes,* and offered vnto thee ; and ſhowe thy
ſelfe in prayſing God a true
Iewe, not by carnall birth, but
by ſpirituall circumciſion of
thy vices, and true confeſſion
of thy ſinnes. Conſider ſecondly, the true cauſe of the
Croſſe was to ſaue thee, to a-
dorne thee with vertues, and
to gouerne thee ſweetly. Pray
thy Lord to ſuffer none to
rule in thee, but only himſelfe.

Therefore many of the Iewes
reade this title, for the place
where Ieſus *was crucified was*
neare the Cittie. Therefore the
Prieſts ſaid to Pilate : *doe not*
write, King of the Iewes *but that*
he ſaid, I am King of the Iewes:
Pilate *anſwered : what I haue*
written, I haue written.

Conſider

COnfider firſt, that many *Iewes* did ſee and reade theſe holy words : but they vnderſtood them not , and therefore ſcorned them : that thou maiſt learne, that none ſcoffe at diuine things, the holy Ceremonies of the Church, the Doctrine & life of Saints, but only they which vnderſtand them not. Therefore becauſe it is written ; *He ſhall mocke the mockers* ; and, *I will laugh in your diſtruction* : do thou take heede, and reſrayne from theſe blaſphemous ſcoffings. Secondly, becauſe the name of *Ieſus* was to be highly honoured, and this tytle to be celebrated ouer the whole world, and the Croſſe it ſelfe to be imprinted in kings foreheads ;

Pro. 1.

heads; therefore it was conuenient to haue it first laughed at and scorned.   For euen
as a brasen vessell doth shine
brightest, after it hath beene
fowled, and rubbed with dyrt
and clay; so he shall be most
glorious, which hath suffered
most shame, and vexation for
Christ.   Yeelde not then to
thy afflictions, nor be dismayed, since there is so great glory prouided for thee : Consider secondly, that Christ was
crucified not farre from the
Cittie : for though hee bee
throwne out by the inhabi-
tants of the Cittie, and of
this world; yet because it is
proper alwaies to him to spare
and to be mercifull, he goeth
not farre, but stayeth hard by,
knock-

knocking continually at the gates of our heart, to trye, if he may be let in. Confider thirdly, that the wicked cannot indure the very name of the kingdome of Chrift: becaufe the Croffe of Chrift is diftaftefull to finners, who choofe rather to haue a delicate king, then one nayled to the Croffe. This was the caufe *Lib. 4.* (as St. *Damafcene* teftifieth) *Act. 11.* why the *Iewes* crucified Chrift *Cap. 13* with his face turned from the Cittie, and looking towards the gentiles; becaufe neither they nor their children fhould euer receiue him for their *Meffias.* Giue thou thankes vnto Chrift, that he would behold the gentiles from his Croffe, thinke vppon thee, and bring

bring thee to the knowledge
of him.   Pray him neuer to
turne his eyes from thee. Consider fourthly, *Pilates* answere.
Hee indeede set on this tytle,
but moued thereunto by the
instinct of God.   Therefore
that ought not to be vndone,
which by God had beene
done : for the glorie of the
Crosse, and the kingdome of
Christ, which is his Church,
wil stand & continue, though
thou shouldest forsake it. For
if thou wilt refuse this King
and his kingdome, another
shall be called and receiue the
Crowne. Remember the ho-
ly Oyntment and consecrated
Oyle in thy baptisme, and
conformation; by which was
imprinted in thee the tytle and
                              signe

Apoc. 3.

signe of the Crosse, that the marke and badge of Christ might remaine in thee (as oyle doth penetrate, is not easily washed off) and that the writing made vppon thee by the finger of God, might alwaies be imprinted in thy soule. Pray then our Lord to ingraue in thee his new name, and the name of his holy Citty, and write thee also in the booke of euerlasting life.

The 35. Meditation of the
first word of
Christ.
But Iesus said,

Onsider first, what thy Lord in these great paines of the Crosse did doe, say or thinke, when as amongst all those

thoſe torments he found no
comfort, neither outwardly
by men, nor inwardly in his
owne ſoule. Yf he moued his
body, the woundes of the
nayles tormented him; if his
head, the thorns ranne in deeper and pricked him; if he ſtirred not at all, his torment was
intollerable ouer his whole
wearied body. Thinke thou
vppon theſe things in all thy
labours and afflictions which
thou ſuffereſt for thy Lord.
Hee reproued no man, al-
though he were ſlaundered
diuers wayes. But becauſe the
mouth ſpeaketh from the a-
boundance of the hart, his
wordes euen vppon the Croſſe
were directed to thy profite
and ſaluation, and doe declare
                                most

moſt manyſeſtly, that he prayed to his Father inceſſantly
for thee, when by reaſon of
his torments he was not able
to vtter one word. Conſider
ſecondly, his ſwan-like ſong,
and note the laſt words of thy
Lord, which he ſpake to thee
at the poynt of death. For e-
uen as the voyce of the Serpent, hyſſing out of the Tree
of the knowledge of good and
euill, inſtilled the poyſon of
ſinne; ſo the laſt wordes of
Chriſt from the Tree of the
Croſſe were very effectuall for
our ſaluation, and full of burning feruour, as proceeding
from the depth of infinite charitie. Hee ſpake with a loud
voyce, and weeping teares;
with great affectió, and deepe
ſighes;

sighes ; in fewe words, but with many teares, mixed with bloud streaming downe from his head. His teares watered his prayers, and his bloud a-dorned them ; his eyes pier-ced his Fathers eares, his sighes moued his heart. Doe thou listen to these wordes, marke them diligently, and gather the fruite thereof. For by these seauen wordes the wordes and formes of the sea-uen Sacraments are sanctified, the seauen gniftes of the holy Ghost are obtained, and the seauen deadly sinnes are dri-uen away. Consider thirdly, *(but Iesus said)* First whilst the *Iewes* were busie in cru-cifying, tormenting, & mock-ing him, Iesus as if he had not

Heb. 5

S   marked

marked thefe thinges, yea rather that he migh render good
for euill, faid. Secondly, thee,
who hetherto in his owne
caufe, to the admiration of all
men held his peace, and could
not be brought to fpeake, but
being adiudged; and had alfo
abftayned from the moft iuft
defence of himfelfe:now inthe
middeft of his torments is not
filent in thy moft vniuft caufe,
but being not intreated, intreateth, yea and intreateth
with moft effectuall wordes.
Iefus faid : who ? the Sonne
of God. To whome ? to God
the Father. Where ? vpon the
Croffe. When ? being ready
to dye,and his vitall fpirits being fpent. How ? not fitting,
nor lying eafily ; but vpright
vpon

vpon his feete, with his hands
lift vp and spread abroad, like
Moses in former times, and all
bleeding. For whome? for
sinners, who were carelesse of
their owne saluation: for
Christ and his frtends pray for
sinners, before sinners pray for
themselues. What? he craueth
mercy, offring his prayers and
supplications, appealing from
this cruell sentence of the
*Iewes (his bloud be vpon vs and
vpon our children)* to a better
sentence and full of mercy,
and desiring, that this cruell
sentence might be made frust-
rate. Before whome? openly,
in the hearing of his enemies,
to teach them mercy & sweet-
nesse; and in the presence of
his Mother, and of his friends,

Exo. 17.

Heb. 5.

S 2   both

both becaufe they fhould bee
witneffes of his pardoning
them, & alfo that they fhould
neuer pray for the reuenge of
this finne. O excellent fpeach
of higheft merite, and worthy
to be imitated by all men, full
of labour, charity, mercy, and
piety! Haue confidence then
in Chrift, and pray him, who
by fpeaking firft for finners,
before he fpake for his Mother, left to vs a teftimonye
how much he efteemeth the
faluation of finners, that hee
will vouchfafe to haue continuall care of thee now in Heauen.

Luc. 23   *Father forgiue them.*

PAufe vpon euery word.
(*Father*) he doth not fay,
Lord, which is a name of
feuerity

seuerity and iustice, but, Father, which is a name of mercy, and of the newe Testamēt, giuen vnto vs in this place by the bloud & merites of Christ: that euen as he would be our Brother, so we should haue all one father in Heauen. He saith therefore O Father, knowe me thy Sonne; the Father will denye nothing to his sonne: I came into the world to this end, that thou shouldest receiue thine enemies for thy children. Heare me then praying for them. For euen as the prayers of the Priestes in the Church shall hereafter be very effectuall, which shall conclude in my name in these wordes, through Christ our Lord: so I doe now pray vnto

S 3   thee

thee my Father, thorough me thy onely begotten Sonne. Therefore as thou louest mee thy Son, so receiue these my prayers. For I ascended this crosse, & haue suffred all these stripes that I might obtaine mercy and pardon for them. If therefore thou doest reiect the prayers of thy sonne, and not hear thy sonne, thou shalt impose a greater torment on mee, then the Crosse it selfe; which I suffer, that I might take away a greater euill, that is, that I might turne away thy wrath from them. Spare therfore the great dolors of thy Son, least he seeme to haue indured them in vaine. Thou giuest reward to others labours; I desire onely this reward for
my

my paines, that thou wilt forgiue thefe men. *(Forgiue)*
heer our Lord doth the office
of a Prieft: for he prayeth for
the finnes of the people, and
he cryeth, not only as a Prieft   Heb. 5.
but as a facrifice, defiring not
a free pardon, but offering a
full fatisfaction. His wounds
crye, his bloud cryeth, his fpittings, his paines, and all his
members crye *(Forgiue* ; *)* accept of thefe torments for
their finnes; I haue paied their
debtes ; I giue my bloud for
the pryce, my paines for the
ranfom, my life in fatisfaction,
my body & foule for a facrifice. Be thou therfore merciful:
for this is a copious redemption. **A** hard thing is required, to wit, ÿ the Father fhould

S 4   forget

forget the death of his onely
begotten Sonne, and of such,
and so great a Sonne: but the
Sonne beggeth, and hee beggeth with his bloud. Secondly hee asketh it not conditio-
nally, as he praied for himselfe
in the Garden, If it bee possible, if thou wilt, if it may bee
done; but absolutely, *(Forgiue:)* Both that thou mayest
learne to pray to God for pardon of thy sinnes, and for his
diuine grace, without any cō-
dition, because that hath alwayes relation to Gods honour: And also that thou
shouldest freely forgiue thy
neighbours faultes without a-
ny condition. Thirdly, hee
prayeth to haue them forgiuē
presently, and not to bee deferred

ferred till after his death. For
hee would not leaue this life,
till peace was made with God.
Parents, when they are dying,
doe often leaue vnto their
children small store of goods,
and those intangled with many difficulties, charges, debts,
and contentions : But Christ
before his death payed all
debts with his owne bloud ;
took away all difficulties, and
charges, and made a peace and
reconciliation with his Father. Hee sayeth therefore,
O Father forgiue, and that by
and by : *For the time of hauing* Psal. 101.
mercy on him commeth, for the
time commeth ; to wit , the
houre of sacrifice, the day of
satisfaction , the time of forgiuenes, the last instant of my

S 5   I fi,

life, in which being presently
to yeeld vp my breath, I now
propound my laſt petitiō, and
intreat onely this ; O Father
forgiue them. Fourthly, hee
ſaith not forgiue the ſinnes already committed; but onely
(*forgiue,*) euen thoſe euills,
which they ſhall hereafter cōmit againſt mee, their irriſions
their blaſphemies, the bitternes of the vineger, my death,
and the wound in my ſide:
that thou alſo ſhouldſt quickly forgiue thy enemies , and
remit all thinges, keeping no
rancor at all in thy heart.
Fiftly, hee ſayth not, I forgiue ;
both becauſe the offence a-
gainſt his Father grieued him
more, then his own torments ;
and alſo becauſe being inten-
tiue

tiue vp on the happines, which
fhould redound to all the
world by this his Paffion, hee
feemed to efteem all the euils,
which the *Iewes* did vnto him,
rather as a benefite, then any
hurt. Like as a man, hauing a
grieuous vlcer in his fide, if his
enemy, thinking to kill him,
fhould wound him in that
place, whereby ỹ vlcer fhould
be opened, and the corrupti-
on let out, would bee glad of
that wound, which was the
caufe of his cure: So defirous
was our Lord of thy faluation, that hee reioyced at thofe
his paines, which were the
caufe of fo great good vnto
thee. (*Them*) Note firft that
hee fayeth not, thefe wicked
Crucifiers, thefe Hangmen,
thefe

these aduersaries and enemies, both because thou shouldest refraine from all euill wordes and reproaches; and also because thy Lord reputeth no man his enemy, who payed the price of his death for all men, and offereth saluation to euery one, louing dearly euen

Rom.11. these very *Iewes* his executioners, not for their owne euill workes, but for their Fathers sakes, who were holy and iust men : and therefore speaking of his stripes, (*I was whipped*

Zach.13. (saith hee) *in the house of them, that loued mee:*) Not by them that loued me, but the Sonnes of them, that loued mee, that good might be done vnto the Children for their holy Fathers sakes. Secondly, *(them)*

in

in the plurall number ; not
onely thofe, which confpire
now againft my death, but alfo to all thofe, who at any
time by their finnes haue giuen caufe of this my Paffion.
For thou fhalt not bee excluded from this prayer, whofe
finnes haue been caufe of our
Lords death; and thou mayft
haue hope of pardon, if thou
wilt ioyne thy prayer with the
prayer of Chrift. For if the
prayer of Chrift did profite
them, which neuer required it
doubtleffe it will profite thee,
requiring it of him, and praying together with him.

For they knowe not what they Luc. 23.
doe.

Onfider firft, that Chrift,
to whome all iudgement
is

is giuen, and whome his enemyes had offended, did not
take vpon him the office of a
Iudge, or an accuser, but rather of a defender & patrone.
The *Iewes* sought how to accuse him, and found nothing
worthy of accusation in him.
Our innocent Lord, that was
offended, seeketh how to excuse the offence; and the malice of the offenee was such,
that nothing could be allead-
ged for the extenuating therof, but onely ignorance. And
yet this ignorance, being voluntary, could no more excuse
the *Iewes*, then him, who wittingly and willingly hideth
his eyes, because he will not
see him, whom he striketh, or
killeth. If Christ then in the
                              midst

midſt of his torments mitti-
gateth the ſinnes of his torturers, will hee not now before
his Father excuſe their ſinnes,
who call vpon his name with
faith, deuotion, and ſorrow
for their ſinnes? Conſider ſecondly, that the Father anſwered not his Sonne by worde;
and yet Chriſt was heard for
his reuerence. For God when
he denyed his Sonnes requeſt,
anſwered in the garden by an
Angell: but, when hee graun-
ted it, hee anſwered not in
worde, but in deede. For firſt
hee reſtrained all creatures
frõ riſing againſt his enemies
in reuenge of his death, all
which would haue fought for
their creator, if this prayer of
Chriſt had not ſtayed them.
                    Secondly,

Heb. 5

Ioan. 19.

Secondly, hee reduced one of the Theeues vnto pennance. Thirdly, at the death of his Sonne he changed the minde of the Centurion, and others. Fourthly, vpon the solemnity of Penticost hee conuerted sometimes three, & somtimes fiue thousand of ẙ same *Iewes* vnto his faith. Therefore God the Father not by outward words, but by inward consent answered his Sonne in this manner : O my Sonne, I grant that, which thou requirest, & laying aside all wrath, I open the fountaines of mercy, and I offer grace, and pardon of sinnes, Iustice, and adoption of children, as wel vnto these, who haue afflicted thee, as also vnto all the Nations of the world

world for euer and euer, so as
they will admit mercy offer'd
vnto them. For I will compell
none against their will, but I
giue power to all to returne
into grace and fauour with
mee, if they will, and to be
made the Sonnes of God, and
to come into my inheritance
in Heauen, so as they will be
partakers of the merit of this
my Passion through faith and
the Sacraments. Doe thou
cry out now with great affliction: great are thy mercyes;
therfore we giue thankes to
thee our Lord God. And
pray him to bestow the guift
of wisdome vpon thee, that
thou mayst know and admire
his bounty and goodnes; and
driuing away all enuy, to giue
vnto

vnto thee the vertue of charity, ẙ thou mayſt bee inflamed with the loue of thy neighbour.

The 36. Meditation of the diuiſion of his Garments.

Ioan. 19

Then the Soldiours, when they had crucified him, tooke his garments, (and made foure partes, to euery Soldiour a part) and his coate. And the coat was without ſeame wouen all ouer.

Conſider firſt the pouerty of Chriſt thy Lord : hee had not change or many ſuites of apparrell, nor the ſame of ſilke and other coſtly matter. but his garments were fewe and poore, to defend him only from the cold, and to couer his nakednes. And by tradition

tion it is deliuered (as *Euthe-mius* witnesseth) that his coate without seame was the worke of the mother of God, which she did weaue with her owne hands for her sonne, when he was a little infant : which grew miraculously as our Lord grewe, and was not worne nor torne out in all that long time : the like whereof is re-hearsed in holy Scripture to haue happened to the children of *Israell* : that thou mayest learne by the example of thy Lord to forsake all curiositie and superfluity, as well in ap-parrell as in other things. Consider secondly, the libera-lity of thy spouse : he had al-ready giuen his body, shedde his bloud, and spent his youth-full

full yeares for thee: and now he giueth a fewe poore garments, leauing nothing for himselfe, but nayles, thornes, spittings, and bloud, clodded on his body. Behold the riches of thy spouse, who hath no place to reſt his head, but on the thorny pillowes of his crowne. Doe thou aske him, *where he feedeth, where he will reſt at noone, in this heate of his charity?* and eſteeming this ignominious pouerty of the Croſſe, to bee the greateſt riches, runne naked to him, that is naked. Conſider ſecondly the ſcoffing of the Soldiours in this diuiſion of his garmēts, and caſting of lotts, when euery one catched a peece for himſelfe, as of the attyre of the

the King of the *Iewes*. Doe
thou also runne and gather vp
at least the hemme of his garment, that is to say, esteeme
highly of all those things,
which any way appertayne to
the passion of Christ, as, his
Sacraments, his wordes, his
Church, and his iustifications.
Consider fourthly, that the
foure executioners of Christ
cut his vestment into foure
partes; that the foure Euangelists should sowe vp our
Lords coate in the foure cor-
ners ot the world : to whome
be thou also an ayde and hel-
per, and by thy holy life and
doctrine ioyne together the
Church of Christ, which is
cut and diuided by many Hæ
resies. Couer the poore of
Christ

Pſal.10.

Chriſt with thy garments, and pray our Lord, *that hee beeing now cloathed with light, as with a garment,* will by the light of his grace cloath thy nakednes, and with mercy adorne thy ſoule.

Ioan. 19
Mat. 24.
Pſal. 21.
Luc. 23
Mat. 16.

Then they ſaid amongſt themſelues, let vs not cut, but let vs caſt lotts for it, whoſe it ſhall be; that the Scriptures might be fulfilled, ſaying : they parted my garments among them, and for my coat they did caſt lotts. Therfore diuiding his garments, they caſt lotts vpon them, which part euery one ſhould take.

Onſider firſt the conſultation of the Soldiours about the diuiding & caſting of lotts for his garments. The counſaile was good (*let vs not*

not cut it) but the aduice was
wicked (*let vs caſt lotts whoſe
it ſhall be*) Thou learneſt firſt,
that God is preſent at $\tilde{y}$ coū-
ſaile of the wicked, that hee
may reſtrayne their malice, as
he infatuated the counſaile of
Achitophell. Secondly, that the
effect of our Lords prayer did
heere appeare, when the garment without ſeame remained
whole : whereby is ſignified,
that the Church ſhall neuer be
diuided by any malice of man,
but that it ſhall continue to
the end of the world whole,
and entyre vnder one viſible
head, neither ſhall the gates
of hell preuaile againſt it. For
although the outward gar-
ments of our Lord may be diuided, that is to ſay, diuers
companies

2 Reg. 17

Mat. 16.

companies and focieties of
men may be diftinguifhed by
diuers lawes, fafhions, and cu-
ftomes ; yet the coat without
feame being next to the body
of our Lord, to wit, the Ca-
tholique Church, wouen all
all ouer throughout, fpread
ouer the vniuerfall world, and
orderly diftinguifhed with feuerall offices in feuerall members, agreeing in the Communion of Saints, wouen as it
were with diuers threedes,
fhall neuer loofe his whole-
neffe and integritie. There
fhall fall from it certaine fmall
boughes or branches, like withered leaues from trees; but
the Coate of our Lord fhall
be purged, and not violated
thereby. Take thou heede,
leaft

leaft thou fall from this vnfea-
med Coate of Chrift, but remaine in it as an excellent
peece of workemanſhip; and
becauſe this Coate was begun
to be wouen in the wombe of
the Virgin Mother, (for there
the Sonne of God ioyned humane nature to himſelfe, and
eſpouſed the Church,) doe
thou commend it to the ſame
mother, by whoſe prayers and
helpe it may remaine vntou-
ched and vncorrupt. Conſider ſecondly their twiſe caſting of lotts for his garments,
to wit, Firſt, for the partes of
his garments, and afterwards,
for his Coate without ſeame.
Whereby is declared, Firſt, ẏ
Chriſt himſelfe, and all things
belonging vnto him , were

T   ſubiect

subiect to the will & scoffings
of wicked men. Secondly,
that wicked men doe obtaine
the coate of Christ, that is to
say, the cure of soules, and also part of his garments, that
is, the externall goods of the
Church, not worthily, but by
chance and fortune, and possesse them by other meanes,
then by the will of our Lord
the true owner of them : for
they thinking of nothing lesse
then of him crucified, deuide
& take away his goods, himselfe looking vpon them, and
holding his peace. Thirdly,
that according to St. *Ambrose*
the partes of the garments of
our Lord, that is to say, his diuine guifts and graces, are di-
stributed and giuen to euery
one

Lib. 10. in
Luc. ca. 23

one by lott, that is to say, by
the secret councell of God,
and not by our owne election; but the Coate, that is,
Faith, is giuen whole to euery
man. If perhaps thou beeft a
Cleargie man, called into the
feruice of our Lord, gather
vnder the croffe of our Lord
that part of his inheritance,
which is giuē vnto thee. Take
heede of feeking many partes
and benefices, & vfe that part
before him crucified, which
thou haft receiued: for he beholdeth thee, and obferueth
howe thou doeft adminifter
his goods. Confider thirdly,
that the Prophets long before
did prophefie of this cafting
of lots for his garments : that
thou mayeft learne, Firft, that
T 2   this

this casting of lottes for his garmentes was a matter of great moment, which so many ages before, Holy men, & Kinges fore-saw & lamented. Secondly, of what thinges the auncient Prophets and Holy men did frame their meditations euen before the comming of the *Messias*, to wit, of the pouerty, nakednes, & reproaches of our Lord, that thou being exercised in the same thoughtes and cogitations, mightest bee incyted to compassion and imitation. Consider fourthly, that these Vestments and holy Reliques of our Lord were permitted to remain in the custody of wicked men, y̌ thou mayst know, first that all men, which are called

called to holy offices, are not Holy men and acceptable to God ; secondly, that holynes is offered to all men in this life. Pray thou vnto God, to impart some of his Sanctitie vnto thee, and suffer it neuer to be taken from thee.

And the Soldiours did these thinges : and sitting kept him, and the people stood beholding.

Ioan. 19.
Mat. 27.
Luc. 23.

C Onsider 1. (*And truly the Soldiours did these things*) as if hee should say, Christ praying in the torments of the Crosse, his Mother suffering ẙ sword of sorrow, his friends weeping a farre off, the Soldiours did these thinges. Whilst the Church suffereth persecutions, whilst the poore perish with hunger , whilst the iust

T 3   man

man is punifhed ; the wicked
play and are merry , they caft
lots and dice , they are idle,
and fpend their time in vanities, neither is there any man,
which fuffereth vpon the con-
trition of *Iofeph*. And what
doeft thou thy felfe , whileft
Chrift, and his Church is afflicted? Confider fecondly, that
Chrift is kept more carefully,
then the Theeues , leaft his
difciples or any others fhould
free him frō his punifhment.
But as it was then, fo now alfo the feruour of Catholiques
is too colde, to aduenture any
danger for ẙ name of Chrift.
Doe thou with all care keepe
Chrift in thy heart, and con-
ferue his grace. Confider 3.
the people ftood beholding,
(for

Amos. 6.

(for so it is to bee read, for, expecting) some of them scoffing, some marking euery thing. Doe thou draw neare, and standing on thy feete, ready to fulfill the will and commaundement of thy Lord, beholde, and constantly looke vppon him fastened to the Crosse. Do not sleightly passe ouer all his members, all his paines, all his reproaches: but beholde him with a constant view, and doe not rest in the outward forme onely, but rather meditate on those things, which lye hidden within. For vnder these wounds, spittings and thornes, lurketh the hidden Manna, which no man knoweth, but hee which receiueth it. Stand then before

T 4   this

this table of the Croſſe, like a little dog before his maiſters table, expecting and obſeruing the geſture of him, that ſitteth, and catching euery thing that is caſt from the table. Doe not imitate the people, curiouſly beholding Chriſt, & going to the church for vanity onely, and hearing diuine ſeruice careleſly : But rather imitate the Virgin Mother, *Who let no worde paſſe, which ſhee did not keepe, obſeruing it in her beart.* And pray thy Lord to caſt large guifts vnto thee from his Croſſe.

Luc. 2

✝
•

The

The 37. Meditation of
his mocking vpon
the Croſſe.

And they that paſſed by, blaſ-   Mat. 27.
phemed him, ſhaking their heads   Mar. 15.
and ſaying : Vah, thou that de-
ſtroyeſt the Temple of God, and
in three dayes doeſt build it a-
gaine, ſaue thy ſelfe. If thou be-
eſt the Sonne of God, come downe
from the Croſſe.

Onſider firſt, that Chriſt
our Lord was mocked
vpon the Croſſe, by 4.
ſortes of people, by
thoſe which paſſed by, by the
Prieſts & Seniors, by the Soldiours, and by the Theeues,
that is, by all ſortes of men;
Iewes, and Gentiles; Prieſts
and lay perſons; Senate and
the people, the executioners

T 5   of

of Iuſtice, and thoſe that were condemned by iuſtice. For wee deride and mocke Chriſt by all kindes of ſinnes, contemning his promiſes, diſpiſing his threatnings, reiecting his benefis, breaking his Cōmandements, and neglecting his councells. Conſider ſecōdly, the difference between the wordes of Chriſt, and the wordes of ẙ *Iewes*; the words of our Sauiour, and the words of the world. Hee being carefull prayeth with teares, they being careleſſe mocke him whileſt hee is praying. For the cuſtom of the wicked is to ſcoffe at all things : and therfore in the Scripture they are called (irriſores) mockers; to whome God doth threaten mocking

mocking againe, when that
shall happen to them, which
they feared. Haue compassion heere vppon the spouse of
thy soule, who in the last
houre of death receiued no
comfort, but mockings: from
which they ought then especially to haue abstained when
he was ready to die, in the
middest of his torments. Consider thirdly, they blasphemed,
Who passed by παραπορευ ομενοι,
which may bee interpreted,
Walking, that he may be said
to haue beene mocked either
by trauellers, or else by such
as walked vp and downe by
the Crosse. Heereby are noted light and vnconstant men,
who carelesly say their diuine
and holy office, who sleightly

ly runne ouer their prayers,
who in the Church at the
time of Masse and of Sermons
haue wandering thoughtes,
whose mindes doe not rest
onely on God, but are carryed
wandering vp and downe after sundry delights and pleasures of the world. Consider
fourthly, what these men did.
First they passed by irreue-
rently. Secondly, they shaked
their heads. Thirdly, by these
very gestures they did blaspheme : for they signified
hereby, that he was worthy of
all reproach that he might, to
be taken from amongst them,
and that his doctrine and life
was to be contemned and despised. Fourthly, *Isaias*, according to the exposition of
St. *Hie-*

St. *Hierome,*fore-shewed two
other kindes of mockinges.
*Ouer whome did yee play? ouer
whome did ye gape, and put forth
your tongue.* Therefore they
vpbrayded him with open
mouth and stretched out
tongue. And euen as Stage-
players in the Theaters vse to
make many sportes before the
Princes, which are placed in
high roomes to behold them:
so these mocking actors vsed
many kindes of scornefull behauiours before this king of
the *Iewes.*Consider fiftly, what
wordes they spake. First they
falsifie his wordes, scoffe at
his preaching,and prophesies,
and wrest his holy wordes to
an euill sence. Secondly,
they iest at his myracles : if
thou

Ísa. 57.

thou haſt wrought true myracles, ſhewe now thy power,
and ſaue thy ſelfe.   Thirdly,
they offer wrong againſt his
perſon, whome they denie to
be the ſonne of God.   Doe
thou beleeue the wordes of
God, admire his myracles,
preſerue thy minde free from
all error in faith, receiue Chriſt
the ſonne of God, and neuer
forſake or paſſe by him.   For
they which in this life paſſing
by Chriſt, doe blaſpheme him,
ſhall in the next world paſſe
by heauen and fall into hell.

In like manner with them did
the chiefe Prieſtes, and the
Scribes, and Seniors deride him;
and mocking they ſaid one to a-
nother : hee ſaued others, him-
ſelfe he cannot ſaue : if he be the
king

Luc. 3.

king of Israel, *let him now de-*
scend from the Croſſe, that wee
may ſee, and beleeue him : hee
truſted in God; let him deliuer
him now, if he will : for he ſaid,
that I am the ſonne of God.

COnſider firſt, that the
Prieſtes religious men,
and Magiſtrates did, contrary
to the dignitie of their order,
inſult ouer a crucified man,
and that they were the leaders
or captaines of the people in
theſe irriſions, For St. *Luke*
ſaith thus : *the Princes derided*
him with them. So great a deſire they had to obſcure the
glory of our Lord, and that
there ſhould neuer after be a-
ny mention made of him; that
all ſortes of people thought
him vnworthy of commiſeration

tion euen in the middeſt of his
torments being ready to
yeelde vpp his ghoſt, and had
contemptuouſly reiected him
as accurſed, and as the ſhame
and ſcorne of the people, to
be mocked both by the noble
and vulgar people. But there
is no councell againſt God,
who chaunged this great ignominy of the people into
greater glory. Conſider ſecondly, that Chriſt was blaſphemed more grieuouſly by
no kinde of people, then by
the Prieſts. For they prouoked one another mutually to
ſcorne him, and alſo abuſed
the wordes of the Scriptures,
which were fore-ſpoken of
Pſal. 21.   theſe blaſphemies by the Prophet, which they recyted by
turnes

turnes like the verſes of a
pſalme. Thou feeſt there-
fore, that the faults of ſuperi-
ors are moſt grieuous, who
alſo ſhall ſuffer mighty torments for their ſinnes. Conſider thirdly, and marke their
wordes : Firſt they vpbraide
him with his good deedes
done to the people, and ſcoffe
at his myracles.   Secondly,
they laugh at his royall dignity.   Thirdly, they obiect a-
gainſt him his truſt in God.
Fourthly, they contemne the
the maieſtie of the Sonne of
God, and maliciouſly mocke
at the things, which ſhould
bring honour vnto Chriſt.
The Magi did adore him in
the ſtable with guiſts, as God,
King, and man : and theſe
men,

ap.6

Mat. 2.

men, after so many myracles
shewed vnto them, to mocke
and deride the sonne of God,
the king of kings, and man
trusting in God. Consider 4.
their euill collections: First,
if hee haue saued others he
ought to saue himselfe also. 2.
If hee be the king of *Israell* he
ought to descend down from
the Crosse. Thirdly, if he trust
in God as the Sonne of God,
God will deliuer him. But
first he did not therefore saue
himselfe ; because he would
saue others by his death. Secondly, he did not therefore
descend downe from the
Wood, because the King of
Israell should raigne from the
Wood. Thirdly, God did
not therefore deliuer his Son,
becaufe

becaufe he trufted, not to be
deliuered by him from the
Croffe, but by the Croffe to
be exalted aboue al creatures,
and to place thee in glory
with him. Confider fiftly,
that euill men giue councell
to defcend, the deuill being
the author, who faid, *If thou*
art the Sonne of God, throwe thy
felfe downe. Whereby thou
mayeft learne, that all thofe
defcend fiom the height of
perfe&tion, which caft away
the Croffe from them. Doe
thou pray deuoutly vnto
Chrift to rule and guide thee
from his Croffe, that is from
his throne of mercy, and alfo to take thee vpp with him
vnto the Croffe.

  The Soldiers alfo mocked him,
        comming

comming, and offering Vinegar, saying. if thou art King of the Iewes, saue thy selfe.

Luc. 23.

Consider first, the great contempt, wherewith our Lord was mocked by these base tormentors both in words and deedes. First (they *mocked him*) vsing wanton and scurrile gestures towards him. Secondly, they came nearer to him being naked, and looked more curiously vpon him, according to that of the Psalmist: *But they considered, and looked on mee.* Thirdly, they offered him vineger, like Cupbearers, offering a cup to their King. Fourthly, in their wordes they allude to the tytle of the Crosse. *King of the Iewes*: they say he is a rediculous

Psal. 21

lous King, which cannot saue himselfe, vppon whome dependeth all the safety of his subiects. Consider secondly, that wicked men do acknowledge no other commoditie or saffetie, but only in this life : but good men desire and seeke after the saluation of their soules, as a thing which is common to them with the Angels; respecting lesse the safetie of their bodies, which the beasts doe inioy, as well as they. Consider thirdly, the infinite loue of Christ thy Lord, and spouse of thy soule towards thee ; who hauing once ascended the Crosse for thy sake, could neuer be moued to come downe from thence, neither by torments,

nor

nor by mockings, nor by the sorowe of his mother standing by him, nor by the teares of *Iohn* his kinsman, nor by the tears of *Marie Magdalen*, nor by any sorrowe of his friends, although he knewe, that thereby he might easily end all their troubles. Doe not thou therfore, when thou hast vndertaken any thing for the loue of thy spouse, and for his honor, leaue it off for any cause, although the world frowne thereat; although thy flesh be repugnant; although thy mother shewe thee her breasts, wherewith shee gaue thee sucke; and although thy olde Father lye in the gate: passe thou on, and tread vppon thy Father; for it is piety,

to

to bee cruell in this caufe.
Pray vnto God, to giue thee
this conftancy of minde, and
fetting before thine eyes him
that was crucified, take courage before him, and in his
prefence determine of all thy
bufines.

The 38. Meditation of
the fecond worde
of Chrift.

   And the fame thing did the   Mat. 27.
Theeues, which were crucified   Mar. 13.
with him, vpbraide vnto him:
and one of the theeues, which
were hanged, blafphemed him,
faying : If thou art Chrift, faue
thy felfe, and vs : but the other
anfwering, blamed him, faying :
Neither doeft thou feare God,
which art in the fame condem-
         nation?

nation? Wee indeede suffer iustly, for wee receiue worthy punishment for our facts, but this man hath done no euill.

COnsider first, the ignominy offered to our Lord in this place, either by one theese, according to St. *Epiphanius*, and St. *Augustine* ; or else in the beginning by both, acording to St. *Chrysostome*, but the one repeting, & the other perseuering. For they were most wicked and infamous men , and did worthily suffer , the accursed death of the Crosse. But it did much more afflict our Sauiours heart, that hee, for whome, and with whom hee did shed his bloud, should presently bee carryed headlong

Hære. 6 8.lib.3.de consi.Eu i. c.16. Ho. 7. ad Phil.

long into Hell.   Learne
hereby, that commonly-hee,
which liueth ill, dyeth ill, as he
liued ill, except he be changed
by Gods speciall grace. For
a sinner is stricken with his   Aug. ser. 3
iudgement, that dying he for-   de num.
getteth himselfe, who liuing
was forgetfull of God. Consider secondly the wordes of
the euill Theefe *(If thou art
Christ saue thy selfe and vs:)*
First he wanted faith, who desired a miracle that hee might
beleeue. Secondly, he desired
temporall life and safety, after
the manner of all sinners, who
haue no care of their euerlasting life to come.   Thirdly, he
spake this perhaps to please
the *Iewes*, which stood by : but
it profited him nothing, to get

V   their

their fauour ; becaufe ỹ world
euer giueth a falfe reward to
her followers. Fourthly hee
once vttered this rayling
fpeach, but being rebuked he
held his peace ; being better
then thy felfe, who art neither
amended by good admoniti-
on, nor well pleafed with him
that aduifeth thee. Confider
thirdly, the mercy of Chrift in
the good Theefe, whofe heart
hee did not onely inftruct by
outward fignes, but alfo did
mollifie it by inward grace, fo
as he profited more in three
houres by hearing him teach
from the chayre of the Croffe,
then the Apoftles did in three
yeares by following our Lord
continually, and feeing his
miracles. For fo great is the
force

force of the croffe of our Lord
that it doth not onely mooue
the fence, but alfo giueth vnderftanding to the hearing,
and addeth affection to the
vnderftanding. Therfore this
good theefe being depriued
of all outward thinges, and
hauing his body ftretched vpon the Croffe, gaue openly all
that was left vnto him, to wit,
hee confecrated his heart and
tongue vnto Chrift. For *hee*
beleeued with his heart to iuftice,   Rom. 10
and with his mouth hee confeffed
to faluation, being made a teacher from the chayre of the
Croffe , openly confeffing
Chrift, and freely reproouing
the vices of the ftanders by.
Confider fourthly the wordes
of the good Theefe, Firft with

V 2   great

great charity hee rebuked his companion, when he sinned, before hee craued any thing for himselfe of our Lord; and hee putteth him in minde of his iminent death, for sinners ought to be repressed with the feare of Hell, when they will not be moued with Gods benefites. (*Neither doest thou feare God?*) a bolde worde, but worthy of a Martyr. None of these (saith hee) feare God; and darest thou imitate them, being now presently to goe before God thy Iudge? Secondly, he confesseth his sinne and receiueth the punishment of the Crosse in satisfaction. For it is a signe of a good man to cōfesse his own faults, & to extenuate the sinnes of other men

men, if hee can. Thirdly hee declareth the innocency of Christ : *But this man hath done no euill*, which saying is true only in Christ, and in his most holy Mother ; for hee hath done no sinne, neither is their any fraude in his mouth. But becaufe he did no sinne, therfore hee ought to beare the sinnes of all men, and suffer the punishment thereof in his body. The good Theefe teacheth vs heere, that we should not complaine in aduersities, but confesse our sinnes, and giue glory to God openly, and conuert our soules earnestly vnto God. Doe thou imitate this theefe : for death is at thy gates, or at least lyeth in waite for thee. And pray our

V 3   Lord

Lord to ftrike his fauing feare
into thy heart.

*And hee faid to Iefus : O
Lord remember mee, when thou
fhalt come into thy Kingdome.*

Luc. 23

Conſider firſt, that this
good Theefe fulfilled the
partes of iuſtice : Firſt hee de-
clyned from the euill, which
he reprehended in his companion ; and then hee did good
turning vnto Chriſt. Secondly, according to the doctrine
of *Micheas* , *Hee exerciſed
Iudgment*, greuouſly accuſing
his ſinne; *hee loued mercy*, admoniſhing his companion to
conuertion ; *and hee walked
carefully with God*, of whome
deuoutly and humbly he craued pardon. Cõſider ſecondly, the ſeuerall fruites of the
croſſe

Michea. 6.

crosse and affliction, according to the seuerall dispositi-
ons of men. The wicked are
not amended, but rather blaspheme : the good confesse
their fault, and come nearer
vnto God. Doe not maruaile
then, if our Lord grant profperity in this world to the
wicked, and affliction to the
good; which hee doth merci-
fully for these causes ; both
because the wicked should
not offend more deepely by
their impatience, & the good
be ioyned more firmely vnto
God; & also ỹ the wicked may
haue some reward in this life,
seeing they are to bee depriued of euerlasting life, & that
eternall reward may be reser-
ued for the good. Consider
V 4   thirdly,

thirdly, euery worde of the
theefe : *(O Lord)* a worde of
reuerence, feare, & fubiection:
I fubmit and promife my felfe
to bee thy feruant and bond-
flaue : hee doth not fay, O my
Lord, For hee fpeaketh to the
Lord, creator, and pofleffor of
all creatures. *Remember mee,*
a modeft & humble petition ;
I aske not a Kingdom, nor any
honous ; but only ỹ thou wilt
remember mee, knowing that
thou canft not remēber me, &
not help me. I dare defire this
remembrance, though I am a
finner. 1. Becaufe thou haft
admitted other finners praying vnto thee. 2. Becaufe thou
haft done fo many & fo great
thinges in fauour of finners.
3. Becaufe I a finner, hauing
giuen

giuen ouer my will of sinning, doe now beleeue in thee
with my whole heart, doe in-
tirely loue thee, and with my
mouth doe openly confesse
thee. 4. Becaufe I ask nothing
but remembrance, and pray
for nothing but mercy. 5. Because it is reason, that hee bee
partaker of thy rest and glory,
whome thou hast vouchsafed
to be a companion with thee
in thy labours, torments, and
death. *When thou shalt come into thy kingdome.* I acknowledg
thee to bee a King, but thy
kingdom is not of this world:
I knowe, that the Angells expect thee at thy death, and a
whole Army of Seruants, who
shall not carry thee, as they
did *Lazarus*, but shall attend

V 5   and

and followe the comming of
thy owne will and power.
Admire thou the faith of this
Theefe, who alone, when all
others blasphemed, did beleeue, and detest thine owne
infidelity, who when $\tilde{y}$ whole
world belieueth, doest scarce-
ly beleeue; and pray Christ to
increase thy faith, and bring
thee into his kingdome with
this theefe.

Luc. 23.
*And Iesus saide to him :
Amen I say to thee, this day
thou shalt bee with mee in Pa-
radise.*

Consider first, that Christ
answered nothing to the
theefe blaspeming; that thou
mightest learne to pacifie thy
anger with the vertue of mildnes : and that hee approued
the

the counsel of the other, who thought it requisite in necessitie to haue recourse vnto Christ ; that thou mayest obtaine the guift of councell. Consider secondly, that Christ as a Priest of the newe Testament did forgiue sinnes, and as a Iudge doth assigne merite and rewardes. For to the iust Theese hee promiseth glory ; and to the vniust, to whom he appointeth no crowne of Iustice, hee declareth by his silence that the fire of Hell was prepared. For Christ giueth glory ; but the paines of hell are not giuen by Christ, but rather proceed frō our sinnes, according as the Apostle saith: *Who shall render to euery one according to his workes : to those truly,* Rom. 2.

*truely, who according to patience
in good worke seeke glory and honour, & incorruption, life euerlasting : But to those which are
of contention, and which doe not
yeeld vnto the truth, but beleeue
iniquity, wrath & indignation :*
that is, it shall be rendred, not
so much by the will of Christ,
as through the malice & merite of sinne. Consider thirdly
the benignity of this King of
the *Iewes.* 1. Hee doth not reiect a man infamous for theft;
who beholdeth not the outward opinion of men, but the
inward disposition of ẙ heart.
2. Hee presently heareth him
confessing, and forgiueth his
sinnes. 3. He giueth more thē
was asked. Remēbrance only
was craued, glory is promised,
and

and the fame to be rendred by
& by, euen the very fame day.
Confider 4. the words of our
Lord *(Amen)* this is a worde
of confirmation : for, that
thou mayft giue credit to my
words, I affirme it by ẙ worde
ẘ I neuer vfe, but in affirming
great and ferious thinges, and
I promife it to thee openly
before all thefe witneſſes. *(I
fay)* I the truth, who cannot
lye, whofe promife is effectuall, I the Lord of the Kingdome difpofe of mine owne,
and of no bodyes elfe. *(To
thee)* not to all , leaft they
might take occafion to de-
ferre their pẽnance to the end
of their life, but to thee alone,
lamenting earneſtly, cõfeſſing
thy fins, & making fatisfactiõ

for

for them by this thy punishment : that if perhaps any sinner at the laſt inſtant of his
death will conuert himſelfe,
hee may by thy example conceiue hope of pardon. For before we ſinne, wee ought to
ſet before our eyes the innumerable ſinners ſtanding before the Croſſe of our Lord,
and yet obtaining no pardon,
leaſt our Lord perhaps leaue
vs , and wee periſh amongſt
them : for hee, who hath promiſed pardon to the penitent,
hath not promiſed repentance
to the ſinner. But after our
ſinne wee muſt remember the
Theeſe , leaſt wee diſpaire.
(*This day*,) preſently after thy
death , that thou mayeſt acknowledge the vertue of the
Croſſe.

Crosse. For euen as a Conquerour carryeth his noble
spoyles in tryumph to shewe
the greatnes of his victory, so
Christ, hauing gotten the victory ouer the Deuill, tooke
this notable prey from him,
and carryed away the spoyle,
and lead this Theefe with him
into triumph, who had before
been a most faithfull slaue to
the Deuill. *(With mee,)* that
thou, which hast beene partner with mee in my paines,
mayest not be depriued of my
Crowne : and that thou mayst
not seeme to haue suffred as a
theefe, but to haue triumphed
as a Martyr with mee. Thus
Christ conuerted the punishment of the Theefe into Martyrdome; so as he which was
brought

brought as a Theefe vnto the Croſſe, did by this his notable and publike confeſſion, receiue the Crowne of his teſtimony, as a Martyr with Chriſt the Prince of Martyrs. (*Thou ſhalt bee,*) to remaine for euer. (*In,*) the ioyes ſhall bee ſo great, that thou ſhalt not comprehend them, but they ſhall receiue thee entring into thē : they ſhall fill thee within, and compaſſe thee without, according to that ſaying : *Enter into the ioyes of thy Lord.* (*Paradiſe,*) hee ſaith not, an earthly Paradiſe, wherwith the ſoules and ſpirits of the bleſſed are not delighted ; but the contemplation of the diuine nature, in which is a full ſatiety and delight of the minde. He calleth

Aug. lib. 4 deami. & eius originie cap. 9.

Mat. 25.

calleth it not a Kingdome, as the theefe had requested, but Paradife, (which name he had neuer vfed before:) Firft becaufe by this key of *Dauid*, to wit, the Croffe of our Lord, the gate of Paradife is opened vnto vs, with the wood of the knowledge of good and euill, being violated by finne, had locked vp. Secondly becaufe after forty dayes he was to afcend into his heauenly manfion, & the place of the bleffed. Behold heer the liberall guift of Chrift thy Lord, & bee of good courage : for hee which promifed a kingdome to the penitent theefe on the Croffe, will render no leffe reward to thee for thy labours fpent all thy life time in his feruice.

But

But becaufe Paradife is not promifed by the crucified, but onely to him that was crucified, doe thou (if thou wilt bee a partner in this Paradife) crucifie thy flefh with the vices and concupifcences thereof; and pray the fpoufe of thy foule to call thee to Heauen, with thefe words at the houre of thy death.

The 39. Meditation of the third worde on the Croffe.

Ioan. 19.

And there ftood by the Croffe of Iefus, his Mother, and his mothers fifter Mary of Cleophas, and Mary Magdalene.

COnfider firft, that when the Apoftles fledde, the women followed our Lord euen

euen vnto the Croſſe. And his
Mother is firſt named, both
becauſe ſhe was more feruent,
then the others, and remained
more côſtant ; & alſo becauſe
it was ſtrange, that a mother
could indure ſo great torments, eſpecially of ſuch a
Sonne ; and laſtly that thou
mayeſt learne hereby, that it is
not comely for womens mo-
deſtie to bee preſent at the
death of guilty perſons, and
yet that it is very glorious for
them to ſtay with the Mother
of our Lord before the croſſe
of Chriſt, and to ſet that alwayes before the eyes of their
ſoule. Côſider ſecondly, why
the Mother of our Lord would
bee preſent at his execution:
ſurely not of curioſity or
light-

lightnes ; but Firſt, that ſhee,
who loued ſuch a Son ſo dearly, and had followed him in all
places, might not forſake him
at his death. Secondly, to be
ready to doe him any ſeruice,
or to giue him any comfort,
w̄ lay in her power. Thirdly,
that ſhee might beholde, not
onely the death of her ſonne,
but alſo the manner of the redemption of man ; by the cō-
templation wherof ſhe might
inflame her zeale of the loue
of God. Conſider thirdly why
Chriſt would haue his Mo-
ther preſent at this ſpectacle.
Firſt, that ſhe ſhould be a witneſſe, that hee had payed the
price for the ſinnes of all man-
kinde. Secondly, that ſhee
might ſee the feruor of his
loue

loue towards vs, & thereupon vndertake to be our Patrone. Thirdly, that the Queen of all Saints ſhould not be depriued of the crowne due vnto Martyrs, but ẙ ſhee ſhould ſuffer ẙ moſt noble martyrdome of all others. For other Martyrs ſuffered their own torments, inflicted vpon thē by the hands of ẙ executioners : But ẙ Mother of our Lord ſuffred ẙ torments of her ſon being deriued vnto her from the body of her ſon, as *Simeon* propheſied of her : *And thine owne ſoule ſhall a ſword pierce.* Fourthly ẙ the preſence of his mother might increaſe ẙ matter of his paine. For the Euangeliſt did not without cauſe ſay (*His Mother*)ſignifying therby the mutuall

Luc. 2.

mutuall affections of them both. Admire thou here two great lights obscured: Christ the greater light, the sonne of Iustice, *which illuminateth euery man comming into this world* ; and the lesser light, *Mary, faire as the Moone. The Sunne is made black* (saith the Apostle) *as a sacke of haire-cloath ; and the Moone is made all like bloud,* the mother bleeding with the bloud of her sonne. Consider fourthly, that shee sate not idly ; nor lay downe, as halfe dead ; nor ran vp and downe amazedly: but she stood. First for reuerence vnto her Sonne, whome shee saw hanging straight vppon the Crosse for thy sake. Secondly, as one ready to obey,

and

Ioan. 1.

Apoc. 6.

and doe any ſeruice. Thirdly,
conſtant, and of a good courage, with an aſſured faith of
the redemption of man, and of
the reſurrection of her Sonne.
Fourthly, as prepared herſelfe
ro goe vp to the croſſe, and, if
need were, to ſuffer death for
ſinners. Conſider ſiftly, that
a fewe others ſtood by the
croſſe with the Mother of our
Lord, a Virgin, a Widdow, and
a Sinner, being ſorrowful and
deſtitute of all comfort : that
thou mayeſt learne, Firſt, that
our Lord crucified on the
Croſſe was giuen vs by God
the Father, to bee a comforte
to the afflicted, a Patrone to
Widdowes, & Orphanes, and
a preſeruer and protector of
Virgins. Secondly, that Chriſt
did

did communicate the feeling
of the griefe of his Paſſion
eſpecially to thoſe, whom he
loued moſt dearely.   Marke
therefore whether thou beeſt
mooued with this paſſion or
not, for thereby thou mayeſt
vnderſtand how much hee loueth thee.   Conſider ſixtly.
There ſtood by the Croſſe of Ie-
ſus. Fewe doe ſtand by the
croſſe of Chriſt. Some onely
walke by it, and lightly paſſe
ouer the myſteryes of Chriſt:
others ſtand a farre off, looking ſo vpon it, as if the myſteries of the Croſſe did not
appertaine vnto them : others
ſtand by the Croſſe of the
Theeues, who ſuffer the troubles of their pride, their ryot,
their couetouſnes, & of their
other

other vices. Neare the croſſe
of Chriſt no ſinners are tolle-
rated, no light behauiour is
committed, nor no pleaſures
are ſought after.   Heere is,
whatſoeuer the world abhorreth, pouerty, ſubduing of the
fleſh, contempt, and reproach:
and all thinges are wanting,
which the world deſireth and
eſteemeth. Come thou to the
Mother of Chriſt, as neare the
Croſſe as thou canſt; becauſe
this way onely leadeth thoſe
that weepe and mourne vnto
Heauen; whilſt others, laugh-
ing, ieſting, and blaſpheming,
fall downe into Hell : And
pray the virgin Mother to aſ-
ſiſt thee at the houre of thy
death, and to comfort thee in
thy troubles, who with ſuch
            X   con-

constancy did ſuffer the ſorrowes of her Sonne.

Therefore when Ieſus ſawe *his Mother, and the Diſciple whome hee loued, ſtanding, hee ſaid to his Mother : woman, behold thy Sonne.*

COnſider firſt, the good order in our Lords wordes, firſt, hee prayed his Father for the ſaluation of ſinners ; next hee gaue ſpirituall goodes to the Thiefe, and aſſigned him Paradiſe ; & laſtly, hee giueth temporal côſort to his dearly beloued Mother. That thou ſhouldeſt learne : firſt, why Chriſt came into the world, and dyed vpon the Croſſe, to wit, to ſaue ſinners, of which number thou art one. Secondly, that thou
ſhouldeſt

Ioan. 19

1 Tim. 1.

fhouldeft be carefull of the
faluation & perfection of thy
neighbours, before thou ap-
plyeft thy minde to worldly
things. Confider fecondly,
that he, who from his child-
hood had followed Chrift,
and had dedicated his youth-
full yeares vnto our Lord,
ftood by his Croffe, when all
the reft hid themfelues, and
did receiue for his reward the
cómendatió of conftancy, and
the keeping of ẙ Virgine Mother, that thou from thy infan-
cy fhouldft honor Chrift, and
his mother, and fhouldft fuffer
the yoake of our Lord euen fró
thy youth. Confider 3. with
what eyes ẙ moft louing Son
beheld his moft deare mother,
& with what countenance fhe

X 2   beheld

beheld him againe. Loue and pitty lifted vpp the Mothers eyes to her Son; and prefently griefe & plenty of teares caft them downe againe. Thinke thou with thy felfe, what the heart of the Son fpake to the heart of the Mother; & what the heart of the Mother an-fwered to the Sonne. Haue compaffion on them both, & to their fpeaches ioyne thy petitions. Confider fourthly, that *Iohn* called not himfelfe by his owne name, but the Difciple whom *Iefus* loued; that thou fhouldeft alwayes fet before thine eyes the be-nefites, wherewith our Lord hath preuented thee, and de-clared his finguler loue to-wards thee. Confider fiftly,

that

that our Lord both by his
countenance & wordes, made
his laſt will and teſtament for
his Mother and his friends.
For beholding his Mother &
his Diſciple, hee gaue vnto
them himſelfe, and all that belonged vnto him ; his crowne
of thornes, his nayles, his ſpit-
tings, his bloud, his contempt
of the world , his mockings
and ſhames ; that wee ſhould
not abhorre theſe enſignes of
Chriſt , but thinke there are
great treaſures hidden in them
and ſeeke them by all diligence & labour ; and that his
Mother might bee moued by
them to take compaſſion vppon vs ; and that wee (being
ſignified in *Iohn*) ſhould vſe
them in our prayers to God,

X 3 and

and to the virgin his Mother, and should beseech them by these spittings, by these nayles and by this bloud. Also by his wordes hee bequeathed his Disciple to his Mother, and his Mother to his Disciple, and to all vs. Consider sixtly euery word of this testament: *Woman:* he sayth not Mother, but Woman: first because hee would not giue occasion to his enemies to mocke her. Secondly because he would not afflict his Mothers heart with a name of loue. Thirdly, that he might shewe that this was she of whome God spake long before: *I will put enmity*

Gen. 3. *betweene thee and the woman, she shall bruize thy head:* for now the body of Christ taken

of

of the Virgine, and giuen
by the Virgine to subdue
the power of the Deuill, did
bruize the head of the Serpent. Fourthly, that we might
knowe the conftancy of his
Mother, to whome the pro-
phefie of *Sa'omon* agreed : Pro. 31.
who shall finde a valiant wo-
man ? Behold : it is not (faith
he) an equall change to
take the Sonne of man for
the Son of God ; or the Son
of a Fisher-man for the Sonne
of fo great a King : but the
guifte ought to be free,
both becaufe it was of neceffity, and becaufe it came
from the Sonne ; and alfo
becaufe in him all man-kinde
was commended. *Son :* I haue
hitherto loued this *Iohn*, and
X 4   in

in him all Chriſtians ; I haue
counted them my children ; I
haue prouided for them as for
children; and I haue fed them
with my fleſh & bloud. Ther-
foſe, ô my Mother, doe thou
account them as thy children
for my ſake. *Thy :* ſo loue
them, as if thou hadſt borne
them in thy wombe. This re-
commending of the Son was
of great force with the Mother. Be thou therefore con-
fident in the benignity of this
Virgin, and flye vnto her, as
vnto thy mother in all thy
neceſſityes.

Ioan. 19.

Then hee ſaid to his Diſciple,
beholde thy Mother, and from
that houre the Diſciple tooke her
as his owne.

Conſider

COnsider first, that *Iohn*, who for ẙ loue of Chriſt had forſaken both Father and Mother, had heere a far more worthy mother giuen vnto him: for ſo our Lord had ſaid *Hee ſhall receiue an hundred folde.* Conſider ſecondly, that virginity and all chaſtity is cōmended by our Lord, and that the wantonnes of the fleſh is repreſſed through the paſſion of Chriſt, and the help of the Mother of God. Conſider thirdly, the piety of Chriſt towards his Mother ; that through the grace of Chriſt thou mayeſt obtaine the guift of piety towards God and thy Parents. Conſider fourthly, the wordes of our Lord. *Beholde :* a great benefite, that

Mat. 19.

X 5   God

God and man fhould both
haue one parent. *Mother :*
whom thou mayft reuerence,
loue, and defend; to whome
thou mayeft flye; in whome
thou mayeft haue hope; who
fhall be a Mediator betweene
me, and you my Children, by
whome I will accept your
prayers. *Thy :* fhe is not onely
patrone of all man-kinde, but
of thee alfo, as fhe that loueth
thee, and gaue her onely begotten Sonne to dye for thee,
fuffering him to be crucified,
whipped, mocked and flaine
for thee. Confider. fiftly, that
Iohn beeing poore, who had
forfaken all, and vowed pouerty with the reft of the A-
poftles, and had left himfelfe
nothing, receiued this newe
Mother,

Mother, not into his houses, lands, or poſſeſſions, but into his dutifull care, ſeruice, and protection. Therfore he tooke care for her, that ſhe ſhould want nothing, prouiding ſuf- ficiently for her out of the almes of Chriſtians. Pray thou our Lord to commaund his Mother, to bee alſo thy Mo- ther, that thou mayeſt defend her honour, increaſe her glo- ry, and ſtanding with her by the Croſſe, mayeſt receiue the guiftes and benefites of the Croſſe.

Au lib. 18 de ciuit. dei cap. 4.

The 40. Meditation of the fourth word on the Croſſe.

And from the ſixt houre dark- neſſe was made ouer the whole earth,

Mat. 27. Mar. 15.

earth vntill the ninth houre, and the Sunne was darkned.

Luc. 23.

Consider first, that in the Passion of thy Lord the Sunne was darkened, and the vniuersal world was compassed with darknes, whereof (as St. *Cyprian* witnesseth) *Amos* had prophesied *The Sunne shall set at noone day, and the day of light shall bee darkened:* and *Hieremias : The Sunne did sett before him, when it was midday.* First, that euen as when the maister of a family dyeth, all the house is hanged with blacke to moue sorrow & lamentation ; so thou when the lightes of Heauen mourne, and darknes ouerwhelmeth the earth, shouldest also morne and lament for the

Lib. 2. ad Quirinu. Cap 23. Amos. 8. Hiere. 15.

passion

paſsion of our Lord. Secondly, to declare, that Chriſt the
true Sunne dyeth, of whoſe
brightnes the light of this our
Sun no leſſe dependeth, then
the light of the other ſtarres
depend vpon the brightnes of
the Sunne. Thirdly, that thou
ſhouldeſt knowe the greatnes
of this ſinne, from which the
Sunne abhorring, did as it
were turne away his face and
withdraw his light, and ſhewed himſelfe ready to reuenge,
and offered to his Lord and
creator to periſh for his death.
Thou learneſt hereby, that e-
uery mortall ſinne is ſo grieuous, that it were better the
Sunne and ſtarres ſhould periſh, then that the maieſty of
God ſhould bee offended by
one

one finne. For by euery mortall finne God is put to death,
whofe death cannot bee recō-
penced with the perifhing of
all creatures. Fourthly, that
thou mayft know, that Chrift
fuffred this death for the great
and thicke darknes of finners,
and of the *Iewes*; ỹ this darknes being driuen away throgh
the death of our Lord, there
might a nowe light of faith &
diuine wifedome be reftored
vnto the world ; as at the 9.
houre the light appeared a-
gaine. Fiftly, that thou mayft
vnderftand, that the fruite of
our Lords death, confifteth in
the cōtempt of the fplendor &
fauour of the world : for they,
ẃ are crucified with Chrift,
reioyce not in Honors & Nobility

bility, but in obscurity, neglect, & contempt. Consider 2.
the manner of this Eclipse, w̄
St. *Dionisius Arcopagita,* being
an eye witnes, hath descri-
bed. 1. The Moone being at
the full and opposite to the
Sun, returned from midnight
to noone. 2. It returned, not
by his ordinary motion, from
the West; but by a contrary
motion to himselfe, from the
East. Thirdly, the Sunne it
selfe lost his light in it selfe.
Fourthly, not in one only part
of the earth (as in other E-
clipses,) but ouer the whole
world this darknesse of the
Sunne was seene, in like manner as of the Moone eclipsed,
and depriued of her light
by the shadowe of the earth
falling

Epist. 7. ad
policarpū
& 11. ad
Apolloph.

falling vppon her. Fiftly, this eclipse continued three whole houres, which vsually lasteth but a small time. All these thinges are not voide of their reasons and considerations. Christ is the Sonne of Iustice, the Moone is the world, and foolish sinners : *For a foole is changed like the Moone.* Therfore our Lord dyed, when the world being opposite to God did shine in glory, riches, and wisdome. The world also came to this eclipse, that is, to the death of our Lord, to w, not onely by other sinnes, but also by this seeking of the death of Christ, it had giuen cause. But because the maiesty of Christ is not subiect to humane power, hee could

Eccles.27

could neuer haue beene obfcured, & put to death by the
power of man, except hee had
bin deliuered to death by the
diuine will of God. Therfore
the Sunne is truly obfcured,
and Chrift is truly flaine, both
by the malice of the world, &
by his Fathers wrath. For our
Lord was like vnto him,
w ftandeth between two men
a fighting, and receiueth both
their fwordes into his owne
body. The world fighteth
with God ; and our Lord receiueth in his body, both the
wrath of God, and the fury of
men. *Thy wrath* (faith hee) Pfal.87.
hath paffed through me, and thy
terrors haue troubled me. Therfore when the Sun of Iuftice
was eclipfed, the Earth was
couered

couered with darknes ; both
becaufe by this grieuous finne
there was newe matter giuen
of lamentation and reuenge ;
and alfo becaufe by the death
of our Lord all power ouer
men was taken away from the
Prince of the world, and in
ftead thereof he was bound in
chaynes of fire, and condemned to ỹ darke prifon of Hell.
But whereas the Moone by a
contrary motion came from
the Eaft to the Sunne in the
South, thereby is fignified that
the *Iewes* without all confideration of equity and iuftice,
haftened the death of Chrift,
contrary to Law, contrary to
the right of nature, and contrary to their owne confcience, and did violently fup-
preffe

preffe all good motions in themfelues. To bee briefe, the Suune was eclipfed three houres, becaufe our Lord lay hid three whole dayes, partly in torments and in the handes of the *Iewes*, and partly in the Sepulcher. Pray thou vnto Chrift to preferue the true light of faith and grace in thy foule.

About the rynth houre Ie-fus cryed out with a loude voyce faying: Eli; Eli, lammafabaßt-ani : which is interpreted: My God, my God, why haft thou for-faken mee ?

Mat. 27.
Mar. 15.

COnfider firft, why thy Lord at the end of his life made this crye : Certainly not to efcape the paines ; like vnto vs, who

who crye out, aſſoone as wee
feele any paine ; for now the
end of his paine approached :
nor to bee reuenged on the
Iewes for this his death ; for
the bloud of Chriſt ſpeaketh
better then the bloud of *Abell*.
But firſt, that hee, who by the
ſpace of three houres, being
couered with darknes, had giuen no ſigne of life neither
by worde nor groane, might
be knowne to bee ſtill aliue.
Doe thou conſider with thy
ſelfe what hee did all the time
of his ſilence in the midſt of
his torments : ſurely hee prayed without ceaſing vnto God
for thee in that admirable ly-
turgie and ſacrifice ; and hee
rehearſed the holy wordes of
the Pſalmes for thy ſaluation,
              ſpeaking

speaking some with a loude voyce, that he might be heard of the standers by. Secondly, least by the continuall silence of Christ, and his admirable patience, and constancy of minde, hee might erroneously be thought to be but a vision and no man, and not to haue felt any paine at all. For hee did truly suffer & feele paines; but the loue of thee restrained him from complaining. Thirdly, to teach thee in all thy miseries, to crye only, and with all affection to almighty God. Fourthly, ẏ thou shouldest learne by this loud voyce to obtaine of God the Father through Christ the fruite of his Passion. Fiftly, that thou shouldst earnestly póder with

thy

Hære. 69

thy selfe, what thinges, & how great ; for whome, and by whome our Lord suffered. For our Lord (saith St. *Epi-phanius*) spake these thinges in the *Syriack* tongue, that all the standers by might vnderstand him. Consider secondly, and marke the wordes. *(O God,)* hee sayeth not, Father ; First, because hee was ashamed, re-presenting the person of all sinners, to call him Father ; that thou, setting aside all pride, shouldest learne humi-lity. Secondly least he should seem as a Sonne to complaine of his Father ; but rather as a naturall man of his affliction. *(My)* that is, though thou art the God of all creatures, yet thou art peculiarly my God, for

for many respectes; both because thou wouldest haue humane nature assumed into the
person of the Son, and mee to
be exalted aboue al creatures;
and because thou with thy
owne handes didst frame this
body in the Virgins wombe;
and also because I haue euer
loued and obserued thee sin-
cerely without any vice. The
repetition (*My God, my God,*)
sheweth the great affection of
this speach: (*Why*)hee asketh
not the cause, least the perfection of his obedience shold be
diminished; but hee complaineth out of a naturall affectiõ.
First, ẏ he is forsaken through
no demerite of his owne: *Are*
(saith he) *the words of my offen-* Psal. 2 1.
ces far from my saluation? ẏ is,
                        doe

doe my sinnes hinder my saluation, and thy helpe ? but I haue committed no sinne. Secondly, of the vnworthines of the cause : that thou mightest (saith hee) redeeme a poor seruant, thou hast deliuered thy Sonne to his enemies. (*Hast thou forsaken*) hee sheweth that hee receiued no helpe nor comfort from the vnion of his Diuinity, and that all the time of his Passion, hee was left as man to his owne power. Hee sayeth not, doest thou forsake, but, hast thou forsaken ; not onely in this passion, but in all my life thou hast not assisted mee in my labours. Amongst the Prophets many thinges were spoken hereof. *I am poore, & in labors*

Psal. 87

from

from my youth. An vnworthy thing : I haue a rich Father, but hee giueth his riches plentifully amongſt wicked men. *For of thy hidden thinges,* that is, of riches, which vſe to bee hidden, *Their belly is filled :* but I thy Sonne am left in the meane time poore and beggerly, & from my child-hood am inforced to great labours. *Thou haſt remoued farre from mee my friend and my neighbour* who might comfort mee in my troubles. *Thy fury is ſetled ouer me, and thou haſt brought all thy floods vpon mee :* thou haſt oppreſſed and drowned mee in calamities. *(Mee)*thy Sonne, whome thou haſt begotten frō all eternity, whom aboue all creatures thou

Pſal. 16.

Pſal. 87

Y　　oughteſt

oughtest to holde most deare.
In these thinges beholde the
iust cause of complaint in
Christ, together with the most
ardent loue of his Father towards thee; who becaufe hee
would heare thy complaint,
refufed to heare the cõplaints
of his Son; whom hee would
haue, not onely to knowe, but
alfo really to feele affliction
and mifery; both ỹ hee might
take compaffion vpon thy in-
firmityes; and alfo beftow on
thee the guift of knowledge,
how to vfe all things to thine
owne faluation.

Mat. 27.
Mar. 15
    *But fome ftanding there, and
hearing, faid : Beholde this man
calleth* Helias.

C Onfider firft, that the Romane Soldiours (accor-
ding

ding to St. *Hierome*) being
ignorant of ỹ *Hebrue* tongue
(for *Eli* is Hebrue, and *Lam-
maſabactani*, Syriack) and hauing heard many times a-
mong the *Iewes*, with whome
they couerſed, mention made
of *Helias*, were deceiued by
the meer ſound of the words,
and thought that our Lord
had called vpon *Elias.* Learne
thou, not to vſe nor interpret
raſhly the wordes of God, w̄
thou vnderſtandeſt not. Conſider ſecondly, that, all thoſe
three houres of the eclipſe,
euery man ſtood amazed,
without motion, and without
ſpeach ; but aſſoone as the
light returned, the wicked alſo returned to their irriſions :
that thou mayeſt learne, Firſt,

that the impiety of wicked
men may bee reftrained for a
time, but cannot be quite taken away, without the fpeciall
fauour of God. Secondly, to
obferue diligently and feare
the miracles and thratenings
of God. For euen as God by
this darknes did forefhew vnto the *Iewes* the iminent darknes, wherin for euer they fhall
remaine, except they repent;
fo by his threatning fignes, by
comets, thunder, earthquakes
peftilence, famine, and other
ftrange thinges and euents, he
forefheweth the calamity and
mifchiefe to come. Confider
thirdly, whereas heretofore ẏ
Iewes required a figne to bee
giuen them from Heauen;
heere they hauing a figne, are
made

made neuer the better : That
thou mayeſt knowe, that they
would not haue beleeued, as
they promiſed, if hee ſhould
diſcend from the Croſſe ; becauſe the deſires of the wicked are not directed to their
ſaluation , but to vanity and
mocking. Conſider fourthly,
what comfort is brought frō
the world ; to wit, mocking,
and contempt ; for how can
they comfort others, which
want true comfort of minde
themſelues ? Conſider fiftly,
that theſe wordes were ſpoken by them, which ſtood by,
and heard : that thou mayeſt
learne, Firſt, ẏ idle men, which
are not occupied in their own
affaires, doe nothing but carp
and ſcoffe at the wordes and
deedes

deedes of others. Secondly that such wreſt Gods wordes, to an euill ſence, which onely heare them, and doe not imploy their time to the ſtudy of vertue. Conſider ſixtly, that the wicked knowe no difference betweene *Helias*,& *Eli*, and the honour, which is due vnto God, and which is due vnto creatures. Therefore ſome leauing God,ſeeke help of his creatures,to which they vſe to flye in all their neceſſities; others giue more honor to men,then to God himſelfe; others thinke thoſe thinges to bee done to creatures, which by them are referred vnto God,as the reuerence & worſhip done to Images & Saints, obediéce to their Paſtors &c.

But

But doe thou better interpret the wordes of Christ, & pray him to informe thy soule with his diuine guift of knowledg.

The 41. Meditation of the fift worde of Christ on the Crosse.

Afterwards Iesus knowing, that all thinges were now consummate, that the Scripture might bee fulfilled, hee saide I thirst.

Ioan.19.

COnsider first, that our Lord in all these torments of the Crosse, did neuerthelesse in his minde reuolue the Scriptures, and diligently view them all, least perhaps there might bee somthing in them vnfulfilled for thy saluation : that thou likewise

Y 4

wise, being alwayes attentiue
to the will of God, and to the
cōmandements of thy Superiours, mayst neuer ouer-stip a-
ny thing belonging to thy office & duty. Consider secondly, that Christ neuer spake,
nor did any thing rashly, but
referred all thinges to this end
that the Scripture might bee
fulfilled. Blessed art thou, if
thou doest nothing, but of o-
bedience, ẇ giueth a great ornament to the dooer, and deserueth an admirable recom-
pence for the worke. Consider
thirdly, that this thirst was
most grieuous; which ẏ king-
ly prophet *Dauid* foresawe so
many ages before ; which
grewe both from the labours
and torments of the Crosse,
and

and frō the continuall streams of bloud, and from his fasting all the day and night before. Mark the wordes of the Psalmist : *My strength is dryed like an earthen pott, and my tongue hath cleaued vnto my iawes, and thou hast brought mee into the dust of death* ; that is, thou hast made mee like to dry ashes. Consider fourthly , why the Scriptnres, that spake of this thirst, were fulfilled last, after all the rest : to wit, First, that the first sinne cōmitted in the wood by intemperāce, which infected all mankinde, might as the greatest prouoker of all the rest, be last of all washed away and abolished vpon the wood of the Crosse. Secondly because this thirst proceeeed

Psal. 21.

Y 5   from

from the decaying of his
strength, and from the losse of
all naturall moisture ; that our
Lord might declare vnto vs,
that hee had with a liberall
hand bestowed all his benefits
vpon vs. Consider fistly, why
being inwrapped & compas-
sed with so many torments &
paines on euery side, he complained onely of thirst. First,
to show, that he did truly and
sharply feele the torments of
the Crosse : for Christ vseth
not to complaine lightly, but
onely in matter of great moment. Secondly, to commend
temperance by his example a-
boue all other vertues, which
doth both lift vp the minde to
God, and bringeth a most certaine remedy for sinnes. 3.
that

That hee, which had fhed all
his bloud for vs, and had giuen vs all his goods, and had
prayed for the finnes of all
men to his Father, might vnderftand, what fign of a thankfull minde men would fhew
vnto him, when he was ready
to depart out of the world. I
defire yee not (faith hee) to
take me from the Croffe, nor
to giue me my cloathes to couer my nakednes, nor to heale
my woundes ; but onely to
giue me one drop of water to
quench my thirft, which is denyed onely to the damned in
Hell : I defire yee onely to
refrefh my drynes : I require
this fauour only of you for all
my labours. Fourthly, that he
might be vnderftood to fpeak

not

not of his bodily onely, but specially of his spirituall thirst. Hee thirsted indeede for our amendment, our perfection, and our saluation; w̄ thirst he had euer from the beginning of his life most burning and to quench the same he left nothing vnattempted, but did all things most liberally, and suffered all thinges most constantly, and both shewed it alwayes by his deeds, and declared it often by his wordes. Therefore hee said to the *Samaritan* woman : Giue me to drinke : And hee said to his Apostles : *I haue to be baptised with a baptisme, and how am I straitned till it bee dispatched?* Also hee admonished *Iudas, that which thou doest, do quickly.*
And

Ioan.4

Luc.12.

And here also at the houre
of his death hee shewed his
thirst more clearly; both because his loue did then shine
more bright vpon vs, like vnto a candle, which oftentimes
giueth more light immediate-
ly before it goeth out, and to a
Swan, which before his death
singeth more sweetly; & also
to shew that hee was ready,
to suffer more for our saluatió
if neede were. I thirst (saith
hee) that is, resteth there any
thing for mee to doe to my
vineyard, which I haue not
done? Beholde whilest I haue
time, I offer my selfe to suffer
more & greater thinges; neither can my thirst be satisfied
by reason of the heate of my
loue, except I drinke aboundantly

Isa. 5.

dantly of the cup of my Paſſion, and transferre the fruite
thereof to my members (that
is) to my Diſciples. And hee
ſpeaketh to his Father, who
knewe the inward deſires of
his Sonne. Admire heere the
loue of Chriſt, which in this
his Paſſion ſent forth a ſweete
ſauour vnto vs, like vnto precious ſpices, which doe then
yeilde forth the ſweeteſt ſent,
when they are moſt bruzed
& broken into powder. Fiftly
to leaue this thirſt vnto vs by
his laſt will and teſtament.
The world thirſteth after riches, honours, pleaſures, and
other vaine delightes, which
put them to a great deale of
trauaile, and yet neuer ſatiſſie
their thirſt and deſire, but like
ſtrong

ſtrong poyſon kill them preſently as ſoone as they haue
drunke thereof, as it happened to the Captaine *Syſara*,
beeing killed by a woman at-
ter he had drunke milke.
Chriſt would haue thee to
thirſt after God, the fountaine
of the water of life, and not
to digge broken Ceſternes,
which cannot hold water. I
would thou diddeſt thirſt after thine owne ſaluation, as
Chriſt thirſted after ir, or as
the Deuill thirſteth after thy
perdition. Be thou the heire
of the thirſt of Chriſt, & pray
him to ſatisfie thee with the
breaſts of his grace.

    *Then a veſſell of vineger was
ſet, and preſently one of them
running, filled a ſponge, which*
                     he

Iudi. 4.

Mat. 27.
Mar. 15.
Ioan. 19

he had with vineger, and set it vpon a reede, and Hysope, and gaue him to drinke.

COnsider first the pronenes of men to mischiefe, who vpon the least occasion offered, make hast to sinne; and also the helpe of the Deuill, who presently affoordeth them meanes to sinne. Heere were all thinges prepared, a vessell, vineger, a sponge, and a reede. Marke what sinners brought into Mount *Caluary*, and into the Church, to wit, instruments for the death of our Lord. Contrariwise holy men with *Nichodemus* and *Ioseph* of *Aramathia* bring thither instrnmēts to take downe the body of our Lord from the Crosse. Thinke thou with thy

thy selfe what instruments
thou dost vse in holy Church,
whether to kill, or to saue
soules. Consider secódly, that
Christ at ẙ houre of his death
had no comfort, neither in
word nor deed, but was denyed euen a droppe of water.
Perhappes according to the
custome there wanted not
wine, which the executioners
themselues had spent through
their cruelty and wantonnes,
according to the prophesie of
Amos : *They sate vpon the*   Amos. 2.
pleadged garments hard by the
Altar (of the Crosse) *and they*
dranke the wine of the condem-
ned in the house of their God;
which was the Mount *Calua-*
ry. Consider thirdly, ẙ sponge
was filled with vineger, and
                                   fastened

Leuit. 4.

faſtned to a branch of Hiſope, according to the cuſtome in their auncient ſacrifices, and ſet vpon a reede, and ſo put to the mouth of our Sauiour to ſucke thereof; which beeing done with a Soldiour-like rudeneſſe, many droppes fell into the wounds of him that was crucified, and with the ſharpenes thereof afflicted his fleſh. Was this the reward of that mouth, which opened ſo often for our ſaluation, and of that tongue, which gaue vs ſo many good leſſons, cured ſo many diſeaſed, & wrought ſo many myracles? But Chriſt who had already ſatisfied God the Father for thy other ſinnes with his other paines, curing thy pride with his great ſhame thy

thy couetoufneſſe with his exceeding pouerty, thy luſt with
his moſt bitter torments, thy
wrath with his incredible patience, thy ſloath with his diligent alacrity; would now
alſo apply a medicine for thy
gluttony and intemperance,
and by this bitterneſſe, as by a
contrary medicine, purge and
waſh thy mouth, which was
infected by eating the apple
in Paradiſe. Behold what
drinke thou vſeſt to drinke
vnto thy Lord, to wit, vineger, and the bottome, & dregs
of wine. To the world thou
giueſt ſweete wine; for her
ſake thou laboureſt earneſtly;
thou ſeekeſt to winne her fauour by all diligence, and ſpa-
reſt neither induſtry, ſtrength,
wealth,

Ha. 5.

wealth, nor any thing, which thou haſt : but to Chriſt, thy God, thou mingleſt all thy worſt things, thy ſloath, thy theft, thy hatred, and thy other ſins, for which our Lord complaineth : *I expected that he ſhould make Grapes, and hee made the wilde Vine.* And the world againe for thy ſweete wine reacheth vnto thee vineger vpon a reede, that is, cold and bitter delightes in a broken and vaine ſoule : for the world hath not, nor cannot giue any true comfort or ſweetnes. Therefore doe thou rather drinke ſweete wine vnto Chriſt, and earneſtly from thy heart conſecrate thy ſelfe, & all that thou haſt vnto him : and euen as thou wilt not offer to

to thy louing Father a withered, but a fresh & sweet smelling flower; so doe thou offer
vnto Christ the flower of thy
age, & thy sweetest labours;
and he will exhibite himselfe
againe to thee, as a sponge,
fastened to the reede of the
Crosse, full of grace and truth,
out of which thou maist sucke
sweete water; & he will communicate vnto thee the guift
of vnderstanding, whereby
thou maist vnderstand, and be
partaker of the delihgts of
thy spouse.

*And he said, let be, let vs
see whether* Helias *come to take
him downe: and the others said,
let be, let vs see, whether* Helias
come to deliuer him.

Mar. 15
Mat. 27.

Consider

COnsider first, the words of the executioners. One of them reaching him vineger, which being dronke by the crucified person, haftneth his death, saith : *let be, let vs see whether* Helias *come :* that is, *Helias* shall not come, for I will preuent him by this deadly cup, and rid this man out of the way. Others by the same words perswaded him to stay the cuppe, that they might see by experience, whether *Helias* would come, and so reproue him as a false Prophet, of vanity, in calling vpon shadowes, & those which were dead. Learn thou heere, first, what those executioners thought of our Lord, beeing euen then ready to dye ; that thou

thou mayeſt eſteeme better of him in thy ſoule. Secondly, that he departed out of this world with great thirſt, and carryed that thirſt of thy ſaluation into heauen with him, where with an ardent, though not troubleſome deſire, hee worketh the meanes of thy ſaluation. Thirdly, that this cold and piercing cuppe of vineger brought death vnto our Lord: for through ſinne death entring into the world, killed all, and ſpared not the very Sonne of God, for whom it was neceſſary to taſte of death, that he might ouer-throwe death. Reſolue thou therefore to flye ſinne, leaſt hauing gotten power to kill thy body, it creepe farther, and

and kill thy foule alfo. Confider fecondly, two kindes of
men : for fome without faith
doe by their finnes deride the
patience of God : *Where* (fay
they) *is his promife, or his comming?* Others haue faith, but
preuent the fting of confcience with haft of finning,
Whofe feete runne to euill. Take
thou heede of both ; and pray
vnto God not to forfake thee
in the houre of death, to bee
mocked by the Deuill.

1Pet.3

     The 42. Meditation of
       the fixt word of our
         Lord on the
           Croffe.

Ioan. 19.

   When Iefus *had taken the vineger, he faid.*

Onfider 1. that this word
aboue all the reft brought
               admirable

admirable comfort to all sinners. For hitherto all that hee said, pertayned for the most part to the executioners, to the Thiefe, to his Mother, &c : but this he speaketh to vs all, declaring, that now our debts are payed, and all things perfected, which seeme necessary to our saluation. Consider secondly, who he is, which saith, it is cōsummate : to wit, Christ God and man; for as man he offereth this payment, and as God he receiueth it. For euen as he that draweth wine, and hee for whome it is drawne, saith there is good measure, we ought to credit them : so we ought to beleeue Christ our Lord, saying : all thinges are consummate. Consider

Z   thirdly,

thirdly, where he ſpake it : as
firſt, vpon the Altar of the
Croſſe, in which the price was
payed vnto God. Secondly,
in a high and eminent place,
ỹ like vnto a cryer, he might
publiſh theſe newe tydings
vnto the world. Liſten thou
vnto it, and be aſſured that the
price is paid. Conſider fourthly, when he ſpake it : which
was when he had drunke the
vineger, and was now ready
to dye : that thou ſhouldeſt
knowe, that he being nothing
moued with our ingratitude,
did confirme his laſt will and
teſtament vnto vs, w̃ ſhall
neuer bee infringed by any
wickedneſſe of man, but who-
ſoeuer will be partaker of this
bloud, it ſhall remaine whole
and

and holy vnto him. Confider fiftly, why he fpake it : namely, for our comfort, who knowe the offence of finne to bee fo great, that no creature was able to redeeme the fame. Our Lord therefore affirmeth, that the enormity of our offences is not fo great, nor the number of our finnes fo many, nor our debts fo infinite, but that he hath fully fatisfied for all. Pray thou vnto him, to comfort thee at thy death with this word, leaft thou beeft affrayd to appeare before God thy creditor thorough the greatneffe of thy debts.

It is confummate.

Onfider firft, he faid not, this or y̆ is confummate ;

but absolutely, it is consummate : that thou maist knowe,
that by this passion of Christ
all things are consummate,
and made perfect in Heauen
and in earth ; as well those
things, which pertain to God,
as those, which belong to
man. For euen as sinne violated all things ; so the bloud
of Christ restored all thinges
againe : that thou maist learn
to seeke all things in the passion of Christ, and with the A-
postle *to glory in nothing, but
in the Crosse of our Lord Iesus
Christ.* Consider secondly,
how those things, which belong to God, are consummate
by Christ. For first, he perfectly obserued all the commaun-
of God the Father, and neuer
trans-

Gal. 6.

transgressed any of them, no,
not in thought. Secondly, he
carefully fulfilled all thinges
committed to him in charge
by the holy Scriptures; neither did one iot or tytle passe,
which was not fulfilled. For Mat. 5.
he had receiued frō his Father
a double charge; one deliuered in Heauen to himselfe, another committed to writing
and communicated to vs.
Thirdly, he ended all figures,
ceremonies, and shadowes of
the old Testament, and commaunded all things to cease,
which signified the death of
the Messias, and the future
mysteries of the Church.
Fourthly, whatsoeuer was imperfect in the old sacrifices,
hee perfected and fulfilled in

Z 5   one

one facrifice of the Croſſe.
Fiftly, by this his death he re-
payred the ruines of Heauen,
which were opened by the
ſinnes of *Lucifer, and gaue*
power to men to bee made the
ſonnes of God, to thoſe, which
be'ieue in his name, and after
this life ſpent in the ſeruice of
God, to repleniſh againe the
ſeates of thoſe Angels, whom
their wickedneſſe and ſinne
had throwne downe into hell.
Behold how thy Lord, ready
to goe to his Father, doth
glory, that he hath left nothing in this world vncon-
ſummate, but that he hath executed all things to the full,
which hee was commaunded.
I would thou alſo at ẙ houre
of thy death, according to the
example

oan. 1.

example of thy Lord, could-
eſt glory, that thou haſt left
nothing imperfect in thy ſelfe.
Saint *Paul* ſaid : *I haue fought
a good fight, I haue conſummate my courſe, I haue kept the
faith :* And Saint *Peter* in the
name of the Apoſtles : *Behold,
we haue left all things and haue
followed thee : what therefore
ſhall we haue ?* What wilt thou
ſay when thou art ready to
dye, who haſt violated Gods
commandements, and haſt receiued thy good in this life ?
What canſt thou offer vnto
God for the reward of eternal
glory ? Thinke earneſtly of
theſe thinges, that thou mayſt
diligently execute the Commaundements of our Lord.
Cóſider thirdly, that by Chriſt

2 Tim. 4

Mat. 19.

Y 4   his

his Paſſion, all thinges like-
wiſe are conſummate, w̄ belong to vs. 1. Sinne receiued
his end; as *Daniel* foreſhewed:

Dan.9.   *All debts are payed, the price of*
all the ſinnes of the whole world
is fully numbred to God the Fa-
ther. 2. *To the faithfull all their*

Cor. 2.   *goods are gotten, that nothing is*
wanting to vs in any grace. 3.
He hath perfected his Church
a new Common wealth, and a
choſen vineyard : for whereas
indeede it was begun to bee
planted from the beginning
of the world, but for want of
good manuring did not proſ-
per ; Chriſt by his Paſſion prepared al things neceſſary for it
he inſtituted a Sacrifice, & Sacraments, he ordained paſtors
he made new lawes he diuided
offices

offices to euery one, hee sent
the holy Ghost into ẙ harts of
ẙ faithfull; to be short, he perfected it in such manner, as he
had spoken before : *I will con-*
sumate my new Testament vpon
the house of Israell, *& vpon the*
house of Iuda. Hee began to
write this Testament many a-
ges past, which now with this
worde, as with the subscriptiō
of his hand, & with his bloud
and passion, as with his seale, is
signed by him. 4. He fulfilled
the desire of the Saints, & hea-
ped aboūdantly his guifts vpō
all ẙ faithfull, whom he would
haue consummated into one,
ioyned together in perfect
charity, & replenished with ẙ
7. guifts of the holy Ghost. Do
thou therfore, who hast recei-

Hiere. 3 1

Ioan. 17

Z 5   ued

ued so many benefites frō thy
spouse, neuer leaue to doe his
will, because *his will is thy*
2 Thes.1. *sanctification :* and bee thou
carefull to keepe whole & vn-
uiolate the white garment,
and grace of the holy Ghost,
which thou didest receiue in
the Sacraments. Consider 4.
that many things are consummate by this passion of Christ
euen in wicked men. First, the
hate of the *Iewes*, w̄ could not
further bee extended. 2. The
malice of ȳ Deuils, who could
doe no more against Christ.
3. The kingdome of the Deuil,
the Prince of this world was
ended, his forces broken, his
spoyles taken away, & he himselfe bound in hel with a chain
neuer to be feared more, but
to

to be laughed at, euen by little
children. Feare not then ý af-
faults of the deuill, who can
only counfel & threaten; but
cannot compell nor hurt. Cōfider 5. that Chrift himfelfe is
alfo confummate for vs, as the
Apoftle faith: *Beeing confum-*
mate, he was made to all that o-
bey him caufe of eternall faluа-
tion. 1. His bloud is confummate, all w̃ he powred out of
his veines for thy fake; his
ftrength is confūmate, which
hee exhaufted for thee; all his
goods are confummate, both
within & without, w̃ he offered
for thee. 2. His paines are confūmate; an end is come of all
his euils; & glory only remaineth. Therefore in this fence,
It is confummate, is a worde
of

Apoc. 11.

Heb. 5.

of reioycing, that his labours
are ouercome. Now (faith he)
all thinges are perfect; *Winter*
is done, the fhower is paft, and
gone; there is an end of all e-
uils, & the begining of good :
For his very Sepulcher *fhall*
prefently after his death bee glo-
rious. Be thou carefull whilft
thou liueft, that thy death may
end all euills, & open the way
to good. Thirdly this mortall
life is confummate : O Father
(faith hee) I now leaue the
world, and come vnto thee.
This word one day fhal alfo be
fpoken vnto thee : *It is cõfum-*
mate: thy life muft be ended, &
thou muft leaue all thinges, w̃
thou haft, thy riches, thy honours, thy parents, thy wife,
thy children, and thy friends.
For

Cant. 1.

Ifa. 35.

For *I haue seene an end of all* | Psal. 118
consummation : and wee, who
brought nothing into this world, | 1 Tim.6.
without doubt cannot carry a-
way any thing. Therefore if
with Christ thou hast nothing
but troubles and crosses, if all
thinges in the world be bitter
and sower vnto thee, the voice
of Christ calling thee will not
be vnwelcome : *It is consum-*
mate : because the houre of
thy redemptiõ draweth nigh.
But O how bitter is the remem- | Mat. 24.
brance of death to a man hauing | Eccle.4.
peace in his substance !

 It is Consummate.

C Onsider first, that Christ
had spoken somthing be-
fore of his consumation, as in
Luke : Behold we goe vp to Hie-
rusalem, and all thinges shall bee | Luc.18.
    consum-

consummate, *which are written by the Prophets of the Sonne of man.* Hee gaue also some beginning to this consummation, when hee saide in his last supper :

Ioan.15

I haue consummate the worke, which thou gauest mee, that I should doe. But in the altar of the Crosse all thinges are consumate ; neither could any thing bee consumate before his passion on the Crosse, because without shedding of bloud there is no remission of sinnes, and a testament is not confirmed, but by the death of

Heb. 9.

the testator. Consider secondly, the manner of his consummation ; to wit, the notable constancy of thy Lord, and his inuincible courage. First, hee perfected all thinges alone : *I*

haue

haue trodden (faith he) *the preſſe
alone, and amongſt the people
there was not a man with mee:* Iſa. 6.
that thou ſhouldſt neuer giue
ouer the ſtudy of piety & deuotion, though thou wert forſaken of all men. For God
ſeeth and helpeth thy endeauours; who becauſe he would
not be wanting to thee in thy
labours, denyed his helpe and
aſſiſtance to his Sonne. Secondly, hee ſubmitted all his
members, & filled them with
torments; that thou ſhouldſt
ſpare no labor for the ſeruice
of thy ſpouſe. Thirdly, hee
perſeuered euen to the end of
his worke. Thou oftentimes
conceiueſt a good worke, but
thou doeſt ſeldome begin it,
and more ſeldome proceed in
                              it,

it, and scarce euer bring it to an end. Pray our Lord, to graunt thee the guift of fortitude, that thou neuer faint in the study of vertues. Consider thirdly, with what liberality hee inuiteth thee to those thinges, which hee hath consummated by these his labors. *My Bulles* (saith hee) *and my Fowles are killed, come to the marriage.* For in this passion, First, *All spirituall daintyes are found for euery man his tast, and necessity* ; as the Scripture reciteth concerning *Manna.* Secondly, it is the medicine of all diseases. Thirdly, it is the payment of all debts. Do thou therefore inioy this liberality of Christ, and being wholy melted into his loue, desire to know

Mat. 22.

Sap. 17.

know nothing else, but *Iesus Christ, and him crucified.* Consider fourthly, ẏ by this word *It is consummate :* God ẏ Father is asked by Christ, whether any thing bee wanting to our perfect saluation; and that also all creatures, yea euen our enemies, are as it were iudicially cyted, to consider what is wanting, and to speake it before the death of Christ. For our Lord professeth, that hee will pay to the full, if there be any punishment yet remaining. Behold the liberall mind of thy Lord. Pray him then, that, laying aside all couetousnes, thou mayest bee indued with this bountiful liberality. Cõsider fiftly, that these great riches of Christ are so prouided

1 Cor. 2.

ded

ded for thee, that thou oughteſt to make application of
them to thy ſelfe. Thy dinner
indeed is ready, but thou muſt
goe to the table, and put the
meate in thy mouth : thy medicine is made, but it is kept
in the ſhop of the Church in-
cloſed in ſeauen boxes, to wit
in the ſeauen Sacraments : the
price is payed for thee, but not
yet applyed vnto thee. Dee
not thou thinke, that onely
Faith (as ſome Heretiques
would haue thee belieue) is
ſufficient for thee; thou muſt
goe with thy feete to dinner ;
thou muſt take thy meate, and
medicine with thy handes ;
thou muſt put them into thy
mouth, and receiue them into
thy ſtomache : that is, thou
muſt

must frequent the Sacraments
and be diligent in the exercise
of vertues, that that, w̅ was
effected & giuen for all man-
kinde, may bee accepted for
thee, applied to thee, and profite thee. Pray thou our Lord
that hee, who spent and consummated all his dayes with
infinite merits of good works
will neuer suffer thee to spend
and passe away thy dayes idly
and in vaine.

The 47.Meditation of the
seauenth worde of our
Lord on the
Crosse.

*And crying againe, he saide
with a loude voyce.*

Mat.27.
Mar 15.
Luc.23.

COnsider first, that as often as Christ spake for
himselfe vnto his Fa-
ther,

ther, hee cryed with a loude voyce; but when he spake to others, or for others, hee vsed a lower voyce, to teach thee, First, that thou must alwayes deale with God with great affection. To others thou openest thy griefes with teares, but when thou speakest with God, thou art so drye, that thou hast scarce any feeling of deuotiō. Secondly, what grieuous paines the Son of God suffered, who with the violence thereof was forced to crye out. Consider secondly, that Christ for diuers causes cryed out in his prayers, when hee was ready to dye. First, to shew that he was Lord of life and death, hauing power to yeeld vp his soule, and to take it

Ioan. 11.

it againe, at his owne will and pleasure. Therfore hee called for death (as *Nazianzen* saith) which durst not come, except it had been called. Secondly, to mooue God the Father to mercy: For seeing all mankinde, being oppressed with grieuous sinnes, was farre off from God, hee, who carryed the person of all men, ought to cal vpon God with a loude voyce, being so farre absent. Doe thou therefore knock at our Lords eares, not so much with loudnes of voice, as with affection of hart. Thirdly, that this voice, being sent through the whole world, might moue mens hearts, and that hearing of the death of God for their sinnes, they might be penitent for

In Christo patiente.

for their offences. For at this voyce the Earth was shaken, the Rockes were cleft in sunder, and the Monuments were opened ; that thy stony heart might also be broken by the force of this worde of God. Not without cause did *Marke* say, *(his voyce being sent forth)* that thou shouldst vnderstand that being sent into the world it worketh still in the heartes of men. Fourthly, that Hell should tremble at this voyce : and euen as at the crye of our Lord, calling *Lazarus*, ẙ soule of *Lazarus* returned without delay into his body ; so now euery one there should prepare himselfe to receiue their Lord, being ready instantly to come vnto them. The holy Fathers

Fathers therefore in *Limbo* reioyced at this voyce : and the Deuils in Hell trembled. Fiftly, to teach thee how to meditate on death, not remisly, or negligently, as of a thing little pertaining to thee ; nor slowly and dully, as of a thing a farre off; but often and earneftly, & of a thing moft certaine, and at hand, & fo much the more feruently, becaufe it is the onely gate to faluation. Confider thirdly, that in the ninth houre our Lord brake forth into this clamor : in the houre (I fay) of prayer, and of the euening Sacrifice. For then the true hoaft was facrificed vpon the Croffe, and being cutt into two partes, that is, into body and foule, was
immo-

immolated to God the Father
by the high Prieſt with a loud
voyce and great labour. Ioyne
thou thy prayers with Chriſt
his prayer, that with his voice
they may pierce the Fathers
eares.

Luc.23. *O Father, into thy handes I
commend my ſpirit.*

COnſider firſt, that Chriſt
prayed not vnto his Fa-
ther vppon the Croſſe, but in
the wordes of the Scripture.
Firſt, becauſe hee knewe, that
theſe wordes were moſt acceptable to his Father, beeing
written by the holy Ghoſt, to
teach vs to pray. Secondly,
to teach thee to worſhip God
not according to thy owne
faſhion & vnderſtanding, but
in ſuch manner, as the Church
                            indued

indued with the holy Ghost
hath appointed thee. Confider secondly, that Christ vsed
this word, *Father*, onely twise
vpō the Crosse, in his first, & in
his last prayer, but in his middle, that is, in his fourth prayer, hee called him not Father,
but, God. First, y̆ thou shouldest like a Son, willingly accept that punishment, which
thy Father sendeth, and in thy
punishment confesse thy own
basenes, who art not worthy
to bee called the son of God,
and like a poore creature call
vpon God thy Creator (for
tribulation and aduersity doe
teach good men their owne
fraile estate, and vnworthines,
and thereby perswade, or rather inforce them to mend

A a   their

their liues,) & that in the end,
hauing ouercome all aduersities, thou shouldest take courage & reioyce as a Son : *For
probation worketh hope , which
confoundeth not*. Secondly,be-
cause the beginnings of Gods
word doe most sweetly affect
the minde ; the progresse is
hard to sensuality ; but the
fruites which are gathered,are
most pleasaunt. The booke
was in ẙ mouth of *Iohn* sweete
as hony, but being deuoured
it made his belly bitter.Third-
ly, because in his first prayer,
when hee prayed for sinners,
hee was to gaine authority to
his prayer through the loue of
a Sonne, for none but a sonne
could bee heard for so great
wickednes : In the middle, he
              com-

Rom. 5.

Apoc. 10

complained as a man : And in this laft, hauing fulfilled his embaffage, he defires as a Son to bee called home to his Father. Confider thirdly, that Chrift made this petition to his Father, not for feare of iudgment, for now his Father had committed all iudgement to him ; nor for feare of the Deuill, whofe forces hee had already broken ; nor for feare of the paines of Hell, which now hee came to take from good men, and to carry away the fpoyles of Hell. But firft, to teach thee, neuer to remit or flacke thy inuincible fpirit from prayer. Secondly, that thou fhouldeft knowe, with what confidence he went vnto his Father. For hee fayeth

Aa 2 not

not anxiously after the māner
of a suppliant, I pray thee, Father, but as it were of mine
owne right and authority, I
commend my spirit. Consider
fourthly,& marke euery word
of this last prayer, which before had bin made by the holy

Psal. 32.   Ghost to this purpose, and is
now recited by the Son to the
Father, with addition onely
of this word, Father. *Father:*
First, I haue remained thy Son
in all these so great torments,
I haue remitted nothing of
my deuotion, & loue to thee.
Secondly, I thy Sonne am returned to thee from this hard
embassage, from this bloudy
battell I carry away the victory, and I bring the spoyles.
What reward wilt thou giue
me,

me, what glory wilt thou prepare for mee, what triumph
wilt thou assigne mee? The
Roman Emperors triumphed
with the victorious Army.
Poore *Lazarus*, ẅ was denyed crūmes from the rich mans
table, was carryed in a trium-
phant Chariot, that is, in Angels hands into *Abrahams* bosome. What glory then wilt
thou giue to me thy Sonne?
I am more honorable, because
I am thy Son; I haue labored
more then the rest, for I haue
spent my bloud; I haue vnder-
gone more danger, for I haue
fought alone with the enemy;
I haue indured more want, for
a drop of water hath been denyed mee; I haue ouercome
more strange enemyes, for I

Luc. 16.

Aa 3   haue

haue subdued the Prince of this world, broken his forces, and thrust him out of possession ; and to bee briefe, I haue taken more noble spoyles, hauing deliuered so many thousand soules from the bondage of the Deuill, and subdued all the whole world vnto thy gouerment. What then wilt thou prepare for so great a conqueror? *Into thy handes:* First, as sacrifices are offered into the handes of God, so I, as high Priest, doe offer my soule, as a most fatt sacrifice into thy handes. Secondly, hitherto the soules, which departed out of this world, went not into the handes of God, but into *Abrahams* bosome, in the places belowe : but now I desire

desire first to be receiued into
thy handes, and my Disciples
hereafter to bee receiued also.
Thirdly, this my spirit, which
is now descending into Hell,
to deliuer the Fathers, shall
not want the diuinity ; but e-
uen as the diuine nature took
the humane nature into the
same person, so it shall remain
both with the body in ỹ sepulcher, & with the spirit in Hell.
Fourthly, I commend it to thy
hands, that thou shouldest en-
dowe it with glory, & adorne
it with rewardes. *I commend,*
or as the Greeke text saieth, *I*
will commend, that is, euen now
I will send it to thee. First,
hitherto neither this body,
nor my soule hath seemed to
bee greatly commended vnto
Aa 4   thee.

thee, because both the body
hath remained in the hands of
enemies, and my soule being
sorrowfull euen vnto death,
was alwaies in my own hands

Psal. 118.   subiect to many miseries, and
death it selfe. Hitherto thou
hast seemed to haue care only
of thy bondslaues, and to neglect thy Sonne : for thou hast
deliuered vp thy Sonne, to redeeme thy seruant : doe thou
now at last receiue my spirit
cōmended vnto thee. Secondly, I commend, that is, I leaue
it with thee, to haue it againe
after three dayes. Thirdly, no
man taketh it from mee, for I
am not compelled to dye a-
gainst my will ; but I willingly yeild it, and deliuer it to thy
custody. *My spirit*, hee saith
not

not my soule, which beastes
possesse aswell as men, but, my
spirit, because the sensual man
(ψυχικὸς) perceiueth not those
thinges, which are of the spirit of God, In Christ, the spirit,
that is, the higher part, had as
it were conuerted the soule
into it selfe, so as the inferiour
man desired, nor coueted nothing, but according to the
rule of reason. Pray thou vnto God the Father, that hee
will receiue thy soule, alwayes
commended, with the spirit of
his Sonne.

*Into thy handes I commend
my spirit.*

COnsider first, that though
the spirit of Christ nee-
ded not to be commended to
ỹ Father, yet it was cõmended

to him ; that all faithfull and holy men should knowe, that they are cómended vnto God by this prayer of Christ. For God calleth those by ẙ name of Spirit , which are indued with his spirit. *That* (saieth hee) *which is borne of the spirit, is spirit :* euen as they which are ruled by the spirit of the Deuill, are called the spirits of Deuils. Doe thou looke into thy selfe, what spirit raigneth in thee, whether of Christ, or of the Deuils : And againe, whether thy soule hath chan-ged the spirit into it selfe, so as thou seemest little different from a brute beast, or whether the spirit of our Lord hath thy soule wholy subiect and obe-dient vnto it. *For the worde of God*

Ioan. 3.

1 Tim.4

Heb.4.

God being liuely and powerfull,
reacheth euen to the diuifion of
the foule and of the fpirit : And
therefore in $\tilde{y}$ houre of death
diligent inquiry fhal be made
what the fpirit hath done, and
what the foule; and they onely fhall bee commended vnto
God, which haue wrought by
the fpirit of God. Confider 2.
if Chrift commended vs to
God the Father , then wee
ought to bee carefull to commend our foules vnto him in
good workes. Therefore let
vs prouide, Firft, $\tilde{y}$ what the
grace of the holy Ghoft hath
wrought in our foules, may be
preferued, framed, & perfited,
as it were by his diuine hands.
Secondly, that our fpirite bee
often conuerfant in Heauen,
and

Rom. 8.

1 Pet. 4

and adhere not too much to any worldly things. For (saith St. *Augustine*) if our mindes be there wee shall haue rest heere. Thirdly, that God will holde vs in his handes, according to that : *The soules of the iust are in the handes of God :* neither can any man take the out of his handes. Fourthly, that our spirits, when they goe out of this world, may bee deliuered to the handes of God to be crowned ; and be commended to his keeping till the future resurrection of our bodyes. Consider thirdly, that the Church of God, which is directed and guided by the spirit of Christ, is so commended to God the Father by this prayer of her spouse, *That the gates*

Ser. 175.
de temp.

Sap. 3.
Ioan. 10

gates of Hell cannot preuaile a-
gainst her. Therefore doe thou
neuer seperate thy selfe from
her, except thou wouldest fall
into thy enemies handes; but
defend the life and safety of
thy soule by the spirit, faith,
grace, and Sacraments of the
same. Consider fourthly, that
there is cōmended vnto thee
by his prayer : First, the guift
of the feare of God ; and next
diligent deuotion against the
vice of slouth. For if Christ
the Son of God did with such
earnest prayer commend his
spirit to his Father : it behoo-
ueth thee not onely to pray,
but also to worke thine owne
saluation with feare and trem-
bling. Pray then vnto our
Lord, to take care of thy soule
and

Mat. 16.

Phil. 2.

and to beſtow rather heauenly guifts vpon thy ſpirit, then
earthly benefites vppon thy
body.

The 44. Meditation of
the death of
Chriſt.

Luc. 23.
Ioan. 19.

And ſaying this, bowing his
head, gaue vp the ghoſt.

COnſider firſt, in what
manner the Spouſe of
thy ſoule ended his life.
The ſtanders by vſe to
obſerue the countenaunce,
geſture, and words of thoſe,
which are to dye : & mothers
alſo vſe to marke the eyes, and
countenaunce of their children, when they goe farre
from them, and to remember
often in their minds the manner of their departure. Doe
thou

thou likewiſe, for whoſe ſake
the Son of God ſuffred death,
come neare vnto the Croſſe;
behold all thinges diligently
with the eyes of thy ſoule, and
let thy ſpeach bee often times
thereof. Conſider ſecondly,
that crying he bowed his ſacred head: firſt, becauſe hee
would call thee, both by his
voyce and becke, to learne the
profite of the Croſſe, and to
receaue the merites and benefites of the ſame. Secondly,
to ſpeake in thy eare, to communicate his ſecretes vnto
thee, & to teach thee his commandements and counſailes.
Thirdly, to ſignifie his con-
ſent to all thy petitions and
prayers, which depend vpon
this his holy paſſion. Fourthly
that

that thou mightest the better viewe his head, and marke euery thing diligently, his thornes, his spittinges, his bloud, his eyes now shutt to thy sinnes, his mouth silent from reuenge, & his face pale with death. Consider thirdly, that the Euangelists wrote this death of our Lord in diuers words. *Iohn* saith, *he deliuered vp his spirite* : Mathewe, *he sent foorth his spirit* : Marke and Luke, *hee breathed out* : that thou shouldest knowe, that Christ died, not like vnto other men, but in a singular, and peculiar manner ; neither did he against his will, or by compulsion, but of his owne free accord render vp his spirite. This word, *hee deliuered,*

sig-

signifieth : first, that he gaue
his spirite into his Fathers
hands to be kept three dayes,
and that from thence all merites, all vertues, all iustice,
and grace should bee gathered for man-kinde. Secondly, that as he had already giuen his body to the executioners, so now also hee would
deliuer his soule for vs, because nothing should be wanting to our felicity and happi-
nesse. He had giuen his garments, he had giuen his honour, he had giuen his body,
hee had giuen his bloud : and
now there remained nothing,
but to giue his soule, that according to the prophesie of
Isaias, the whole Sonne might be | Isa. 9.
giuen. 3. That he deliuered vp
the

the full price of our redemption. For hitherto something
was wanting, and he had payed as it were but in part : but
now he made an absolute and
full payment : that thou maist
knowe, that now thou art not
thine owne man, but Chrifts,
who hath bought and redeemed thy members with his,
thy powers with his, thy honours and riches with his, thy
body with his, and thy soule
with his. If thou doeft confider these things rightly, thou
shalt learne, first, not to abuse
thy selfe, & thy goods to thy
owne pleasures ; nor to spend
them according to the will of
the Deuill ; no nor yet to vse
them as thine owne, but to
referre all to the honour of
Chrift,

Chrift, to whome all thinges belong and appertayne. Secondly, feeing thou haft gotten Chriftian liberty, and art deliuered out of the power of the Deuill, neuer to yeilde to him againe. For hee hath no right to thee, whome Chrift hath fo dearely redeemed with his bloud. Do thou giue thankes vnto thy Lord, and offer vp thy felfe, and all that thou haft, freely vnto him.

He breathed foorth.

COnfider firft, that by this word is fignified, that Chrift breathed foorth his laft fpirite: by which fpirite and holy breathing, firft hee purged the ayre, being infected with deuils; by vertue wherof the Deuills alfo are driuen

away

Mar. 15.
Luc. 23

away in exorcismes and exsufflations. Therefore as the earth is sanctified by the holy body of our Lord, and the element of water, and all lyquors, by the holy bloud and water yssuing from his side: so by the diuine spirite of Christ the ayre is sanctified, ẏ it may the more profitably carry and inspire into our sences the word of God, and his holy mysteries. Secondly, hee cõmunicated vnto this world his inward guifts and graces, not onely through the holy wounds of his body, but also by his mouth. Consider secondly, that Christ for many causes would suffer, not onely paine and torments, but also death. First, to offer vp himselfe

selfe by his death as a sacrifice, and Holocaust vnto God. Secondly to redeeme eternall death, due vnto thee, through this his death of infinit value. Thirdly, to confirme by his death all his Sacraments, and the newe Testament. Fourthly, that by this his death as by the death of the high Priest, according to the old figure, he might recall thee into thy heauenly countrey. Fiftly, to let thee knowe, y̆ thou oughtest to bee his, who dyed for thee, and not to submitt thy selfe to the Deuill, who suffered neither death, nor wound for thy saluation. Sixtly, that thou shouldest account thy selfe dead to the world with Christ, and mortifie thy vices and

Num. 15.

and affections: *For if* (saith the Apostle) *one dyed for all, therefore all are dead.* Consider thirdly, that Christ dyed in his flourishing age, being three and thirty yeares old, when his sences were fresheft, his heat greateft, and his strength beft to indure labour. First, becaufe he was willing to beftowe all his moft flourifhing things vpon thee, to preferue the heate of his loue in thee, and with great forces to prepare many benefites for thee. Secondly, that thou fhouldeft not prolong the change of thy life, till thy withered and decayed old age, but confecrate thy youthfull yeares & ftrength vnto Chrift. Confider fourthly, that our Lord was

nayled

nayled to the Croſſe in the ſixt houre; and in the nynth houre, when the day began to growe to an end, hee dyed. Firſt, becauſe he, which in the precedent ages had beene immolated in the figures of the ſacrifices, did in this fourth age of the world dye truly for vs. Secondly, that thou, who hitherto perhapps haſt ſpent the reſt of thy life vnprofitably and wickedly, mayeſt at the leaſt in the end of thy life flye to the death of our Lord. A great comfort is heere giuen vnto ſinners, who languiſhing, either with age, with ſicknes, or in minde, are not able, by exacting grieuous puniſhment of themſelues, to ſatisfie for their ſinnes, may haue the

paines,

paines, bloud, and death of
Chrift to offer for their offences. Giue thankes vnto God,
and difpife not fo great a treafure.

Hee fent forth his fpirit.

Ioan.19

COnfider, that heere alfo
mention is made of the
liberty & freedome of Chrift
to dye. For euen as in former

Gen.8

times *Noe* fent the Doue out
of the Arke, which after a few
dayes returned, bringing in
her mouth a boughe, with
greene leaues : So Chrift fent
foorth his fpirit, to returne a-
gaine after three dayes, with
an army of flourifhing Saints.
Emifit (faieth hee,) hee fent
forth ; and not, *Amifit*, he loft :
that thou fhouldeft not loofe
thy fpirit amongft the wicked.
Con-

Confider fecondly, how the Deuills expected this fpirite, being ready to come foorth, that by the cómon law of all it might bee ioyned to other foules in Hell. For the Euangelift feemeth to fignifie fo much, when hee faid, the Deuill went from him for a time, as though at this time of his death, hee would returne againe. But becaufe the Prince of this world had nothing in Chrift, hee was boúd by Chrift the Conquerour with moft ftraite chaynes, & carryed into Hell, to bee condemned to eternall prifon. Confider 3. the glorious company of Angels, which did not fo much carry, as followe the foule of Chrift defcending vnto Hell.

Luc. 4.

B b   Con-

Confider 4. that by Chrift his
comming to Hell, thofe fearfull darke places were indued
with a new light, that the ho-
lyFathers came flying to meet
him, and to giue him thankes
for themfelues, and for their
vngratefull children; that the
they were all clothed in a new
garment, and admitted to beholde the diuine nature; and
that Hell was filled with bleffed foules, before Heauen, the
feate of the bleffed. Confider
fiftly, what thy Lord did heere
thefe three dayes. Hee beganne to exercife the power
(which hee receiued from his
Father both in Heauen and
Earth,) in the lowest part of
the world. Firft, hee inflicted
worthy punifhment vpon the
Deuill

Deuill, with the rest of his e-
nemies, whome hee had ouercome with great wisdome &
power. Secondly, hee made
new lawes to Hell, and prouided, that none of the Saints
should euer bee carryed thither againe. Thirdly, hee stop-
ped the mouth of that stin-
king place, and shut it so close
that none of that deadly sa-
uour should breath vnto mortall men. Fourthly, he brought
saluation, promised so many
yeares before to the holy Fa-
thers, *and preached to those Spi-*   1 Pet. 3
rites, which were in prison, That
is, brought tydings of peace,
euen vnto thē, who being punished by the deluge, & other
miseryes, for their incredulitie
& sin, were seriously cōuerted
            Bb 2   before

before their death. Pray thou
our Lord, that at the time of
thy death hee will subdue the
Deuill, and bring to thee true
peace and comfort.

The 45. Meditation of the signes in the death of Christ.

And behold the vaile of the Temple was slitt in two peeces, euen from the top to the bottome.

Mat. 27.
Mar. 15.
Luc. 23.

COnsider first, that when
Christ sent foorth his
spirit with a loude cry,
all creatures, reioycing with
their Creator for his noble victory ouer his enemy, made
great noyses & shoutings for
ioy; in like manner as we vse
to shewe publike ioy by dis-
charging great gunns and or-
dinance

nance of warre. Consider secondly, that by this noyse all thinges were opened; the Tabernacle, the Earth, and the stones were resolued, and (as St. *Athanasius* saith) the very Mountaines were cleft in sunder. 1. Because the sacke of grace, being opened by so many woundes, did by our Lords death poore out his guiftes most aboundantly and inuited all men to open the vessels of their hearts. Looke thou therfore to thy selfe, & withdrawe not thy selfe out of this holy showet. 2. Because all creatures, shewed themselues ready to bee reuenged vpon the wicked, and offered euen their bowels vnto God. Consider thirdly, that the vaile of the

Lib. de in carnatione verbi.

Bb 3   Temple

Temple was rent. 1. Becaufe
by this death of our Lord all
the myfteries of the olde Te-
ftament, fhadowed and couered fo diuerfly vntill this time,
did now at laft (the vaile being taken away) fhine moft
cleerly, and were manifefted
and fulfilled by the 7. wounds
of Chrift, of his handes, feete,
fide, head, and whippings of
his whole body; and that the
Temple it felfe, and all the le-
gall Sacrifices, remained prophane, and deftitute of all holynes and fanctity. 2. Becaufe
now was opened the way in-
to *Sancta fanctorum*, that is, the
kingdome of Heauen. 3. To
fignifie, ẏ the Temple it felfe,
for the Synagogue, lamented
the death of Chrift, & detefted
               the

the great blafphemy of the
Iewes; and, to ſhew her griefe
and anger, cutt her vaile or
garments. 4. That thou, re-
membring the death of thy
ſpouſe, ſhouldeſt remooue the
vaile of all excuſes from thy
heart, and open thy inward
thoughtes to our Lord, without any vaile or colour, hi-
ding nothing from the Prieſt
in confeſſion, nor couering
thy ſinnes with the pretence
of piety. For moſt certainly
the vaile of thy body ſhall
ſhortly be broken by approa-
ching death, and thy wickedneſſe ſhall bee reuealed to the
whole world.

And the Earth was moued,
and the Rocks were cleft a ſun- | Mat. 27.
der.

Bb 4 Conſider

Onfider firſt, that at the death of our Lord ẙ earth was mooued and trembled. 1. For the horror of ſo great a ſinne. 2. Becauſe the Prince of the world, who was wont to ſhake the earth with ſeditions and wickednes, was with great violence throwne headlong into Hell. 3. Becauſe God of infinite Maieſty entred into the bowels of the earth, at whoſe comming into the Mount *Syna, the mountaine it ſelfe* (as it were honoring him) *trembled and ſmoked.* 4. Becauſe by the death of our Lord all the earthly heartes of men were to be moued, and carried out of their places vnto Chriſt. 5. Becauſe the new Law of the Goſpell was to bee brought into

Ex 19.20

into the world. If thou therefore, when the whole Earth shaketh, art nothing mooued by the death of Christ, thou art more drye and colde, then the earth it selfe Consider secondly, the Rocks were cleft. 1. Because Christ the corner stone, who was also signified in the old rocke, was now cut asunder, his soule being pulled from his body, and his body beeing torne with diuers woundes. 2. Because mens heartes, being more hard then the very stones, were to bee molified in ỹ bloud of Christ, the true Goate, prefigured in the typicall Goate ; euen as the hardnes of an Adamant is said to bee molified and made soft by the bloud of a Goate.

Ephe. 2.
1 Cor. 10.

Bb 5   Con-

Confider 2. that ẙ ftate of finners is fitly declared by ftones. For euen as the earth is colde, filthy, & bafe, and without the labour & induftry of men, becómeth barren & beareth nothing but weeds ; & as a ftone is likewife hard, heauy & troublefome : fo finners polluted with diuers crimes are grieuous and troublefome to all men, yea euen to themfelues. Pray thou our Lord, to open thy heart to bring forth fountaines of teares, & to diffolue it into very duft, that it may bee framed according to the will of God and drinke in the liquour of his diuine grace.

Mat. 27.   *And the Monuments were opened, & many bodyes of Saints which had flept, rofe : and going*
out

out of the monuments after his
refurrection, entred into the holy
Citty, and appeared to many.

Confider firft, that by this
figne, being the greateft
of all other, is fignified: Firft,
that Chrift thy Lord, opening
by his death the gates of Hel,
did fet at liberty the holy Fathers there imprifoned , and
brake hell gates, fo as neuer
any Saint hereafter fhould
bee detained there. Secondly,
that by the fame death the
ftinking clofets of our heartes
are to bee opened , that all
the ftinche of finne and death
may vapour out , and bee
difperfed. Thirdly, that the
bodyes of the iuft fhould rife
againe, & liue for euer. Confider fecondly, that though
the

Col. 1.
Rom. 4.

the Sepulchers were opened,
yet the Saints did not rise before Christ, who is the first begotten of the dead : for, as the
Apostle faith, *Our Lord was
delivered vp or slaine, for our
sinnes ; and rose againe for our
iustification :* That is, by his
death hee hath payed the price
of our sinnes; but rising again
hee hath applyed this price
vnto vs, by the preaching of
the Apostles, by our faith of
his death & resurrection, and
by the Sacraments and other
meanes left vnto vs after his
resurrection. Consider thirdly,
that these Saints, whether
being to dye againe, as the ancient Doctors thought, or to
liue for euer with Christ, as
many late writers doe thinke,
            assumed

assumed their bodyes againe, and appeared to many, that they might bee true witnesses of the resurrectió of our Lord who was able as easily to reſtore his ſoule to his body being lately dead, as to raiſe vp the bodyes of the Fathers being conſumed to aſhes so many ages before : that thou in all thy difficulties ſhouldſt haue confidence in God, to whome nothing can bee impoſſible. Conſider fourthly, ẙ they appeared not to all, but to many : for all are not worthy of ẙ fellowſhip of Saints. Conſider fiftly, that they came into ẙ holy Citty (for the dead were buryed abroad) that is, *Hieruſalem*, ſanctified by the religion of the Temple, and
of

of sacred thinges : for nowe
through Christ the way vnto
the heauenly *Hierusalem* was
opened vnto them. Consider
sixtly, that in these fiue signes
are contained the fiue effects
and fruites of our Lords passion, which the worde of God
worketh in the soule of a sinner. For first, the vaile being
broken, and the darknes of ignorance being driuen away, ŷ
truth appeareth more plainly,
the seuerity of the iudgement
to come is set before our eyes
and the most cruell and euerlasting torments of Hell are
seriously & frequently thoght
vpon. Secondly, the earth is
shaken, when the minde of
man is terrified, and strucken
with feare through the re-
mem-

membraunce and meditation
of thefe thinges. Thirdly, the
ftony heart is made foft vnto
pennance. Fourthly, by confeffion of finnes all the euill
fauour doth euaporate and
vanifh away out of the opened Sepulcher. Fiftly, the
minde is reftored to a fpiritu-
all life, which is outwardly
feene by the goodnes of his
actions, to the comfort, of all
good men, who with the
Angels of Heauen reioyce at
the conuerfion of finners.
Pray thou our Lord, that thou
mayeft rife with him, and
that hee will not fuf-
fer thee to dye
in
finne.
* *
*

The

The 45. Meditation of the
conuerſion of the
Centurion.

And the Centurion, *which ſtoode ouer againſt him, and they which were with him, keeping* Ieſus, *ſeeing that thus crying he dyed, and hauing ſeen the earthquake, and thoſe thinges which were done, they feared greatly.*

Mat. 27.
Mar. 15
Luc. 23.

Conſider 1. how quickly the bloud of Chriſt ſhewed forth his forces, eſpecially being offered with ſo effectuall prayer to God the Father, in which hee prayed for his crucifiers. For ſuch thinges as were ſignified by the earthquake and by other ſignes, were heer fulfilled in the mindes of men. Thou mayſt therfore be well aſſured
that

that hee will neuer forsake
thee, which recalled euen his
executioners to repentance.
Consider secondly, who were
the first, which were conuerted to the faith by our Lords
death. 1. *The Gentiles, wor-*
shippers of Idolls : for euen then
our Lord began to loue the
Church of the *Gentiles*, to the
which, forsaking the *Iewes*, he
resolued to transferre his mysteries. 2. *Executioners, Soldi-*
ours, infamous men, to shewe
vnto thee, that no man committeth so great a sinne, which
our Lord is not ready presently to forgiue ; and also to let
thee know his great mildnes,
who as he shewed no signe of
anger against his enemies, so
with great loue and affection
he

hee drewe them firſt of all vnto him. Thirdly, the *Romanes*;
for becauſe the Romane faith
and religion was hereafter to
rule and gouerne the vniuerfall Chuch, it was conuenient
that it ſhould bee confecrated vnder the Croſſe of our
Lord by the bloud and death
of Chriſt. Fourthly, *The Centurion ſtanding ouer againſt
him, with the people, which kept*
Ieſus ; for the Romane Princes and Emperours, as in the
beginning they indeauored
by moſt grieuous perſecuti-
ons to ſuppreſſe the Faith of
Chriſt; ſo after they had once
receiued it, they enlarged it by
their Authority, and defended
it by their Armes. Confider
thirdly , the cauſes and manner

ner of their conuersion. First,
standing ouer against him,
they kept *Iesus.* Secondly,
they heard his crye, when hee
yeilded vp the ghoast. Thirdly, they saw the Earthquake,
and other testimonyes of
Gods power. Therefore if
thou wilt bee conuerted, First,
marke diligently the måners,
gesture, life; and wordes of
Christ : For *all thinges, which
are written, are written for our
learning.* Secondly, admire
his most feruent loue, who
tooke all this paine and labour for thee, and for thy
saluation, in hope onely,
that thou wouldest followe
him to beatitude, calling
thee so earnestly. Thirdly,
consider his omnipotencie,
and

Rom. 15

tencie and maiesty, to whome
all creatures obey, that thou
mayest be moued to pénance
at least through feare. Confider fourthly, that the *Centurion* was conuerted with his
people, that thou mayest vnderstand of how great mo-
ment the example of a Supe-
riot is, to the conuersion of
those ẙ are vnder his charge.
Cósider fiftly, that all of them
were afraide : For *the feare of*
our Lord is the beginning of
wisdome, and the beginning of
our conuersion proceedeth
most commonly from feare.
Pray thou our Lord to reduce
thee by their example to a
better course.

And they glorified God, saying : Verily this man was iust :
verily

Pro. I.

Luc. 23.
Mat. 27.

verily this man was the Sonne of God.

Mar. 15.

COnsider first, that the first fruit of our Lords crosse was, that God was glorified in perfect faith , euen by his executioners. Great was the vertue and goodnes of God, which so suddainly changed the cruelty of his tormentors into mildnes, and would haue his praises, being the office of Angels, to bee celebrated by his executioners. Consider secondly, that those Romanes did beleeue in their heart to iustice, when through true faith, they were much afraide; and with their mouth they confessed to saluation, that Christ was true man, with spot of sinne & true

Rom. 10.

Sonne of the true God : because afterwards it was to bee
the office of ý Roman church,
to keep & preserue the whole
and entyre faith, and to spread
it ouer all the world. Consider thirdly, the great myracle,
that in this infamous and most
cruel death the *Gentiles* shold
acknowledge him to be God,
who for his deformity scarce
seemed to bee a man. For the
bloud of Christ induceth vs
to beleiue those things which
exceede all humane capacity.
Pray thou our Lord to confirm
and increase thy faith through
the merite of his bloud.

And all the troupe of them,
which were present at this spect-
tacle, saw what thinges were
done,

done, returned, knocking their breastes. But all his acquaintance stood a farre off, and many women looking on him a farre off, which followed Iesus *from* Galile, *ministring vnto him:* among whome was Mary Magdalene, *and* Mary *Mother of* Iames *the lesse, and of* Ioseph, *and* Salome, *Mother of the sonnes of* Zebedee, *and many other, which came together to* Hierusalem.

Mat. **27**.
Mar. **15**.

Onsider first, the goodnesse of God, who converteth the euill intentions of men to their owne profite. They came to behold, to mocke, and to blaspheme; but changing sodainly their mindes, they returned sorrowfull, and striking their breasts.

Haue

Haue thou confidence, that
thy good workes through his
goodnes ſhall turne to thy
ſaluation, ſince their euill acts
through his mercy were profitable vnto them. Conſider
ſecondly, that whileſt the Romane ſoldiours praiſed Chriſt
the *Iewes* were ſilent; becauſe
hereafter the *Gentiles* ſhould
gouern the Church of Chriſt,
and the *Iewes* ſhould holde
their peace. Conſider thirdly
that they ſtroke their breaſts;
becauſe hee, that will drawe
the fruite of the Paſſion vnto
himſelfe, muſt vndergoe ſome
pennance. For euen as aſhes,
beeing moiſtened with ſome
liquor, doe make a greater
quantity, then if beeing drye
they were powred into the
water:

water : so hee, who like vnto
Christ, suffereth some labour
and pennance, shall reape the
greater profite by his Passion.
Consider fourthly, that these
Iewes did know the dignity of
Christ,& the greatnes of their
owne sin ; but yet they would
not confesse it in their words.
For there are many , which
feele indeed the prick of conscience ; but beeing hindered
either by pride or malice they
refuse to confesse their sinnes.
Cōsider fiftly, that his friends
and acquaintance stood a farr
off, and those women, which
had serued our Lord in *Galilee.*
That thou shouldest knowe :
First, that Christ rewardeth
almes with this benefite, that
they shall perseuere euen vnto

C c   the

Tob.4.	the Croſſe. *For Almes addeth confidence, and ſuffereth not the ſoule to goe into darknes.* Secōdly, by what meanes Chriſt rewardeth his friendes in this world : to wit, that through many tribulations they ſhould enter into the Kingdome of God. But *they ſtand farre off :*
Actor.14.	for that which they ſuffer is very ſmall, if it bee compared to the Paſſion of Chriſt. Pray thou vnto Chriſt, to ſign thee with his Croſſe, and to ioyne thee to ỹ nūber of his friends.

The 47. Meditation of the opening of Chriſts ſide.

Ioan.19.	*Then the Iewes (becauſe it was the* Paraſecue *) that the bodyes might not remaine vpon the Croſſe*

*Crosse on the Sabaoth (for that
was a great Saboth day) intreated* Pilate, *that their leggs might
bee broken, and they might bee
taken away. The Soldiers therfore came, and indeed they brake
the legges of the first, and of the
other, which was crurified with
him.*

Onsider first, that by the commandement of the Law, such as were han-ged on ỹ tree, were wót to bee buryed at night, when as such, as were put to death by any other meanes, were (as vnworthy of buriall) either couered with stones, or left to bee deuoured by beasts. First because God, the soueraigne Law-maker, knewe, that his Sonne should dye that death.

Deut. 21

C c 2   Second-

Secondly becaufe God in his mercy would not, that guilty perfons fhould bee punifhed twice for one and the fame fault : For, becaufe *euery one was accurfed which hanged on the Tree*, hee ordained that at leaft after their death they fhould haue the honor of buriall. Thirdly, that all fuch as fuffer the Croffe (that is the punifhment of Chrift) in this life, may be affured, that there is great glory referued for thē with Chrift in the next life. Confider fecondly , that the *Iewes* were not moued by this Lawe, but by the folemnity of the next day : for wicked men doe often times many thinges well, not becaufe they defire to obey God, and to ferue his honour ;

honour; but to preserue their owne fame and estimation. Consider thirdly, that the dead bodyes ought not to bee left on the Crosse on the Sabaoth day; that thou shouldst neuer carry a dead soule about thee, but at the least on the Holy dayes thou shouldest purge it from all sinne and wickednes. But thou notwithstading dost not onely carry a dead soule, but also doest defile it more vpon Holy dayes, consecrated to the seruice of God, then vpon any other dayes. Consider fourthly, that the *Iewes*, vnder pretence of seruing God, desired another matter; to wit, that they might take away the life of Christ, (whom they knewe not to bee yet

Cc 3   dead)

dead) with more grieuous torments : that thou maist learn,
First, that the impiety of wicked men (who maliciously
are seperated from God) is
daily increased according to
the Apostle : *But euill men,*
and seducers shall prosper to the
worse. Secondly, how cruell
the enemy of man-kinde will
bee in his owne kingdome a-
gainst wicked men, which ra-
geth so much in anothers
kingdome by his Ministers.
Doe thou therefore take heed
of his tirány, wherein there is
neither measure, nor end. Cósider siftly, that the good and
the euill Theefe did not both
suffer one punishment : For
the one wiped away his sinnes
by his paines, and obtained
glory

Tim. 3

glory to himselfe; the other changed his temporall punishment with the euerlasting torment of Hell. Learn hereby what reward the world, and the Deuill doe giue to their seruantes, to witt, grieuous paines, and euerlasting torments in Hell. For this Theese who to please the *Iewes* blasphemed against Christ, was as much tormented by them, as if hee had praised him. See that thou adhere vnto Christ, and according to the example of the good Theese recciue all thy torments in full satisfaction for thy sinnes : and pray vnto God, to afflict thee here, and not to punish thee euerlastingly.

But when they came to Iesus,

*and sawe him already dead, they
did not breake his legges ; but
one of the Soldiers with a speare
opened his side, and presently issued forth bloud and water.*

COnsider first, that the Soldiours, assoon as they had
receiued cōmandement from
the President, made hast to the
Crosse, and diligently obserued, whether there was as yet
any signe of life in Christ : for
if they had perceiued any,
they would haue inflicted the
same torment vpon him. Consider secondly, what manner
of wound this was. For the
Scripture saith not, hee stroke
his side, or hee wounded his
side ; but hee opened his side,
(as St. *Augustine* noteth)that
the

the cruelty of ỹ wound might
bee signified thereby, which
opened his side so much, that
St. *Thomas* was bidden by our
Lord to put his hand into it.
Cōsider thirdly, why our Lord
would receiue this wound,
being now dead for vs. First,
that hee might shew that by
his death hee abated nothing
of his loue towards vs, and ot-
fered himselfe ready to suffer
againe and againe for vs, if it
were thought necessary for
our saluation. Secondly, that
according to St. *Ciprian*, hee
might power out all the moisture remaining in his body
and all the bloud residing in
his heart, and reserue nothing
to himselfe. Thirdly, that hee
might ingraue the signe of

Ioan.20

Ser. de du-
plici mar-
tirio.

Cc 5   thy

thy loue in his heart, & neuer blot thee out againe. Fourthly, that as out of the side of *Adam* sleeping, *Eua* was taken ; so out of the side of our Lord sleeping, the Church should bee deduced. For out of his side issued bloud & water, by which both Baptisme is signified, whereby the faithful are regenerate, washing their body with water, and purging their soule with bloud ; & also the Sacrament of ẙ Eucharist, by which the faithfull, being regenerate in Christ, are as it were strengthened with meat, & preserued aliue. Fistly, that thou mightest enter into the inmost parte of his heart as it were by a gate in the side of a Tower. For by this wound onely

onely is the way opened into the Church, and into the wine Cellar, that is, into the secret mysteries of Christ. Sixtly, ỹ hereafter we should make no more doubt of the humanity of Christ, seeing we finde heer the 4. Elements, and the 4. vitall Humours, plainly shewed by the bloud and water. *For there are three,* (saith the Apostle) *which giue testimony in the earth,* of ỹ humanity of Christ, *the Spirit, the Water, and Bloud.* Seauenthly, that his Resurrection might bee the more admirable, whē he should come to liue againe, whose breast and heart the Soldiour had pierced with his launce; and that thou shouldest not doubt of the resurrection of thy own body.

Gen.6

1Ioan. 5.

body. Come thou hither, and, according to ȳ councel of the Prophet, drawe the flowing springes of water from this mysticall & true Rocke ; and sucke good nourishment, as frō thy Mothers breastes : and pray our Lord to wash thee with the water of his side, and to strengthen and maintaine thee with his bloud.

And hee which sawe it hath given testimony, & his testimony is true ; and hee knoweth, that he saith true ; that yee also may beleeue : for these things were done that the Scripture might be fulfilled: Yee shall not break a bone of him : and againe another Scripture saith : They shall looke on him, whome they pierced.

Consider

Ioan. 19

Exo. 12.

Zach. 12

COnsider first, that these three thinges spoken of before, to wit, that the legges of our Lord were not broken; that his side was opened; and that there issued foorth bloud and water, are proued by a three-fold testimony of *Moses*, of the Prophet, and of the Apostle, who declareth by many words, that he was an eye witnes hereof; that thou shouldest knowe, that this was a matter of great weight, from the meditation whereof thou shouldest not easily depart. Consider secondly, that the Commandement giuen in *Exodus* touching the paschall Lambe, is fitly applyed in this place vnto Christ. For he is the true Lambe; who beeing so

cruelly

cruelly facrificed, tooke away the finnes of the world, with whofe flefh thou oughreft to fatisfie thy felfe with all fpeed and defire. Therefore thofe thinges, which are commanded about the eating of the Lamb in the figure, ought alfo to bee obferued diligently in the holy Communion. And firft we muft take heed, that we breake not a bone, that is, that wee fearch not into his diuine power, nor breake our brotherly charity. For euen as the dinine nature and Maieftie (which is fignified in a bone)fuffred no euil vpon the Croffe : fo in the Communion of this moft holy Sacrament, nothing, concerning the Diuine power ought to be curioufly ously searched into, or doubted of. And as by the passion of our Lord the power of the Church was not broken, or taken away, but augmented and increased: so by receiuing of the Eucharist, the forces of the Church ought to bee vnited and strengthened, and her charity not to bee abated and weakened. Consider thirdly, that *Zacharias* the Prophet, heere cyted by the Euangelist, spake of the future comming of Christ to iudgement. For then shall all the wicked see the Iudge comming marked with his holy wounds, shewing to the good his bowels of charity powred out for them; and vpbrayding to the wicked the manifold sinnes, wherewith

with they had wounded him,
together with the number of
benefites, which hee had bestowed vpon them. Pray thou
our Lord to open, and shewe
vnto thee his wounds, to the
comfort and saluation of thy
soule.

The 48. Meditation of
his taking downe
from the
Crosse.

When the euening was come,

Mat. 27.

because it was the Parascheue,
which is before the Sabaoth, *be-*
Mar. 15.

hold there came a certaine rich
man from Aramathia, *a Cittie*
Luc. 23.

in Iurie, *called* Ioseph, *who was*
Ioan. 19

a Senatour, a good man and a
iust; who himselfe also was a
Disciple of Iesus, *but secret, for*
feare of the Iewes.

Consider

Onsider first, that Christ our Lord, who about the nynth houre of the day, that is, about three in the after noon, had yeilded vp ẙ ghost, did hang at the least 2. houres dead vpon the Crosse : that thou with the eyes of thy soule shouldest continually meditate vpon him both aliue and dead ; and shouldest neuer forget this so great a benefite of his death. Consider secódly, by whom, & by what manner of man he would be taken down from the Crosse : to wit, by him, whose riches, nobility, and authority, gaue courage to demaund the body of Christ, (for hee was rich, noble, and a Decurion, that is, a Senatour of *Hierusalem*), and

and whofe integrity of life commended him vnto God. Confider thirdly, the power of the bloud of Chrift, which gaue courage to a noble man, and one that was timerous, to confeffe Chrift openly, and to take him downe from the Croffe with his owne hands. Pray thou our Lord to confirme thy ftrength, to perform thofe thinges couragioufly, which feeme hard and difficult to nature. Confider fourthly, what manner of man Chrift would haue thee to bee, that he might commend his body vnto thee, & that thou mighteft preferue it profitably in the fepulcher of thy heart. Firft, *Rich*, not to the world, leaft thou fall into the fnare

of

of the Deuill, but hauing thy
treasure layed vp in Heauen.
Secondly, *Noble*, a worthy
Sonne of God. Thirdly, *a Decurion*, which word in this
place signifieth not a man of
warre, but a Counsailor, or
Senatour, that thou shouldest
order thy life according to the
wholsome counsailes of God.
Fourthly, *of Aramathia, a
Citty of* Iurie, which was the
countrey of the Prophete *Sa-
muell. Aramathia* signifieth
high ; & *Iudæa*, or *Iurie* con-
fession and praise : that thou
shouldest alwaies be conuersant with thy mind in the high
Heauens, that is, in the countrey of the Saints, & confesse
thy sinnes vnto God, & sing
his praises vnto him with his
holy

holy angels. Fiftly, *Ioseph*, which was the name of that Patriarch, who long before prepared with great pomp the funerall of his Father *Iacob*; and the name also of the Virgins spouse, who was the first man, that tooke the infant *Iesus* in his armes, and cherished and brought him vpp. This name signifieth increase: for God would haue thee to increase in vertues, to proceed in deuotion, and with great charity alwaies to helpe thy neighbours. Sixtly, *a good mā*, that in thy selfe thou shouldest be indued with grace, and leade an vnspotted life. Seauenthly, *iust*, and vpright towards thy neighbour. Eightly, *the Disciple of Christ*, to whose

whose doctrine & rule thou
must cóforme thy life. Ninth-
ly. *secrete*, that for feare of the
Deuills, who alwaies lye in
waite against good workes,
thou doest neuer vaunt of thy
good deedes, nor seeke vaine
glory by them. Pray thou our
Lord, to indue thee with these
ornaments, ŷ thou maist worthily receiue his holy body.

He had not consented to their
counsaile and acts, for he also ex-
pected the kingdome of God. He
boldly went into Pilate, *and de-*
maunded the body of Iesus : *but*
Pilate *wondred, if he were alrea-*
dy dead: and hauing sent for the
Centurió, *he asked him if he wer*
already dead: & when he knewe
of the Centurió, *he was content,*
and cómanded the body of Iesus
to be giuen him.   Con-

Luc. 23.
Mar.
Mat. 27.
Ioan. 19.

Onfider firft, foure other quallities of *Iofeph*, w̄ it is neceffary for thee to imitate, if thou wilt haue the body of Chrift profitably committed vnto thee. 1. Not to confent to the councell & actes of the wicked. 2. To expect ȳ kingdome of God, and to thinke long for the Heauenly countrey. 3. To performe thofe thinges conftantly, which aduance the glory of God. 4. To require the body of *Iefus*, that is, neuer to be feperated from the Church, the myfticall body of Chrift, & to come with great deuotion to the holy Eucharift. Confider fecondly how much it doth profite a man to auoide the fociety and company of wicked men ; for hee,

hee, which flyeth euill, shall
easily be brought to do good.
Consider thirdly,. that hee, w̄
expecteth the kingdome of
Heauen, ought most of all to
flye wicked company. Therefore if thou seekest this Kingdome , forsake quickly the
world, and all that is in the
world. For the blessed Apostle teacheth, that *Nothing is
found in it, but concupiscence of
the flesh, and of the eyes, & pride
of life.* Consider fourthly, that
Pilate maruailed ; whereby
thou mayest vnderstand that
our Lord suffered much more
grieuous torments, thē either
the Euangelists did expresse,
or our vnderstanding can conceiue. For whereas the crucified persons liued three whole
dayes,

1Ioan.2

dayes, and Chriſt liued little aboue three houres vpon the Croſſe; it appeareth plainly, that more torments were inflicted vpon him, then commonly was vpon other crucified perſons. Giue thou thanks to thy Spouſe for his great bounty, and offer vp thy ſelfe likewiſe freely to his loue and ſeruice. Conſider ſiſtly, that the holy body of *Ieſus* was required of *Pilate* beeing a Heathen; that thou mayeſt not meruaile, if in the Church the ſame ſacred body, and other holy myſteries be committed ſometimes to the diſtribution of wicked men. Pray thou our Lord, ſo to deliuer his body vnto thee, y̆ through any fault of thine it may neuer be taken from thee. *But*

But Ioseph *hauing bought a cleane piece of linnen, tooke down the body of* Iesus, *and laying it downe, wrapped it in the cleane linnen.*

Mar. 13
Mat. 27.
Luc. 23.
Ioan. 19

COnsider first, with what reuerence this holy Senator came to the Crosse, and pulled out the nayles with his owne handes, tooke downe the holy body from ẏ Crosse, Saint *Iohn* perhappes and the women, but specially our Lords Mother, running to helpe him : who comming all neare, and beholding his sacred countenance, vpõ which the Angells desire to looke, what wordes doe they vtter? what sighes doe they send foorth? what teares doe they powre out? Behold then his

D d   Mother.

Mother, lifting vp her handes, & earneſtly begging her ſons body of *Ioſeph*, and receiuing it reuerently : Come thou to the virgine and comfort her, who lamented euery wound. For although, contrary to the cuſtome of Parents, ſhee refrayned from vnſeemely crying, and womaniſh geſtures ; yet ſhee felt the inward griefe of minde, and a moſt ſharpe ſword piercing her hart. Conſider ſecondly, that *Ioſeph* bought a cleane piece of linnen, wherein the body of Ieſus ſhould bee wrapped : in ſtead whereof thou oughteſt to haue a cleane conſcience, bought with the price of pennance, and made fit to receiue the body of Chriſt. Conſider thirdly,

thirdly, that heere is no mention made of the seruants, because holy men doe those
things themselues, which per-
tayne to the seruice of God,
and by their seruauntes they
dispatch their worldly busi-
nesse : whereas contrariwise
wicked men doe Gods seruice
by their deputies, applying
themselues wholly to temporall affaires. But let such men
take heede, least by their deputies they obtaine eternall
glory, and by themselues bee
throwne into euerlasting
fire. Pray thou our Lord
to make thy consci-
ence a worthy
shroud to re-
ceiue his
sacred body.

The 49. Meditation of the buriall of our Lord.

Ioan. 19. *And* Nichodemus *also came, who had come first to* Iesus *in the night, bringing a mixture of* Myrrhe, *and* Aloes, *about a hundreth poundes. And they took the body of* Iesus, *and bound it in linned, with spices, as the custom of the* Iewes *is to bury.*

Ioan. 3. Consider first, how much *Nichodemus* profited by this bloud of Christ, which was shed. Hee came before to *Iesus* in the night; now openly: then he brought nothing but questions and words; now he bringeth precious spices, and helpeth to bury him: that thou mayest learne to increase in vertues, and to shake off all base

base and seruile feare. Consider secondly, that neither of
them came without their
guiftes. For *Ioseph* bought a
linnen sheete, and a noble sepulcher. And *Nichodemus*
brought Myrrhe and Aloes
in great plenty for the vse of
the dead body. First, that thou
shouldest not say with *Iudas*,
why is all this losse? when
thou seest much spent about
the honour & seruice of God.
Secondly, that thou by their
example shouldest bring thy
guiftes to Christ, who dyed
for thee, and offer vp all thy
labours to his honour. Consider thirdly, what manner of
duty they did to the holy body of our Lord. First, when it
was taken downe, all of them

Mat. 26.

Dd 2   toge-

together, with the Mother of our Lord, ſtood reuerently beholding, and contempla-ting the ſame body with their eyes, and mindes. And heere againe ponder with thy ſelfe what teares they ſhedd, what wordes they ſpake, and what thoughts they had; & caſting away al vaine feare, come neer and ioyne thy words & pray-ers vnto theirs. Beholde this chincke of the Wall (the wound, I meane, of his ſide) behold the holes of the Rock (the foure wounds of his hāds and ſeete) behold the crowne of Thornes, remayning yet vpon his holy head, wouen with many boughes(as it may be ſeene in *Paris* in the Kings chappell, where it is kept with great

great reuerence) behold like-wiſe his whole body, blewe with ſtripes, and torne with wounds. Pray our Lord, firſt, to hide thee in theſe holes of the Rocke, and in this chinck of the Wall, that thou neuer thinkeſt, nor deſireſt . any thing, which tendeth not to the glory of him crucified. Secondly, that he neuer looke vpon thee, but through theſe wounds, or windowes of his hands, feete, and ſide , nor haue any other proſpect, but through theſe crannies, that is, theſe wounds of his whole body & head, through which hee cannot ſee but with the eyes of mercy. Secondly, they tooke off his crown of thorns from his head, and perhappes

Dd 4   being

being tangled in his haire and
sticking in the flesh & ioynts
of the bones, they hardly pluc-
ked out the thornes entyre:
and taking a bason, they reuerently washed off the spittings, bloud, and filth, which
stucke vnto the same. Thirdly, with great honour they
washed, according to the
custome of the *Iewes*, the
holy body of our Lord,
and gathered together all the
foulenesse, as most holy and
sacred reliques, & kept them
with great care ; which in
continuance of time waxing
hard, and being reduced into
a bloudy substance, mingled
heere and there with a watery
colour, was sent by *Baldwin*
King of *Hierusalem* from *Pa-
lestina*

lestina to *Bruges* in *Flaunders*
by the Abbot of St. *Bertins*,
where it is kept, and reueren-
ced most deuoutly by the
Brugeans, and hath been preserued by Gods help, and their
singular care from the fury of
the *Genseoms*. Fourthly, they
wrapped the body in the
sheete, and after the manner
of the *Iewes* couered it ouer
with spices. Marke thou euery thing, and conuert it to thy
owne benefite. Thy Lord is
bound, who looseth thee
bounden: his hands are boūd,
least they punish thee : his
feete are bound, least they
runne to reuenge : his face is
couered, least he see the foule-
nes of thy sinnes. Pray vnto
him, to season thee with the
spices

spices of vertues, and to burie thee together with him.

   And there was in the place, where hee was crucified, a Garden, and in the garden, a Monument, which Ioseph *had cut out in a Rocke, in which neuer any was yet laide. Therefore, for the* Parasceue *of the* Iewes, *they laid* Iesus, *because the Monument was hard by. And* Ioseph *rowled a great stone to the mouth of the Monument, and went his way.*

Onsider first, that Christ our Lord was not left without Sepulture, but was buryed like vnto others : First that hee might seeme to haue omitted nothing, pertaining vnto men. Secondly; y̆ thou being buried with him, shouldest

Ioan. 19.
Luc. 23.
Mat. 27.
Mar. 15.

deſt neither regard nor know thoſe thinges, which are done in the world. Cóſider ſecondly, that the Prophet foretolde, that the Sepulcher of our Lord ſhould be glorious. This Sepulcher may bee taken three wayes. Firſt, for this whereof wee now ſpeake, which being cut out in the Rocke was reſerued for an honorable man. Which was made more glorious, becauſe two Senators being Noble men, and one of them, a Maiſter in *Iſraell*, and a Doctor of the Lawe, executed the office of buriall with their owne handes ; and becauſe none but iuſt & holy men touched the ſacred body of Chriſt, which with great coſt they annoynted, and ſeaſoned.

Iſa. 11.

Ioan. 3

foned. Secondly, for his Sepulcher in the Church , where
the true body of Chrift, being
thought indeede liuing , yet
like vnto his dead body is referued vnder the forme of dry
and immoueable bread, the
filuer and golden veffels being as it were a Sepulcher,
wherein it is kept. And this
Sepulcher is glorious, becaufe
it is reafon, that wee exhibite
to this body, that once dyed
for vs, as much honour and
glory, as lyeth in the power
of man to giue. Thirdly, for
the Sepulcher of our heartes
and bodyes, wherein commu-
1 Cor. 12 nicating wee receiue the holy
hoaft. For as often as we receiue this Heauenly bread, by
this very action, we fhew and
declare

declare the death and buryall of our Lord. Let therefore this Sepulcher bee also glorious, to wit, illuminated with the grace of God, & adorned with all vertues : for *All the glory of the Kinges Daughter is from within* ; and our Lord by his comming addeth a greater brightnesse vnto our soule. Consider thirdly, with what funerall solemnity our Lord was carryed to his Sepulcher , when the holy men did beare him, and his Mother and the Holy women, and his Disciple *Iohn* followed him. Therefore as often as thou shalt see the holy Hoast carried in procession, imagine that thou doest follow this body of Christ to buryall ; and re-membring

Psal. 44.

mēbring his paſſion & death,
cōmend thy ſelfe and the neceſſities of the whole cōmon
wealth vnto him by the ſame.
Pray alſo thy Lord, to giue
vnto thy heart the ſtrength
and conſtancy of a ſtone or
rocke, and to prepare a ſepul-
cher therin for himſelfe, *Where*

Cant. 1.   *hee may lye in the middꝭ*, and
graciouſly ſuppreſſe the heate
of thy temptations.

    And Mary Magdalene, *&*
Mary *of* Ioſeph *were ſitting*

Mat. 27.   *there againſt the Sepulcher, and*
the women which came with him

Mar. 15.   *from* Galilee, *and followed him,*

Luc. 23.   *beheld where the body of* Ieſus
was laide ; and returning, they
prepared ſpices and oyntments :
and on the Sabaoth they reſted
for the Commandement.

                 Conſider

Onsider first, the sorrowe both of the other women and also of the Mother of Christ, when they must bee drawen from the sight of so sweet a Lord. There seemeth to be no mention made of the Virgin *Mary*, not because she was absent, but because shee w stood by him at his death, could not bee absent herselfe from this office & duty. Consider secondly, these women sate ouer against the Sepulcher, and diligently marked, what was done. First that thou in all thy needs shouldest flye vnto the holy Eucharist of Christ, and sitting as it were by the Sepulcher of our Lord, meditating & pondering vpon his death & passion, shouldest

dest shew forth all thy griefes and receiue remedy and comfort for thy afflictions. Secondly, that thou with these women shouldst mark, where the body of *Iesus* was laide. First, in a Garden, both because by the death of our Lord the way is open to the garden of delightes, from whence we were excluded by the sinne of *Adam* ; and also that thou shouldest not lay vp thy Lord in any other place then in the flowers of vertues. Secondly *In a new monument*, both because hee desireth all thinges to be new in thee. For *New wine is not powred into olde vessels* ; and also because he came to make all thinges newe. Thirdly, *In which neuer any was laide,*

Mat. 9.

laide, least perhaps not Christ, but some other might be said to haue risen from death; and that thou shouldest suffer no other to rest in the sepulcher of thy heart. For he teacheth, that our Lord alone will possesse thee wholy, and that hee will suffer no companion of his Kingdome in thy soule. Fourthly, *In a Stone*, both to take away all suspition of the stealing away of his body; and also because from thence-foorth hee had determined to pierce the stony hearts of *Gentiles* and sinners. Fiftly, *In a-nothers Monument* that by his death hee might commend that pouerty, which he had so often praised in his life: for hee, whose Mother had no place

place wherein to lay her Son, when hee was borne; and he who had not where to rest his head, when he liued; was buryed in another mans Sepulcher, when hee dyed. Besides, it was conuenient, that hee, which dyed not for his owne fault, but for others, should be buryed not in his owne, but in another mans Sepulcher. Sixtly, *In a place hard by*, both because no man should say, hee was stollen away, if the place had beene farre off; and also because both aliue and dead our Lord would not bee far from his seruants, but alwaies remaine amongst his people. Seauenthly, *In the Sepulcher of a iust man*, both because hee dyed, that hee might indue vs
with

with Iustice; and also because
no man ought to receiue him
in the holy Communion but
a iust man. Consider thirdly,
that the womē rested the next
day, and ceased from their
worke and duty by reason of
the Commandement: where-
by the vertue of obedience is
commended vnto vs, which
teacheth vs, that for God e-
uen the seruice of God somtimes is to bee omitted; that
is, that many workes of deuotion, and Heauenly comforts
are to bee pretermitted, when
the Superiour so cōmaundeth.
Pray thou our Lord, that hee,
who exercised obedience e-
uen till his death, will graunt
thee the perfection of that
vertue.

The

The 50. Meditation of
the keeping of the
Sepulcher.

And the next day, which is after the Parasceue, the chiefe Priests & the Pharises came together to Pilate, *saying : Maister wee remember, that this seducer saide, whilest he liued : after three dayes I will rise againe: Commaund therefore that the Sepulcher may bee kept till the third day; least perhaps his Disciples come and steale him away, and say to the people hee is risen from death : and the last error will hee worse then the first.*

Mat. 27.

COnsider first, what the care of these men was vpon the Sabaoth, and vpon this Sabaoth also, being the solemnitie of their Pasch :

Pasch : to wit, to obscure the
glory of Christ : and that day,
wherein they should speake
with God, they spend in busines with a prophane man :
whome thou doest often imitate , spending thy time in
worldly busines, when either
the Sacraments ought to bee
handled, or some other thing
to bee done with God. Consider secondly , that the Sabaoth is not named the
next day after the Parasceue :
First, because the true solemnity of the Saboath and of the
Pasch was to bee transferred
to the next day by the new resurrection of Christ. Secondly, because holy dayes, being
prophaned by sinne, are not
feastiuall & profitable to sinners

Theoph. in Mat. 27.

ners, but rather hurtful & prophane. Confider 3. *Maifter*, they, which refused the *Meſſias* for their Lord and Maifter, are worthily compelled to accept a vile Idolater for their Maifter. For the Deuill and the world ſhall rule ouer him, ouer whom Chriſt ruleth not. Confider fourthly, that Chriſt was called by the wicked a ſeducer : For the Deuill euen at this day indeauoreth by his ſeruants to perſwade, ẏ Chriſt is a Seducer, and that they are ſeduced to errors and wickednes, whom Chriſt doth either conuert to the true faith, or exhort to a better kinde of life ; whereas Chriſt doth ſeduce no man, but leadeth them from the wide way of Hell

Hell to the ftraite and nar-
rowe pathe of eternall life.
Confider fiftly, that the wicked feared Chrift being dead;
how much more then ought
he to be feared being liuing,
and comming with Maieftie
to iudge the quicke and the
dead ? Heere thou feeft two
kindes of the feare of God;
one in the *Centurion*, and the
reft which went away, ftriking
their breafts, and for feare of
future euils thinking of the a-
mendment of their liues ; the
other of wicked men, who labor to infringe the councells
of God, and this feare is proper to the deuill, and to all the
enemies of God.   Confider
fixtly, that the great care and
diligence of thefe wicked
                              men

men did much increafe the glory of Chrift. For by this diligent carefulnes of them, the rumor of the foresaid refurrection of Chrift was the more publifhed, and caufed very many to hope and expect the fame, and alfo tooke away all fufpition of ftealing him away, feeing there was with fuch diligence a company of fouldiers appointed to watch him. Confider feauenthly, that they feared, leaft the Difciples of Chrift fhould fteale away his bodie. Doe thou receiue it openly, for it is giuen to thee, borne for thee, and crucified for thee : and pray our Lord neither to depart from thee himfelfe, nor to fuffer any creature els to take him from thee.   *Pilate*

Pilate said to them, ye haue a guard, goe, and keepe him, as ye knowe.

COnsider first that *Pilate*, who had once consented with the *Iewes* to the death of Christ, did now assigne them a guard, to wit, the Garrison soldiours, appointed for the watching of the Cittie. For whosoeuer doth once yeild to the will of the wicked, shall hardly withdraw himselfe after from their will and importunity; wherof they haue experience, who intangle themselues with the vnlawfull loue of women: and the Deuill also, hauing once got the vpper hand, bringeth men into miserable bondage. Consider secondly, that *Pilate*

who

who before had diligently defended the caufe of Chrift,
doth now confpire with the
Iewes againft the glorie of
Chrift. *Goe* (faith he) *keepe
him, as ye knowe*; that is, be diligent in watching him : for
a man doth fo eafily fall out of
one finne into another, that
he alfo becommeth an author
and prouoker of fin in others.
Confider thirdly, that *Pilate*,
when he heard mention made
of his refurrection, waxed a-
fraid, both of the inconftant
people, and alfo of *Cæfar*,
without whofe commaunde-
ment he had condemned an
innocent man to death. For
this is the fruite of finne, that
it bringeth feare, care, and
difquiet of minde. Therefore
doe

doe thou auoide sinne, and with a secure and quiet Conscience be thankfull vnto God.

And they going away garded the Sepulcher, marking the stone with Watchman.

Mat. 27.

COnsider first, the diligent watching of the Sepulcher. For First, they marked the stone with a seale, least the Souldiers should vse any subtiltie or deceipt. Secondly, they appointed a Garde, that is, a sufficient number of Soldiours, both because the fauourers of Christ should be able to offer no violence, and also least a sewe might fall asleepe, and in the meane time, be stolen away. Consider secondly, that Christ permitted

E e 2　　　them

them to vfe all this diligence and induftrie, that his refurrection might be more publifhed and knowne, being proued euen by the teftimony of his enemies. Thou feeft firft, that there is an admirable treafure of goods hidden, in Chrifts Sepulchre, which by all meanes thou oughteft to endeauour to keepe. Secondly, that thy heart, in which our Lord doth reft, ought to bee kept moft carefully. Thirdly, that thou needeft not to feare the wicked, who by their perfecutions do nothing elfe, but keepe and watch the hidden treafure of thy foule ; leaft by any vanity or pride it fhould bee ftollen from thee. Confider thirdly, that

that the markes of the wicked
are nothing but impure spots,
whereby they labour to infect
and pollute the cleane creatures of God. Doe thou mark
thy heart with Christ his seale
and pray him to guard and
preserue thee with his Angels
in his true faith and seruice : which Almighty
God grant vnto mee
also through
thy
intercessions
and
Prayers.

Laus Christo, Virginiq́, Matri.
Ad maiorem Dei gloriam.

FINIS.

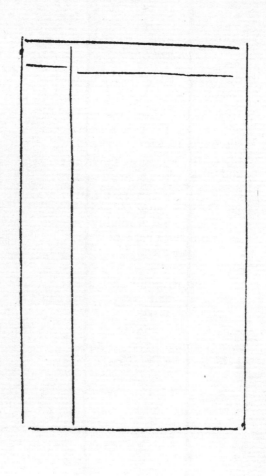

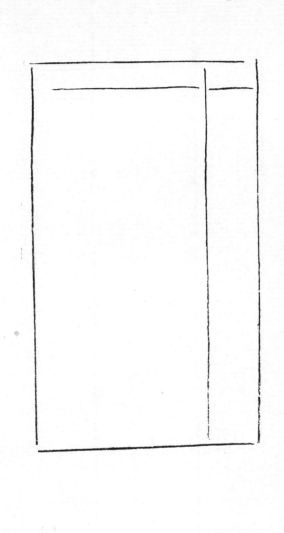

APPENDIX

verily this man was the Sonne of God.

Mar. 15.

Consider first, that the first fruit of our Lords crosse was, that God was glorified in perfect faith, euen by his executioners. Great was the vertue and goodnes of God, which so suddainly changed the cruelty of his tormentors into mildnes, and would haue his praises, being the office of Angels, to bee celebrated by his executioners. Consider secondly, that those Romanes did beleeue in their heart to iustice, when through true faith, they were much afraide; and with their mouth they confessed to saluation, that Christ was true man, without spot of sinne & true God, the Sonne

Rom. 10.

Sonne of the true God : becaufe afterwards it was to bee
the office of ϛ Roman church,
to keep & preferue the whole
and entyre faith, and to fpread
it ouer all the world. Confider thirdly, the great myracle,
that in this infamous and moſt
cruel death the *Gentiles* fhold
acknowledge him to be God,
who for his deformity ſcarce
ſeemed to bee a man. For the
bloud of Chriſt induceth vs
to beleiue thoſe things which
exceede all humane capacity.
pray thou our Lord to confirm
and increaſe thy faith through
the merite of his bloud.

Luc. 23.   *And all the troupe of them,*
which were preſent at this ſpect-
acle, and ſawe what thinges were
done,